L O C K E

JOHN LOCKE, LL

G. KNELLER Eques. PINXIT 1697.

L O C K E

BY

ALEXANDER CAMPBELL FRASER

KENNIKAT PRESS
Port Washington, N. Y./London

LOCKE

First published in 1890
Reissued in 1970 by Kennikat Press
Library of Congress Catalog Card No: 71-103188
SBN 8046-0825-3

Manufactured by Taylor Publishing Company   Dallas, Texas

PREFACE.

Two hundred years have elapsed, in this March of 1890, since the first publication of Locke's 'Essay concerning Human Understanding.' The philosophy of the intervening period has probably been more affected by its direct or indirect influence than by any other similar cause, and indeed the effect seems in excess of the author's speculative depth and subtlety, or grandeur of character. Perhaps no philosopher since Aristotle has represented the spirit and opinions of an age so completely as Locke represents philosophy and all that depends upon philosophic thought, in the eighteenth century—especially in Britain and France. Reaction against his real or supposed opinions, and therefore indirectly due to his influence, is not less marked in the later intellectual history of Europe, wherever the influence of Leibniz, and then of Kant and of Hegel has extended ; in Britain the reaction is marked in Coleridge.

The bicentenary of this memorable book may be taken as a convenient occasion for a condensed Study of Locke —biographical, expository, and critical—and of his historical function, which is now more important than his own philosophical conclusions. In these two centuries the ' Essay ' has been subjected to the most opposite interpretations at the hands of its numerous critics, from Stillingfleet, Lee, Leibniz, and others who were Locke's contemporaries, to Cousin, Webb, and Green. Its intellectual flexibility, in admitting the most opposite interpretations, is due partly to imperfection in its intellectual scheme and manner of expression; but this nevertheless may be one cause of its influence in the development of philosophy.

What strikes one about Locke and his fortunes, besides the large place which he fills in the history of modern opinion—religious and political as well as metaphysical—is the difficulty of interpreting his philosophy without reading into it the history of the man and his surroundings, and also the abundance of imperfectly used materials for this purpose which exist.

There is no adequate edition of his Collected Works,[1] in which the parts are compared with one another, with the purpose which pervades the whole, and with his extensive published and unpublished correspondence and other literary remains.

As regards his Life, the " Éloge Historique de feu M. Locke " by Le Clerc, which appeared in the ' Bibliothèque Choisie,' in 1705, about a year after Locke's death, has been the foundation of subsequent memoirs. Le Clerc found his materials in his own and Limborch's personal intercourse with Locke in Holland, and their correspondence with him afterwards; in a letter by the third Lord Shaftesbury; and in an interesting letter by

[1] Bishop Law's edition, 4 vols. (1777), is the best.

Lady Masham, lately recovered by Mr Fox-Bourne. A letter published about the same time by M. Pierre Coste, Locke's amanuensis, gave a few additional details. For a century and a quarter after the death of Locke the meagre biographical sketches which appeared were drawn from these sources.

In 1830, Lord King, the lineal descendant of Locke's cousin and executor, Lord Chancellor King, wrote a 'Life' which contains a small part of the abundant correspondence, journals, commonplace-books, and other manuscripts that he inherited,—now at Horseley Park, in possession of his son the present Earl of Lovelace. In 1876, Mr Fox-Bourne produced two large volumes which add many facts previously unknown, collected with much care and industry. To his extensive and painstaking researches all who are interested in Locke owe a debt of gratitude.

Much correspondence and other matter in manuscript remains still unused. The interesting collection which belongs to Lord Lovelace, and which by his kindness I was some years ago allowed to see, is a mine only partially worked. There is also a large collection of letters to and from Locke, from 1673 till his death, in possession of Mr Sanford of Nynehead, near Taunton, the representative of Locke's friend, Edward Clarke of Chipley in Somerset, which, through Mr Sanford's kindness, I saw some years ago, and some of them I understand may soon be published by the Historical Manuscripts Commission. The Locke relics, kept till lately at Holme Park, I have likewise seen. In this volume I have availed myself of these fresh resources, as far as narrow space has permitted.

It is much to be desired that an exhaustive edition of Locke's Works, freed from errors which have crept into successive editions, collated, with the needful annotations, dissertations, and historical and biographical accompaniments, should some day form a national monument to the most typical of English philosophers. At one time I contemplated an annotated edition of the 'Essay,' and collected materials for the purpose; but the progress of the work showed now inadequate a commentary on the 'Essay' alone would be, as a substitute for a suitable edition of the Collected Works, and for this, even if I were otherwise competent, my day is too far spent.

Perhaps the attempt made in this small volume to show Locke's characteristic office in the succession of modern philosophers, to keep steadily in view the main purpose of his life as a key to the interpretation of his 'Essay,' and to place his 'Essay' and Philosophy in a new light, may not be without use, as an introduction not only to Locke, but through him to the intellectual philosophy of Europe since March 1690—the Era which the 'Essay' has inaugurated.

A. C. F.

GORTON, HAWTHORNDEN,
March 1890.

CONTENTS.

THIRD PART.

ADVANCED LIFE: CONTROVERSY AND CHRISTIANITY (1691-1704).

L O C K E.

———•———

FIRST PART.

EARLY AND MIDDLE LIFE: A PREPARATION FOR PHILOSOPHICAL AUTHORSHIP
(1632-89).

———

CHAPTER I.

YOUTH IN THE PURITAN REVOLUTION (1632-60).

NEAR the little market town of Pensford, six miles south-east from Bristol, and ten west from Bath, on the side of one of the orchard-clad hills of Somerset which enclose the fertile vale of the Chew, the modest mansion of Beluton may still be seen. Early in the seventeenth century it was the home of the author of the 'Essay on Human Understanding,' in his boyhood. The Beluton Lockes had migrated into Somerset from Dorsetshire. In Elizabeth's reign, a certain Nicholas Locke, the descendant of a middle-class family of the

name, who owned Canon's Court in that county, came to
live in Somerset. He settled as a prosperous clothier,
first at Pensford, and afterwards at Sutton Wick in
the neighbouring parish of Chew Magna, where he
died in 1648.[1] The house and the little property of
Beluton, purchased by his industry, was before 1630
occupied by his eldest son John; who in that year
married Anne Keene (or Ken), the daughter of a substantial tradesman in the neighbouring parish of Wrington. John Locke, the philosopher, was the eldest son
of this marriage. It was at Wrington, not at Beluton,
that he was born, in the same beautiful county of Somerset, under the shadow of the Mendip Hills. In the
register of that parish the following entry appears among
the births : "1632, August 29—John, the son of John
Lock." A few yards from the parish church, against the
churchyard wall, still stands the two-storeyed thatched
cottage in which he first saw light. It was then the
home of his uncle, Anne Keene's brother, and she, it
appears, was in that August on a visit at Wrington.

When the future philosopher of England awoke into
life in August 1632, in that humble Somerset cottage,
Charles I. had passed through seven years of his
troubled reign. The great antagonistic forces, whose
antagonism in due time caused the temporary over-
throw of the social order in England, followed by the
"faithless cynicism" of the Restoration period, and ending in the compromise of 1689, were then beginning to
show their strength. The birth at Wrington was the
beginning of a life that was to be passed amidst that

---

[1] In the seventeenth century younger members of families of good
birth not seldom went into trade.

long and memorable struggle, in the course of which
England exchanged monarchical or personal for the par-
liamentary government which has since developed into
a democracy.   The normal functions of the constitution
were in a state of suspense at the time of Locke's birth ;
for the last of Charles's three short Parliaments had been
dissolved in 1629, and the next was the Long Parliament,
summoned eleven years after.   The Church, too, was becoming an influential factor in the incipient commotion.
Laud, in 1632 Bishop of London, and Archbishop of
Canterbury in the year after, in uncompromising temper,
was resisting the Puritans on behalf of that sacerdotal
ideal of the great Anglican communion, as a reformed
branch of the one visible and historical Church, which,
in the more tolerant and humane spirit of the nineteenth
century, is again a conspicuous influence in English life.
Faith in the divine right of the king, and faith in the
divine authority of the one Catholic Church, — each
in collision with faith in the supreme right (divine or
other) of the people,—were forces destined to convulse
the England through which the child born at Wrington
in August 1632 had to make his way as an actor and
thinker.   The seventy-two years of his life were to correspond with that crisis of dramatic interest in the affairs
of Church and State which occupied the interval between
the First Charles and Anne, between Strafford and Marl-
borough, between Laud and Burnet.   In its course the
State was violently convulsed, insufficiently restored,
again disturbed, and finally settled ; while the Church,
alternately persecuted and dominant, was, towards the
end, the subject of ineffectual endeavours after a comprehension which should reconcile within its ample pale

the whole English people on the basis of a reasonable
Christianity.

The year 1632 was, throughout Western Europe as
well as in England, a stage in that memorable transition
from authoritative belief to free inquiry, which was
going on in the sixteenth and seventeenth centuries.
Bacon died six years, and Shakespeare sixteen years
before the August in which Locke was born, and
Richard Hooker had been a contemporary of Bacon and
Shakespeare. There was still in England the spiritual
freshness of the great Elizabethan age, with its remainder, too, of medieval philosophy and theology,
and its metaphysical poetry. Lord Herbert's 'De
Veritate,' in which long afterwards Locke was to find a
representation of the dogmatism assailed by him under
the name of "innate" knowledge, had appeared in
1625. In 1632, Descartes was pondering in Holland
the thoughts which afterwards, during Locke's boyhood
and youth, he was giving to the world. Hobbes, then
approaching fifty, was unknown as an author till about
the time when Locke was going to school. Of those,
moreover, who were to influence thought in Locke's
own lifetime and after, two entered life in the same
year that he did,—Richard Cumberland, one of the
least recognised of the really significant English moralists of the seventeenth century ; and Spinoza, whose
thoughts, overlooked or misunderstood by his contemporaries, more apt to be assimilated now, thus belongs
rather to the nineteenth than to either of the two preceding centuries.

Not much that explains his own individuality can
be traced back to Locke's Puritan ancestors, of whom

personally almost nothing is known. Of his mother,
Anne Keene, we have only this dim glimpse in Lady
Masham's memoranda : " What I remember Mr Locke
to have said of his mother, expressed her to be a very
pious woman and affectionate mother." It seems that
she died when her son was still a boy. The father,
who was a country attorney, survived her, and died in
1661,—by precept and example a considerable influence
in the formation of his son's character. " From Mr
Locke," Lady Masham says, " I have often heard of
his father that he was a man of parts. Mr Locke
never mentioned him but with great respect and affection. His father used a conduct towards him when
young that he often spoke of afterwards with great ap-
probation. It was the being severe to him, by keeping
him in much awe and at a distance when he was a boy,
but relaxing still by degrees of that severity as he grew
up to be a man, till, he being become capable of it, he
lived perfectly with him as a friend." Both parents
seem to have inherited the severe piety, prudent, self-
reliant industry, and love of liberty that were common
in English Puritan families of the middle class in the
seventeenth century. The family at Beluton was small.
Thomas, the only other child of the elder Locke and
Anne Keene, was born there in August 1637, bred
in his father's profession, married, and died of consumption childless in early life. The father and the
two sons formed the family when Locke was a boy.

The first fourteen years of the elder son's life were
years of home training in this rural Puritan household,
where the boy, according to his own report to Le Clerc,
was carefully schooled by the father. In peaceful times

he might have been sent in due season to the neighbouring grammar-school at Bristol. Perhaps the disturbed
state of Bristol at that time—first violently seized and
ruled by Cavaliers, then violently wrested from them
by Parliamentarians—may have confined young Locke
so long within the family life at Beluton, and limited
his social experiences in his first fourteen years to his
Somerset relatives and neighbours, in the country parishes
of Pensford, Publow, Sutton Wick, and Wrington.

Even home training must have been in many ways
interrupted in these troubled years, especially in this
little household. In August 1642, when the boy was
just ten years old, the Civil War broke out. The
elder Locke, then clerk to a neighbour justice of peace,
Francis Baker of Chew Magna, joined the army of the
Parliament, and was advanced by his neighbour, Colonel
Alexander Popham of Houdstreet, near Pensford, to be
a captain in the service, after he had publicly announced
in the parish church of Publow his assent to the protest
of the Long Parliament. The Pophams were among
the few Somerset gentry who took sides against the king.
After the first crisis of the war Colonel Popham represented Bath, and was well known among the political
leaders of the West.

Thus, from his tenth till his fourteenth year, we may
picture the youth living in the midst, of the exciting
drama in which his father was for a time an actor.
The Star-Chamber prosecutions, the Scottish war and
the Covenant of 1638, the opening of the Long Parliament in 1640, Edgehill, the surrender of Bristol to
Rupert, the trial and execution of Laud, Marston Moor,
and the final defeat at Naseby, were all within the

troubled years ; while Bristol, six miles away, was one of the headquarters of the war. We may conjecture, for we have no recorded facts, how the boy's mind opened at Beluton, in his father's frequent absences, amidst such surroundings. The elder Locke suffered so considerably in the Civil Wars that he left a smaller estate to his family than he had inherited, and he seems somehow to have returned to home life after less than two years of service.

Other than home training at Beluton followed at the end of four years of civil war. Through the influence of Colonel Popham, young Locke was in 1646 admitted to Westminster School, where he was kept during the next six years. The School, then under Puritan control, was at the headquarters of the Revolution. The political movement does not seem to have relaxed its traditional scholastic discipline, under the stern Dr Busby, its master at the time and long after. Locke's condemnation in later life of the verbal learning that was forced upon him at school, reveals his matured judgment of these Westminster experiences. But the influences at work during the years spent there, cannot have been wholly of the verbal pedagogic sort. There was something that he could not fail to derive from companionships ; perhaps still more from awe - inspiring public events. John Dryden and Robert South were both then at Westminster, but there is no sign of intimacy with them. William Godolphin (brother of Sydney), Thomas Blower (who became incumbent of a rural parish), Needham and Mapletoft (afterwards physicians), were his intimates, but none of them reached fame in later life. Then, during these Westminster years, the Assembly of Puritan

divines was debating knotty questions in Calvinistic
theology a few yards from the school in which Locke
was learning Latin.   A part of the boy's Westminster
experience, too, may have been as an eyewitness of the
tragedy on the memorable morning, in January 1649,
when Charles and Bishop Juxon walked together from
the palace of St James's to the palace of Whitehall, and
when, an hour after, in front of the banquet-room window, the streets and roof thronged with spectators, the
king's head was held up by the executioner, amidst the
groan of horror from the assembled crowd.

Less than four years after this tragedy, we find Locke
in Oxford.   At Whitsuntide 1652 he was elected to
a Junior Studentship in Christ Church, and he matric-
ulated in the following November.   He is designated
"generosus" in the register of Christ Church.   There-
after, for thirty years, Oxford was more or less his home.

When he entered Christ Church he found himself
under the well-known John Owen, the newly appointed
Puritan Dean, who was also Vice-Chancellor of the
University.   Cromwell himself had the year before succeeded the Earl of Pembroke as Chancellor.   Oxford
had ceased during the Civil War to be the august centre
of learning and spiritual influence in England.   At first
it had been the headquarters of the Cavalier army; and
when it surrendered to the Parliament in 1646, "there
was scarce the face of an university left," all things
being so out of order and disturbed.   Throughout
Locke's undergraduate life the Independents were dominant there.   In the persons of Owen and Goodwin,
unlike the Presbyterians, they were advocates of toleration, and among the first in England to recognise the

right of the individual to the free expression of his religious beliefs.

Faint light falls here and there upon Locke's undergraduate life in the city of colleges on the Isis, in the years when Cromwell was ruling England. There are no signs in his temperament or otherwise that either its external beauty or its historic glory touched his unimaginative mind. According to Anthony Wood, he was consigned to the care of "a fanatical tutor," a certain Thomas Cole, a pervert to Independency, who rose to be Principal of St Mary Hall. The Puritan revolution had not in Oxford more than in Westminster displaced the "verbal exercises," inherited from the past, which in the lapse of time had degenerated, according to an adversary of the scholastic discipline, into "childish sophistry." The reaction against this sophistry, which his whole life afterwards expressed, showed itself thus early in a strong disposition to rebel, in the interest of utilitarianism, against tradition and empty verbal disputes. According to his college friend James Tyrrell, he spent no more time than he could help at "the disputations"; for he never loved them, but was always wont to declaim against the practice, as one invented for "wrangling and ostentation rather than to discover truth." "I have often heard him say," Lady Masham records, "that he had so small satisfaction from his Oxford studies,—as finding very little light brought thereby to his understanding,— that he became discontented with his manner of life, and wished that his father had rather designed him for anything else than what he was there destined to." "I myself," says Le Clerc, "heard him complain of his early studies; and when I told him that I had a tutor who was a disciple of Descartes, and was a man of very clear intelligence, he said that he had not that good fortune (though it is well known he was not a Cartesian); and that he lost a great deal of time at the commencement of his studies, because the philosophy then known at Oxford was the Peripatetic, perplexed with obscure terms and useless questions." In Spence's 'Anecdotes,' it is told that he "spent a good part of his first year at the university in reading romances, from his aversion to the disputations then in fashion." This "discouragement," Lady Masham adds, "kept him from being any very hard student at the university, and put him upon seeking the company of pleasant and witty men, with whom he took great delight in corresponding by letters; —and in conversation and these correspondences, according to his own account of himself, he spent for some years much of his time."

It is perhaps not without meaning that the Oxford tutor whom Locke singled out for special regard, and with whom he afterwards lived in friendship, was Edward Pococke, professor of Hebrew and Arabic, the most prominent and outspoken Royalist in the university. This suggests a mitigation already of his inherited Puritanism, aided as such influence was by his often expressed revulsion from the intolerance of Presbyterians, and an unreasoning enthusiasm among the Independents, in the stormy time through which he had been living. The comprehensive spirit of the philosophical divines of the Church of England of the Cambridge school, probably conspired with these early influences when he was ripening into manhood. His Oxford friendships were at least as much amongst

Royalists and Churchmen as among Republicans and partisans of the sects. But, as at Westminster, none of his Oxford intimates ever reached a foremost place in learning or in public life. The friendship and correspondence of at least three of them followed him in after-years. One was Nathaniel Hodges, in due season a prebend of Norwich; another was David Thomas, later on a physician, first at Oxford and then at Salisbury; the third was James Tyrrell, son of Sir Thomas Tyrrell of Shotover, near Oxford, who became a barrister of some repute, as well as author of a 'History of England,' and of a 'Treatise in Public Law,' and who in old age expounded the ethics and political philosophy of Richard Cumberland.

Another Oxford influence must not be forgotten. Dr John Owen, the head of Christ Church, was at one with Milton and Jeremy Taylor in proclaiming and defending the then unrecognised religious duty of toleration. In 1649 Owen had abandoned his youthful Presbyterianism for Independency; and though freed from the danger of persecution, with his sect now in the ascendant, he was an exception to his own experience, of having failed to find any one earnestly contending for a toleration of Dissenters who was not himself at the time outside the establishment. To Owen's sermon on the death of the First Charles, to whom he certainly showed no toleration, there is appended a defence in which he argues that the magistrate has no right to interfere with the profession of any religion which does not expressly require its follower to disturb the social order. Of his own tolerant practice as Vice-Chancellor there is abundant evidence. The precept and example of Owen may

have had its influence on Locke, in inspiring his steady
support through life, by argument and example, of the
principle of a free toleration of discordant religious beliefs within the same State, as an indispensable condition
of the happiness of its members, of its own prosperity,
and of the advance of truth in the world.

The "new philosophy" of free inquiry determined
by experience, was then finding its way into Oxford
through books, if not through college lectures. Descartes,
Locke's great philosophical predecessor, died just before
Locke left Westminster,—the 'Method,' 'Meditations,'
and 'Principia' having issued from Holland when he
was a boy at Beluton; and Leibniz, his great philosophical contemporary and rival, was born in the year in
which he went to Westminster. Hobbes had produced
his 'Treatise on Human Nature' in 1642, and his
'Leviathan' in 1651. These books were followed a few
years later by Gassendi's exposition and defence of the
system of Epicurus. Cartesianism never took root in
Oxford, which remained faithful to the Aristotelianism
of the schools, till this was partly supplanted long after
by Locke's own writings; Cambridge alone encouraged
the new French philosophy. But the books of Descartes
and Hobbes, as well as Bacon's 'Advancement of Learning' and 'Novum Organum,' were directly or indirectly
affecting leading minds in England; and Locke afterwards acknowledged the influence of Descartes upon
himself. "The first books which gave him a relish for
philosophical things, as he has often told me," says Lady
Masham, "were those of Descartes. He was rejoiced in
reading these; for though he very often differed in opinion
from this writer, yet he found what he said was very

intelligible,—from which he was encouraged to think that his not having understood others had possibly not proceeded from a defect in his own understanding." This attraction of Locke to the lucidity of Descartes is characteristic of his disposition to revolt against empty verbalism and mystical enthusiasm. The Englishman found the mind of the Frenchman like a revelation from heaven, and an inspiration of intellectual liberty; —though he afterwards used the freedom in which Descartes had encouraged him by controverting many principles of Cartesian philosophy.

On the whole, we find that at the Restoration in 1660 the inherited Puritanism of the young student of Christ Church was in process of disintegration, under these manifold influences; his spirit was in revolt from the intolerance or the enthusiasm of the sects, and boldly in sympathy with the sober reasonableness which was the genuine outcome of masculine common-sense, wherever it could be found. This, we may infer, was partly the effect on a mind like his of the strange Oxford of the Commonwealth, and of Westminster during the "Great Rebellion." But after all, our direct and indirect means of knowing what Locke was and did, as well as his personal surroundings during these twenty-eight years of opening life, present only a faint and almost invisible picture.

CHAPTER II.

MEDICAL EXPERIMENTS, AND PROBLEMS IN SOCIAL
POLITY—A CAREER (1660-70).

In one of Locke's commonplace-books, towards the end
of 1660, he thus characteristically welcomes the Restoration, and treats with sarcasm the "liberalism" of the
sects :—

"I no sooner perceived myself in the world but I found
myself in a storm, which has lasted almost hitherto ; and
therefore cannot but entertain the approaches of a calm
with the greatest joy and satisfaction. This, methinks,
obliges me, both in duty and gratitude, to endeavour the
continuance of such a blessing by disposing men's minds
to obedience to that government which had brought with
it the quiet settlement which even our giddy folly had
put beyond the reach not only of our contrivance, but
hopes ; and I would men would be persuaded to be so
kind to their religion, their country, and themselves, as
not to hazard again the substantial blessings of peace and
settlement in an over-zealous contention about things
which they themselves confess to be little, and at most are
but indifferent.

"I find that a general freedom is but a general bondage ;
that the popular asserters of public liberty are the greatest

engrossers of it too, and not unjustly called its keepers.
I have not the same idea of liberty that some have, but can
think the benefit of it to consist in a liberty for men at
pleasure to adopt themselves children of God, and from
thence proclaim themselves heirs of this world ; not a
liberty for ambitious men to pull down well-framed constitutions, that out of the ruins they may build themselves
fortunes—not a liberty to be Christians so as not to be
subjects."

It is characteristic of Locke that he should prefer
liberty of individual thought to collective liberty of a
multitude or of a sect. For the collective power was
made then, as often before and since, an instrument to
crush the intellectual freedom of the individual.

He continued to live at Oxford, now restored to its
Royalist traditions, and with the Church once more
dominant. His academical and social position there
soon after the Restoration stands out pretty clearly.
He had taken his master's degree two years before
the return of the king. His tenure of the Junior
Studentship, which carried him from Westminster to
Christ Church, had ended in 1659 ; but his election
that year to a Senior Studentship, tenable for life,
fixed his connection with Oxford. Soon after he was
appointed lecturer in Greek and in rhetoric, and he
also held the censorship of moral philosophy for three
years after 1661—offices usually assigned to those in
holy orders. About this time, too, the little Somerset
property became his by inheritance ; for his father
died in February 1661, leaving to him the house at
Beluton, with the small domain around it (still called
"Locke's mead"), while the rest of his property went
to the other son Thomas.   The death of Thomas soon

after may have increased the share of the elder brother, so that a few years after his father's death Locke appears to have owned houses and land in and near Pensford, at an annual rent of nearly £80 ; corresponding to about £200 a-year now. Although I find no express record of visits to Beluton from the time he went to Westminster in 1646 till his father's death in 1661, his allusions to intercourse with his father, and other circumstances, imply that he was sometimes there, with less frequent visits perhaps after Beluton became his own. But he never forgot his native Somerset ; some of its friendships, as we shall see, lasted through life.

The modest income afforded by the Senior Student-ship, with other emoluments at Christ Church, supple-mented by the rents from Somerset, hardly formed a sufficient provision for the future, and Locke began about this time to look to some professional career. There is a surmise that he contemplated ecclesiastical life in the Anglican Church. His religious as well as his meta-physical disposition always attracted him to theology. His revulsion from Presbyterian dogmatism and Con-gregationalist fanaticism favoured friendly connection with latitudinarian Churchmen. Soon after the Re-storation, Whichcote, the Cambridge divine, was his favourite preacher, and in later life his closest intimacy was with the Cudworth family. But though Locke has a place among the lay theologians of England, his natu-ral dislike to ecclesiastical impediments to free inquiry, as well as a growing taste for experimental research among natural phenomena, directed him into another course. Some of his objections to accept ecclesiastical preferment are expressed in the following characteristic answer to an offer of advancement in the Irish Church, which seems to have reached him in 1666, after he had engaged in a different enterprise :—

"The proposals in question are very considerable ; but consider, a man's affairs and whole course of life are not to be changed in a moment, and one is not made fit for a calling in a day. I believe you think me too proud to undertake anything wherein I should acquit myself but unworthily. I am sure I cannot content myself with being undermost, possibly the middlemost of my profession ; and you will allow on consideration that care is to be taken not to engage in a calling wherein, if one chance to be a bungler, there is no retreat. . . . I cannot think that preferment of that nature should be thrown upon a man who has never given any proof of himself, nor ever tried the pulpit. . . . Should I put myself into orders, and by the meanness of my abilities grow unworthy such expectations (for you do not think that divines are now made, as formerly, by inspiration and on sudden, nor learning caused by laying on of hands), I unavoidably lose all my former study, and put myself into a calling that will not leave me. Were it a profession from which there were any return, you would find me with as great forwardness to embrace your proposals as I now acknowledge them with gratitude. The same considerations made me a long time reject very advantageous offers of several very considerable friends in England."

Locke was thirty-four when this letter was written. He had already felt the influence which, after the Restoration, was drawing England and many in Oxford to observation of the qualities and laws of matter, much animated by the utilitarian desire to enable men so to accommodate themselves to these qualities and laws as to increase their own physical comfort. "The year 1660," says Lord Macaulay, "is the era from which dates the ascendancy of the New Philosophy. In that year the Royal Society, destined to be the chief agent in a long series of glorious and salutary reforms, began to exist. In a few months experimental research became all the mode. The transfusion of blood, the ponderation of the air, the fixation of mercury, succeeded to that place which had been lately occupied by the controversies of the Rota. All classes were hurried along in the prevailing sentiments. Cavalier and Roundhead, Churchman and Puritan, were for once allied. All swelled the triumph of the Baconian philosophy." Scientific inquiry was indeed, both in England and on the Continent, taking the place which, for a century after the Reformation, theological controversies had held in the minds of men and in the main movement of history. It was at Oxford itself that the Royal Society was founded in the year of the Restoration. There Wallis and Wilkins, and afterwards Boyle and Wren, with Barrow and Newton at Cambridge, helped to substitute experiment in chemistry and meteorology and mechanics for the "vermiculate" questions of the schoolmen. In 1663 we find Locke an inquisitive student of chemistry. Anthony Wood, who could not fail to be an unsympathetic reporter, tells that he was himself a fellow-student with "John Locke of Christ Church, now a noted writer. This same John Locke," he adds, "was a man of a turbulent spirit, clamorous and discontented; while the rest of our club took notes deferentially from the mouth of the master, the said Locke scorned to do so, but was ever prating and troublesome." The ages of faith were passing away, and he was becoming the spokesman of the new questioning spirit.

In the course of the six years which followed the Restoration, Locke was gradually drawn to physical inquiry, and especially to medical experiments. His correspondence and commonplace -books in these years are filled with the results of chemical and meteorological observations. Meteorology attracted him all his life, and some of his observations were afterwards published in the 'Philosophical Transactions.' Boyle's 'History of the Air' contains Locke's "register of changes measured by the barometer, thermometer, and hygrometer, at Oxford, from June 1660 till March 1667." Observations of diseases, too, in their relations to the materia medica, abound in these manuscript memoranda of his Oxford life. And so it came about that before 1666 he was more or less engaged in a sort of amateur medical practice in Oxford, in partnership with his old friend Dr Thomas. Though he never graduated as a doctor, nor even as a bachelor in medicine till 1674, he was now and afterwards known among his friends as "Doctor Locke." But his professional connection with the faculty was always rather loose and uncertain. It may have been that the philosophic temperament made professional trammels and routine irksome, and that he instinctively preferred the hazards of freedom to submission to rules which might compromise the development of his individual genius. His health even now was constitutionally indifferent. He inherited a delicacy which ended in chronic consumption, with periodical attacks of asthma, against all which he contended through life with characteristic forethought and contrivance. To the end he was an amateur medical inquirer, and was ready upon occasion to advise his friends about their health, long after he had abandoned the idea of living by the practice of medicine. The habits thus formed must be taken into account in interpreting his later intellectual career. "No science," Dugald Stewart remarks, "could have been chosen more happily calculated than medicine to prepare such a mind as that of Locke for those speculations which have immortalised his name ; the complicated, fugitive, and often equivocal phenomena of disease requiring in the observer a far greater amount of discriminative sagacity than those of physics strictly so called, and resembling in this respect more nearly the phenomena about which metaphysics, ethics, and politics are conversant." Appreciation of such phenomena was at any rate in harmony with the method of investigation in philosophy which Locke afterwards adopted ; so that he was perhaps too much disposed to deal with the ultimate questions of human knowledge as if *they* also could be treated adequately by methods of matter-of-fact science, and in subordination to mechanical categories.

But the phenomena and laws of the material world, in their relation to the human organism, did not absorb all Locke's attention in these years. He early gave signs of strong human interest in the practical problems of politics and of the government and organisation of society. His commonplace-books between his twenty-eighth and thirty-fourth year throw welcome light on this bent of his thoughts and tastes. These records of his inner history during this part of his life contain characteristic revelations. Among them is a fragment on the " Roman Commonwealth," which shows how

soon ideas about civil and religious liberty, and the relation of the State to religion, were forming in his mind.
For example, the formation of the Roman State is attributed to a virtual if not an express compact among its
individual members; according to which, for the sake
of their common happiness, they surrendered their individual liberty to rulers who arranged a constitution
which, if it had been maintained according to its ideal,
would have been "the noblest as well as the most lasting limited monarchy that ever was seen in the world.
The generous principle of tolerating all religions in the
commonwealth," he continues, " was what above all else
fitted Numa's system to the chief design of government ;
for the rise and progress of Roman greatness was wholly
owing to the mighty confluence of people from all parts
of the world, with customs and ceremonies very different
from the Romans, who would never have settled without
an allowance of the free exercise of their religions. The
government of religion being in the hands of the State,
was a necessary cause of this liberty of conscience. For
there is scarce an instance in history of a persecution
raised by a free Government. A State that has the
command of the national conscience will never indulge
in persecution at the expense of the public good. The
religious institutions of Numa did not introduce into
the Roman religion any opinions inconsistent with the
divine nature ; nor did he require the belief of many
articles of faith, which create heresies and schisms in
the Church, and end in the ruin of religion. For if
schisms and heresies were traced to their original causes,
it would be found that they have sprung chiefly from
multiplying articles of faith, and narrowing the bottom

of religion, by clogging it with creeds and catechisms, and endless niceties above the essences, properties, and attributes of God. The common principles of religion all mankind agree in, and the belief of *these* doctrines a lawgiver may venture to enjoin ; but he must go no further if he means to preserve an uniformity of religion." The ideas partly of Hobbes and partly of the latitudinarian Churchman appear in sentences like these, rather than the dominant conceptions or language either of the Puritan or of the disciple of Laud. They are an interesting anticipation of some of Locke's teaching throughout his later life.

His early dislike to sac otalism comes out plainly in another fragment, headed "Sacerdos," in which the idea of a priesthood, whether in Rome or in Geneva, is described as the one widespread perversion of the original simplicity of Christianity. "There were," he says, "two sets of teachers among the ancients,—those who professed the arts of propitiation and atonement, who were their priests, and those called philosophers, who professed to instruct in the knowledge of things and the rules of virtue,—founded severally upon the supposition of two distinct originals of knowledge, namely, authoritative revelation and reason. The priests never for any of their ceremonies or forms of worship pleaded reason. The philosophers pretended to nothing but reason. Jesus Christ, bringing by revelation from heaven the true religion, reunited those two, religion and morality, as inseparable parts of the worship of God. Those ministers of Christianity, who call themselves priests, have assumed the parts both of the heathen priests and the heathen philosophers, which hath been the cause of more disorder, tumult, and bloodshed than all other causes put together; the cause of which hath been everywhere, that the clergy, as Christianity spread, laid claim to a priest-hood derived by succession from Christ, and so inde-pendent from the civil power." To reunite religion and morality through an exposition of the reasonableness of Christianity as a guide of conduct, in contrast to the magical power of a priesthood, was the chief enterprise of Locke in the closing years of his life.

The most remarkable of the commonplace-book revela-tions of those early Oxford years is entitled an 'Essay concerning Toleration.' It seems to have taken shape in his hands in 1666, and was first published by Mr Fox Bourne, who found it among the Shaftesbury papers. It anticipates positions for which Locke argued in his books nearly thirty years later, in defence of a social ideal which it was the chief aim of his life to see realised. This juvenile essay is partly a plea for wide ecclesias-tical comprehension in a national Church, by restoring Christianity to its original simplicity, and thus remov-ing reasonable grounds for nonconformity; and partly a vindication of this civil and ecclesiastical toleration, on account of the folly of persecution.

"What efficacy force and severity hath to alter the opinions of mankind, I desire no one to go further than his own bosom for an experiment to show whether ever violence gained anything upon his own opinion; whether even argu-ments managed with heat do not lose something of their efficacy, and have not made an opponent more obstinate—so chary is human nature to preserve the liberty of that part wherein lies the dignity of a man. . . . The introducing of opinions by force keeps people from closing with them, by giving men unavoidable jealousies that it is not truth that is cared for, but interest and dominion. But though force cannot master the opinions men have, nor plant new ones in their breasts, yet courtesy, friendship, and soft usage may. For men whose business or laziness keep them from examining take many of their opinions upon trust, but never take them from any man of whose knowledge, friendship, and sincerity they are not well assured—which it's impossible they should be of one that persecutes them. And inquisitive men, though they are not of another man's mind only because of his kindness, yet they are the more apt to search after reasons that may persuade them to be of his opinion whom they are obliged to love. He that differs with you in opinion is only so far at a distance from you ; but if you use him ill on account of that which he believes to be true, he is then at perfect enmity. Force and ill-usage will not only increase the animosity but the number of enemies ; for the fanatics, taken all together, being numerous, are yet crumbled into different parties amongst themselves, and are at as much distance from one another as from you ; their bare opinions are as inconsistent with one another as with the Church of England. People, therefore, that are so shattered into different sections are best secured by toleration ; since, being in as good condition under you as they can hope for under any, 'tis not like they should join to set up another whom they cannot be certain will use them so well. But if you persecute them, you make them all of one party and interest against you."

In these passages the policy is apparent which Locke would have recommended at a time when Acts of Uniformity were passed by those who had just worked out their own deliverance from the persecutions of fanatical sects. These thoughts regarding the folly of persecution and excommunication, as means for the advancement of truth in the minds of men, matured as his life advanced. Mainly through his influence they have now become part of the common-sense of mankind, although

the strength of the lower tendencies in human nature
makes reiteration of them expedient.

A prudential utilitarianism, ultimately resting on a
theological basis, which characterised Locke's ethical
philosophy, appears already in passages of the commonplace-book. His fundamental rule for testing human
conduct is there founded on the principle that " it is a
man's proper business in life to seek happiness and avoid
misery; happiness consisting in what delights the mind,
and misery in what disturbs and discontents it." But this
pursuit of happiness is not a pursuit of "whatever pleasure
offers itself." It is the preference of lasting pleasures to
short ones. Health, reputation, knowledge, the luxury
of doing good to others, and above all, the expectation
of eternal and incomprehensible happiness in another
life, are mentioned as " the five great and constant
pleasures " which we must steadily pursue. (This is a
scanty list of permanent pleasures. It takes no account,
for instance, of the pleasures of imagination in poetry,
music, and external nature.) The chief part of the art
of conducting life is " so to watch and examine that one
may not be deceived by the flattery of a present pleasure
to lose a greater." But the idea that there may be something higher than happiness, even as happiness is higher
than a transitory pleasure, is not even conceived by
Locke ; nor the faith that there is something which
may be ours in all circumstances, and which puts a new
meaning upon the most extreme physical suffering.

Locke's tutorial lectures, medical experiments, and
meditations on social polity, were unexpectedly varied
during the winter of 1665-66 by a temporary engage-

ment which took him away from Oxford for some months. For we find him suddenly employed in the diplomatic service, as secretary to Sir Walter Vane, who was an embassy to the Elector of Brandenberg at Cleve that winter. It was Locke's first introduction to life out of England, and to affairs other than local and academic. How the appointment came in his way, or why he accepted it, is not clear. He scarcely appears to have looked to it as a first step in a diplomatic career; at least, after his return from Cleve, in February 1666, he declined an offered appointment as secretary of the Spanish embassy—"pulled both ways by divers considerations," however, before he finally resolved. Then, after spending part of that spring among his relatives in Somerset, and with his friend Strachey at Sutton Court, we have him as before at Oxford. His letters to Strachey and to Boyle, from Cleve, contain shrewd and humorous observations on the Elector's Court, German manners, Lutheran, Calvinistic, and Catholic religious life.

It was in the summer after his return from Germany that an incident occurred which finally determined Locke's career, during middle life, in the direction of public affairs, admitting him into "the society of great wits and ambitious politicians," so that henceforward "he was often a man of business, and always a man of the world, without much undisturbed leisure." This change from amateur work at Oxford in the medical profession was due, as it happened, to one of his occasional engagements in the practice of medicine. Lady Masham thus repeats his own account of the most remarkable external event in his life :—

"My Lord Ashley (who became, a few years after, the first Lord Shaftesbury) designing to spend some days with his son at Oxford, had resolved at the same time to drink Astrof's medicinal waters there, and had, accordingly, writ to Dr Thomas to provide them against his coming. The doctor, being obliged to go out of town, could not do this himself, and requested his friend Mr Locke to take the care of getting the waters against my lord's coming. Mr Locke was in no way wanting in this case; but it so fell out, through some fault or misfortune of the messenger employed by him for this purpose, that my lord came to town, and the waters were not ready for his drinking them the next day, as he had designed to do. Mr Locke, much vexed at such a disappointment, and to excuse from the blame of it Dr Thomas, found himself obliged to wait upon my Lord Ashley, whom he had never before seen, to acquaint him how this had happened. My lord, in his wonted manner, received him very civilly, accepting his excuse with great easiness; and when Mr Locke would have taken his leave of him, would needs have him to stay supper with him, being much pleased, as it soon appeared, with his conversation. But if my lord was pleased with the company of Mr Locke, Mr Locke was yet more pleased with that of Lord Ashley. My lord, when Mr Locke took leave of him after supper, engaged him to dine with him the next day, which he willingly promised; and the waters having been provided against the day following, and Mr Locke having before had thoughts of drinking them himself, my lord would have him drink them with him, so that he might have the more of his company. When my lord went from Oxford, he went to Sunninghill, where he drank the waters some time; and having, before he left Oxford, made Mr Locke promise that he would come to him thither, Mr Locke within a few days followed him to Sunninghill. Soon after, my lord returning to London, desired Mr Locke that from that time he would look upon his house as his home, and that he would let him see him there in London as soon as he could."

This accidental meeting with Lord Ashley was the beginning of a lasting friendship, sustained by their common sympathy with civil, religious, and intellectual liberty. In the following year Locke exchanged his home at Christ Church for one at Exeter House, in the Strand, as medical adviser and confidential agent of this mysterious politician, and tutor to his son. Although he retained his Studentship at Christ Church, and sometimes visited Oxford and his little estate in Somerset, he shared fortune and home, during the fifteen following dark years, with the most remarkable man of affairs in Charles the Second's reign.

The change probably secured Locke against sundry "idols of the den," to which professional or even exclusively academic life is exposed. It trained him in habits of business, and brought him into personal intercourse with those who were at the springs of political action. His place as the confidential friend of the most sagacious and powerful statesman in England, could not fail to affect the growth of his own character. The demands of his new office do not seem at first to have interrupted his experiments in natural science, while the social experience, of which he fully availed himself, was all in the line of his previous inquiries. "Mr Locke grew so much in esteem with my grandfather," the third Lord Shaftesbury (author of the 'Characteristics') writes, "that, as great man as he experienced him in physic, he looked upon this as but his least part. He encouraged him to turn his thoughts another way ; nor would he suffer him to practise physic except in his own family, and as a kindness to some particular friend. He put him upon the study of the religious and civil

affairs of the nation, with whatsoever related to the
business of a minister of state; in which he was so
successful, that my grandfather soon began to use him
as a friend, and consult with him on all occasions of
that kind."

Among Locke's offices soon after he entered Exeter
House, was that of secretary to the founders of the
North American colony of Carolina, of whom Lord
Ashley was the most active. The curious scheme for
the government of that colony, of which a draft in
Locke's handwriting exists, dated June 1669, in the
preparation of which his advice must have had weight,
contains characteristic provisions when read in the light
of his earlier and later writings. "Religion," it is proposed to enact, "ought to alter nothing in any man's
civil estate or right. No person shall disturb, molest,
or persecute another for his speculative opinions in
religion, or his way of worship." At the same time,
"no man shall be permitted to be a freeman of Carolina,
or to have any estate or habitation within it, that doth
not acknowledge a God, and that God is publicly to be
worshipped;" but "any seven or more pastors agreeing
in any religion shall constitute a Church, to which they
shall give some name to distinguish it from others."
Words which record a conception of religious liberty to
which England was then unaccustomed.

Locke did not lose his interest in medicine, or his
love of natural science, when he came to live in London.
It happened that the year in which he was introduced
to Lord Ashley was the year after the Great Plague
in London. This supplied a motive to medical experiment. His new home introduced him to Sydenham,

with whom he continued in intimacy during the remaining twenty years of the life of the great London
physician. In these years at Exeter House he was in
the way of going to see remarkable cases in Sydenham's
practice, which provided the sagacious physician with
opportunities for penetrating the uncommon character
which Locke's modesty had hitherto concealed from
general view. "You know," Sydenham writes in the
dedication of his book on 'Fevers' to their common
friend Mapletoft,— "you know how thoroughly my
method is approved of by an intimate and common
friend of ours, and one who has closely and exhaustively
examined the subject—I mean Mr John Lock—a man
whom, in the acuteness of his judgment, and in the
simplicity, that is, in the excellence of his manners, I
confidently declare to have amongst the men of our
own time few equals and no superior."

The friend of Ashley and Sydenham, hitherto unknown except among a few intimates, was now about
to undertake the work which has made his name illustrious in Europe, in the history of philosophy and of
human progress.

CHAPTER III.

WE now approach the turning-point in Locke's intellectual career. Like his meeting with Lord Ashley, it was
due to an accident. One accident had already carried
him into the centre of public life and affairs; the other
was to carry him into philosophy, and into a philosophy largely determined by the interests of political life
and the struggle for liberty in the England of his own
generation.

In November 1668 Locke became a Fellow of the
Royal Society. In thus connecting himself with the
leaders of experimental research, he showed his sympathy with the spirit and methods of the mechanical
sciences. Soon after he was admitted, his name appears in a committee of eleven "for considering and
directing experiments;" but he took little part then
or afterwards in the proceedings of the Royal Society.
For he found more satisfaction in occasional reunions
of a few intimate friends which he helped to form
at different periods of his life. It was at one of
these informal meetings, probably at Exeter House, or
perhaps at Oxford, which he often visited, that Locke

was led to devote himself to that enterprise which directed the main current of his thoughts during the remainder of his life. To the results of that enterprise his reputation in the world is chiefly due; for it inaugurated the philosophy that was to remain dominant in Britain for more than a century after his death, and which, through further developments and by reactions against it, has so affected the thought of the world ever since, that the last two centuries might be termed the Lockian epoch in the intellectual history of Europe.

This memorable meeting took place on some unknown day, probably in the winter of 1670-71. Its outcome was the famous 'Essay concerning Human Understanding,' which was published nearly twenty years later. Here is Locke's own account of the circumstances, given in the "Epistle to the Reader" that is prefixed to the 'Essay':—

"Were it fit to trouble thee with the history of this Essay, I should tell thee that five or six friends, meeting at my chamber, and discoursing on a subject very remote from this, found themselves quickly at a stand by the difficulties that arose on every side. After we had a while puzzled ourselves, without coming any nearer a resolution of those doubts which perplexed us, it came into my thoughts that we took a wrong course, and that, before we set ourselves upon inquiries of that nature, it was necessary to examine our own abilities, and see what objects our understandings were or were not fitted to deal with. This I proposed to the company, who all readily assented; and thereupon it was agreed that this should be our first inquiry. Some hasty undigested thoughts, on a subject I had never before considered,[1] which I set down against our next meeting, gave

---

[1] Mr Fox Bourne quotes a fragment "in Locke's handwriting,"

the first entrance into this Discourse ; which, having been begun by chance, was continued by entreaty, written by incoherent parcels, and, after long intervals of neglect, returned again as my humour or occasions permitted ; and at last, in a retirement where an attendance on my health gave me leisure, it was brought into that order thou now seest it."

Locke himself does not tell what the "subject" was —"very remote" from an investigation into the resources and limits of a human understanding of the universe—which at this epoch-making meeting puzzled the assembled friends, and thus led Locke to make an essay in intellectual philosophy the chief work of his life. But we are not left quite in the dark. It so happens that James Tyrrell, one of the assembled "friends," has recorded it in a manuscript note on the margin of his own copy of the 'Essay,' now preserved in the British Museum. The "difficulties" which perplexed them arose, according to this record, in discussions regarding "the principles of morality and revealed religion." This was a subject not, after all, "very remote" from an inquiry into the extent of our human power of dealing intellectually with the universe ; rather one which, whether for intellectual satisfaction, or for relief from mysteries which may embarrass conduct, inevitably mixes itself with all profound ethical and theological inquiry. The logical or epistemological problems to which Locke now addressed himself, press for settlement, when we inquire into the ultimate

found in his father's memorandum-book, on "Philosophy," which seems to have been written before 1660. The contents show that philosophical inquiries of a very general kind were not quite new to him in 1670.

rationale of action, and the possibility of supernatural
revelation, more than perhaps in any other inquiry in
which man can engage. It may be that the result is
not the removal of mystery. Reflection upon the constitution and limits of human knowledge may discover
that the ultimate questions of ethical and religious
thought cannot be solved by the merely generalising
understanding, judging according to the data of sense.
To "solve," as Coleridge somewhere says, "has a scientific, and again a religious sense; and in the latter
a difficulty is satisfactorily solved, as soon as its in-
solubility for the human mind is proved and accounted for." Thought on these, as on all subjects, must
not, of course, be self-contradictory; and must also
be in harmony with those universal judgments of reason which our physical and our moral experience can
be shown to presuppose. Reason itself, moreover, forbids us to reject practical beliefs, hitherto permanent,
though often dormant in individual men, which are
found to meet wants in human nature, so long as
they are not proved to be inconsistent with the constitution of reason.

Locke tells his "reader," that when he "first put
pen to paper," in fulfilment of his promise, he thought
that "all he should have to say on the matter would
be contained within one sheet of paper," but that "the
further he went the larger prospect he had—new discoveries leading him on,"—till, in the course of years,
the work gradually "grew to the bulk it now appears
in.' The germ of the 'Essay' was in certain "hasty
and undigested thoughts set down against the next
meeting." The 'Commonplace-Book' contains a few

sentences, with the date 1671, which perhaps correspond to this original draft. At any rate they are worthy of being transcribed :—

"Sic cogitavit de Intellectu humano Johannes Locke, anno 1671.

"Intellectus humanus cum cognitionis certitudine et assensus firmitate.

"First, I imagine that all knowledge is founded on, and ultimately derives itself from Sense, or something analogous to it, and may be called Sensation ; which is done by our senses (organs of sense) conversant about particular objects, which gives us the simple ideas or images of things ; and thus we come to have ideas of heat and light, hard and soft, which are nothing but the reviving again in our mind the *imaginations* which these objects, when they affected our senses, caused in us—whether by motion or otherwise it matters not here to consider—and thus we do observe, conceive [*i.e,* have ideas of], heat or light, yellow or blue, sweet or bitter ; and therefore I think that those things which we call *sensible qualities* are the *simplest* ideas we have, and the *first* object of our understanding."

The philosophical enterprise in which Locke was thus led to engage, and in which the writing of this interesting fragment was probably the first step, was undertaken in a spirit, and by methods like those to which he had already become accustomed in natural science. He was thus led to look at a human understanding as a fact among other facts in the universe,—a fact supreme above others, it is true, the fact of facts indeed, which illuminated all others,—but still to be approached by solid calculating observation, and not in an *a priori* way. A human understanding of the universe, and the extent to which it could go, was for him something concrete, that had to be determined by what he might find. It was the kind and amount of contingent knowledge that is adapted to our actual human capacities for knowing things, not any abstract theory of knowledge or existence, or of the relation of the universe to a knowledge other than human, that Locke now set to work to report upon. It was a plain matter-of-fact inquiry about man ; not an *a priori* criticism of the rational constitution of knowledge as such, and of the metaphysical essence of things. Moreover, as his commonplace-books, and the whole tenor of the enterprise show, it was engaged in with the moral purpose of correcting certain prevailing intellectual faults and fallacies of mankind ; not in order to satisfy purely speculative curiosity, nor in any way to minister to the intellectual conceit that looks too high to be able to see the human facts of the case. Some of the prevailing evils, the removal of which was the end in his view, may be gathered from his commonplace-books about this time, and in the general tenor of his correspondence in the years when the 'Essay' was in progress, which all afford indispensable help in the interpretation of the great philosophical work of his life. Thus a fragment, 'De Arte Medica,' dated 1668, while it illustrates Locke's continued interest in the phenomena of disease and the functions of the human body, is even more important as evidence of the spirit in which he was at this time searching for truth, and of the tests which he was accustomed to employ :—

" He that in physics shall lay down fundamental questions, and from thence drawing consequences and raising disputes, shall reduce medicine into the regular form of a science (*totum teres, atque rotundum*), has indeed done something to

enlarge the art of talking, and perhaps laid a foundation
for endless disputes ; but if he hopes to bring men by such
a *system* to the knowledge of the infirmities of their own
bodies, or the constitution, changes, and history of diseases,
with the safe and discreet way of their cure, he takes much
what a like course with him that should walk up and down
in a thick wood, outgrown with briers and thorns, with a
design to take a view and draw a map of the country. . . .
The beginning and improvement of useful arts, and the
assistances of human life, have all sprung from industry and
observation. True knowledge grew first in the world by
experience and rational observations ; but proud man, not
content with that knowledge he was capable of, and which
was useful to him, would needs penetrate into the hidden
causes of things, lay down principles, and establish maxims
to himself about the operations of nature, and then vainly
expect that nature—or in truth God—should proceed according to those laws which *his* maxims had prescribed to him ;
whereas his narrow weak faculties could reach no further
than the observation and memory of some few facts produced
by visible external causes, but in a way utterly beyond the
reach of his apprehension ;—it being perhaps no absurdity to
think that this great and curious fabric of the world, the
workmanship of the Almighty, cannot be perfectly comprehended by any understanding but His that made it. Man,
still affecting something of Deity, laboured by his imagination
to supply what his observation and experience failed him
in ; and when he could not discover [by experience] the
principles, causes, and methods of nature's workmanship, he
would needs fashion all those out of his own thought, and
make a world to himself, framed and governed by his own
[narrow] intelligence. This vanity spread itself into many
useful parts of natural philosophy ; and by how much the
more it seemed subtle, sublime, and learned, by so much the
more it proved pernicious and hurtful—by hindering the
growth of practical knowledge. Thus the most acute and
ingenious part of man being, by custom and education, engaged in empty speculations, the improvement of useful arts

was left to the meaner sort of people. . . . Hence it came to pass that the world was filled with books and disputes ; books multiplied without the increase of knowledge ; the ages successively grew more learned, without becoming wiser and happier. . . . They that are studiously busy in the cultivating and adorning such dry, barren notions are vigorously employed to little purpose, and might with as much reason have retrimmed, now they are men, the babies they made when they were children, as exchanged them for those empty impracticable notions that are but the puppets of men's fancies and imaginations, which, however dressed up, are, after forty years' dandling, but puppets still, void of strength, use, or activity."

These words show the state of mind in which, two years after they were written, Locke proposed, by a matter-of-fact examination of human understanding, to guard men against errors, especially in morality and religion. He set to war against *a priori* abstract assumptions, and against the abuse of words void of meaning, yet protected under the assumption of their meaning being "innate,"—all in order to liberate the minds of men from this bondage ; to get them out of the "thick wood" of prejudice into the open day of actual facts and experience ; even although, at our human point for understanding the universe, the only possible scheme one could make of the whole might turn out to be, as Bacon says, "abrupt," and not a system. But we must not forget the crude empiricism of medicine in the seventeenth century in estimating the influence of his medical studies upon this undertaking.

Locke engaged in his intellectual enterprise at the point of extreme opposition to the medieval ideal of obedience to authority, and of system verbally consistent with itself, expressed in strictly defined terms. A hunger for facts,—for agreement between the ideas or laws that are in things and his own individual ideas,—which as nearly amounted to a passion for truth as was possible for his cool and considerate temperament,—was joined to a deep and modest conviction that he needed to bring about this agreement for himself in the exercise of his own reasoning insight, not in deference either to tradition or to contemporary opinion. This is the manly individualism that belongs to a representative Englishman, encouraged by institutions in Church and State favourable to personal freedom. In England, as Hume remarks, " the great liberty and independence which every man enjoys, allows him to display the manners peculiar to himself. Hence," he adds, " the English of any people in the universe have the least of a national character ; — unless this very singularity may pass for such."

The sources of Locke's philosophy are therefore to be looked for in himself, and in the unconscious influence of the age and country into which he was born ; not in an adoption of the philosophical opinions either of preceding or of contemporary thinkers. Of these, indeed, his constantly avowed indifference to such " learning " left him comparatively ignorant. Proper names seldom occur in his writings. They have this feature in common with the English philosophical literature of the epoch which he inaugurated—in remarkable contrast to the abundant references to authorities which one finds in books of the seventeenth and preceding centuries, as well as of the present generation. Hobbes, in a like spirit, is reported to have said, " that if he had read as many books as other men, he would have been as ignorant as they." But in other respects Locke and he had little in common. Although Hobbes, and Bacon too, are often represented as Locke's predecessors in the succession of "English empirical philosophers," they differed widely from one another, and from him, in their strongly marked individualities and in their conceptions of life. The sentiment of Hobbes, now referred to, would have been adopted by Locke, while it receives no countenance from the copious bibliographical allusions and quotations in which Bacon delights.

The sources of the 'Essay' and of Locke's philosophy are not to be sought in the books of his own or preceding generations, so much as in the reaction of his sagacious intelligence against the bondage of books, and his cool and independent observation of the facts of human nature. Among books, those of Descartes no doubt gave impulse, and encouraged his passion for thinking for himself; while the 'Port Royal Logic,' its plan, and its constant sympathy with life, is not to be forgotten in accounting for the plan and contents of the 'Essay.'

The "reality" for which Locke always hungers is that to which his early habits had accustomed him, and which he found in all the data of experience. He was like Bacon and Bacon's English successors at least in this; for he turned away with aversion from scholastic Aristotelianism, just because he saw in it security only for verbal consistency, and not for truth of fact. It seemed to him to encourage the two chief hindrances to the intellectual liberty of the individual, against which his whole life was a steady protest—empty verbalism and unverified assumption. It was with this aim that for seventeen years he maintained a cautious and considerate observation of his own understanding of things and that of other men; testing the significance of their words, which he often found to be void of ideas, and the grounds of their judgments, for many of which only blind submission to authority could be pleaded. The 'Essay concerning Human Understanding' was the issue of seventeen years lived in this state of mind,—often disturbed, indeed, by troubled politics and by ill health, so that the 'Essay' was "written in incoherent parcels, and after long intervals of neglect resumed again, as humour or occasions permitted." And average common-sense was always kept in his view. What he wrote was expressed for the most part in the language of the market-place. The terminology formed to express the subtle concepts of the schools was on principle avoided, although he indulged in some degree in a terminology of his own.

The ultimate problems of chief human interest with which philosophy is concerned, have to do severally with Matter, Man, and God. Each of these is so connected with the other, that while an individual philosopher puts one of the three in his foreground, it is found to be inseparable from the other two. The second, or rather one branch of it, was in Locke's foreground. The enterprise in which he now engaged was an attempt, for purposes of human life, to delineate the intellectual resources and capacity of Man.

CHAPTER IV.

PUBLIC AFFAIRS—RETIREMENT AND STUDY IN FRANCE
(1671-79).

SOME of those "intervals of neglect" which interrupted
from time to time the progress of that inquiry into the
nature and limits of a human understanding of the
universe, in which Locke now engaged, must have
occurred in the four years that followed the memorable
meeting of the "five or six friends at his chamber."
Early in 1672, Lord Ashley, risen in Court favour, after
filling for a short time the office of Chancellor of the
Exchequer, was created Earl of Shaftesbury, made
President of the Board of Trade, and in November,
Lord Chancellor of England. This accumulation of
official responsibilities brought Locke into still closer
relation with public affairs. The new Lord Chancellor
in that same year made him his secretary for the
presentation of benefices, with an annual salary of
£300 ; and in the following year he was advanced to
the Secretaryship of the Board of Trade, with an income
of £500. The records of the Board illustrate Locke's
diligence in the details of business, and his habit of
methodical administration. This official work was not

sustained without difficulty. The asthma from which he suffered so much in middle and more in later life, after previous premonitory symptoms, began to show itself decisively about this time; in consequence, a retreat to the south of Europe was contemplated even in 1671. In October of that year he wrote from Sutton Court in Somerset, expressing gratitude to his friend Dr Mapletoft for "concernment for my health, and the kindness wherewith you press my journey into France. I am making haste back again to London," he adds, "to return you my thanks for this and several other favours; and then, having made you judge of my state of health, desire your advice what you think best to be done;— since nothing will make me leave those friends I have in England, but the positive direction of some of those friends for my going. But however I may dispose of myself, I shall enjoy the air either of Hampstead Heath or Montpellier, as that wherein your care and friendship hath placed me."

The journey abroad "for his health" was not imperative in 1671. He was able for some years to do the work of secretary with exemplary exactness, until a turn occurred in political affairs which set him free to betake himself to some retirement, where attendance on health should give also leisure for study. In March 1675 Shaftesbury ceased to be Chancellor; after he had quarrelled with the Court, and put himself at the head of the Country party in Parliament. Locke had to quit office, but his patron and friend was not forgetful of his services. He endowed him with £100 a-year as a pension for life—"a relief," as he says, "to one now broken with business," and suffering more than ever from his chronic malady. The project of a visit to the south of Europe could now be carried out. So after seeing his friends in Somerset, he made his way into France in November 1675. The three following years were spent partly at Montpellier and partly in Paris, in a meditative quiet to which he had been a stranger for many years.

We have now for the first time in his life means for tracing his history almost from day to day, in the circumstantial record of them in his Journal. The chronological arrangement of his movements in France by this means comes out distinctly. About a month after he left London we find him at Montpellier, on Christmas Day in 1675. Montpellier—a resort in cases of consumption and the seat of a famous medical school—was Locke's home till April 1677, when he returned to Paris, where he lived till July 1678. In autumn of that year he returned to Montpellier, after an abortive attempt to visit Italy and Rome, which was barred against him by those snows of Mont Cenis, where "old winter kept guard," that were encountered by Berkeley on his way to Italy more than thirty years later. The following winter Locke spent in Paris. In April 1679 we find him in London, brought back on the eddy tide in public affairs which had carried Shaftesbury again into power.

The daily journal of Locke's life in France, which sometimes takes the form of a commonplace-book, contains sagacious observations regarding Frenchmen and their works, with vigilant and inquisitive investigation of natural phenomena. Medical experiments, too, combined with prudent study of his own health, often recall the Oxford professional pursuits of former days. But

the chief intellectual interest is its exhibition of the
inquiry into human understanding now in progress, for
one here sees the 'Essay' in process of formation.
During the first sixteen months in which Montpellier
was his home, Locke was busy revising and expanding notes for the 'Essay,' which had accumulated even
in the three or four previous busy years of official life
in England.   At Montpellier Thomas Herbert, afterwards Earl of Pembroke, to whom the 'Essay' is dedicated, happened to be his neighbour; and with him,
then and ever after, he was much in friendly intimacy.
Locke afterwards reminded him in the Dedication,
that the book, "grown up under your lordship's eye,
has ventured into the world by your order, and does
now, by a natural kind of right, come to your lordship for that protection which you several years since
promised it;" and then, according to the fashion of
dedications, he speaks of the results of his own seventeen years of search as having "some little correspondence with that nobler and vast system of the sciences
which your lordship has made so new, exact, and instructive a draft of."   This philosophic Lord Pembroke,
to whose friendship and encouragement Locke, thus and
otherwise, acknowledged his obligations, was afterwards
the patron and friend of Berkeley.   The 'Principles of
Human Knowledge,' as well as the 'Essay concerning
Human Understanding,' entered the world under his
protection.

Locke's least interrupted leisure and most exclusive
devotion to the preparation of the 'Essay' was probably
during these years in France.   His manuscripts at this
time show how much his mind was then engaged with

the multiplying problems which an answer to his own
question, propounded at the memorable meeting years
before, required him to deal with, and also discover
more fully the moral purpose that kept him so steadily
in quest of them. This revelation is full of instruction.
It helps to a more just interpretation of the 'Essay'
itself and of Locke's philosophy. Here is part of a
paper, begun in March and finished in May 1677, in
which Locke represents empty words and deference to
authority, as the two tempters that are apt to bewilder
men and lead them out of the way in the exercises of
the understanding :—

"First to be guarded against is all that maze of words
and phrases which have been invented and employed only
to instruct and amuse people in the art of disputing, which
will be found perhaps when looked into to have little or no
meaning ;—and with this kind of stuff the logics, physics,
ethics, metaphysics, and divinity of the schools are thought
by some to be too much filled. This, I am sure, that where
we leave distinctions without finding a difference in things ;
where we make variety of phrases, or think we furnish ourselves with arguments without a progress in the real knowledge of things, we only fill our heads with empty sounds.
Words are of no value or use but as they are the signs of
things ; when they stand for nothing they are less than
ciphers, for, instead of augmenting the value of those they
are joined with, they lessen and make it nothing ; and where
they have not a clear, distinct signification, they are like un-
usual or ill-made figures that confound our meaning. Words
are the great and almost only way of conveyance of one
man's thoughts to another man's understanding ; but when
a man thinks within himself it is better to lay them aside,
and have an immediate converse with the ideas of the things.
He that would call to mind his absent friend does it best by
reviving in his mind the idea of him, and contemplating

that ; and it is but a very faint, imperfect way of thinking of one's friend barely to remember his name, and think upon the sound he is usually called by."

Blind deference to other men's opinions, and consequent desire to know what these have been, with dogmatic assumption that this sort of knowledge is the most important part of learning, is the other vice in the exercise of a human understanding which, according to this revelation of his mind at work, loomed largely in his view :—

"Truth needs no recommendation," he continues, "and error is not mended by it. In our inquiry after knowledge, it as little concerns us what other men have thought, as it does one who has to go from Oxford to London to know what scholars walk quietly on foot inquiring the way and surveying the country as they went — who rode forth after their guide without minding the way he went—who were carried along muffled up in a load with their company, or where one doctor lost or walked out of his way, or where another stuck in the mire. If a traveller gets a knowledge of the right way, it is no matter whether he knows the infinite windings, byways, and turnings, where others have been misled; the knowledge of the right secures him from the wrong, and that is his great business. And so methinks it is in our intellectual pilgrimage through this world. It is an idle and useless thing to make it our business to study what have been other men's sentiments in things where reason only is the judge. I can no more know by another man's understanding than I can see by another man's eyes. Yet who is there that has not opinions planted in him by education time out of mind, which must not be questioned, but are looked on with reverence, as the standards of right and wrong, truth and falsehood ; where perhaps those so sacred opinions were but the oracles of the nursery, or the tradition and grave talk of those who pretend to inform our childhood, who receive them from hand to hand without

ever examining them ? . . . By these and perhaps other
means, opinions came to be settled and fixed in men's minds,
which, whether true or false, there they remain in reputation
as truths, and so are seldom questioned or examined by
those who entertain them ; and if they happen to be false,
as in most men the greatest part must necessarily be, they
put a man quite out of the way in the whole course of his
studies, which tend to nothing but the confounding of his
already received opinions. . . . These ancient preoccupations
of our minds are to be examined if we will make way for
truth, and put our minds in that freedom which belongs and
is necessary to them."

Locke finds that most men can hardly be said to think
or to have ideas at all, at least ideas of their own, on
any important subject. They profess the phrases which
they have been taught, without putting meaning into
them, either from laziness, or from fear to examine
critically words invested with sacred associations. The
desire to bring their individual thoughts into harmony
with things,—with the divine ideas, shall we say, of
which things are the manifestation,—in a word, the love
of truth, as distinguished from superstitious regard for
idealess phrases, is foreign to their habit.

Empty words, and dogmatic assumptions blindly
sustained by authority, are always present to Locke's
mind as the two chief obstructions to a human understanding of things. Both evils were encouraged, as it
seemed to him, by an oversight of the necessary limits
of human understanding, and of the immense disproportion between the universe and man's power of interpreting its phenomena. So men try to cross the gulf
by help of words that are really empty of meaning ;
aided by assumptions which, if not meaningless, are

at any rate without warrant in facts. This weakness or " disproportion " of human understanding is the one fact which Locke returns to again and again at this time. In a paper dated at Montpellier in February 1677, he writes :—

" Our minds are not made as large as truth, nor suited to the whole extent of things. Amongst the things that come within its reach, it meets with not a few that it is fain to give up as incomprehensible. It finds itself lost in the vast extent of space ; the least particle of matter puzzles it with an inconceivable divisibility ; and those who deny or question an eternal omniscient Spirit run themselves into a greater difficulty by making an eternal and unintelligent Matter. If all things must stand or fall by the measure of our understanding, and that be denied to be wherein *we* find inextricable difficulties, there will very little remain in the world, and we shall scarce leave ourselves so much as understanding, souls, or bodies. It will become us better to consider well our own weakness and exigencies, what we are made for, and what we are capable of ; and to apply the powers of our bodies and faculties of our souls, which are well suited to our condition, in the search of that natural and moral knowledge which, as it is not beyond our strength, so is not beside our purpose, but may be attained by moderate industry, and improved to our infinite advantage."

That the true end of any knowledge that is within the reach of man is wise action, and communication to others of what is found ; and that if we study only for the pleasure of knowing, this is rather amusement than serious business, and so to be reckoned among our idle recreations,—are favourite ideas of Locke, seldom long out of view, according to these memoranda of his studies at Montpellier and Paris :—

" The extent of things knowable is so vast, our duration

here is so short, and the entrance by which the knowledge of things gets into our understanding is so narrow, that the whole time of our life is not enough to acquaint us even with what we are capable of knowing, and which it would be not only convenient but very advantageous for us to know. . . . The essence of things, their first original, their secret way of working, and the whole extent of corporeal being, is as far beyond our capacity as it is beside our use. And we have no reason to complain that we do not know the nature of the sun or stars, and a thousand other speculations in nature; since, if we knew them, they would be of no solid advantage to us, nor help to make our lives the happier, they being but the useless employment of idle or over-curious brains. . . . All our business lies at home. Why should we think ourselves hardly dealt with that we are not furnished with compass and plummet to sail and fathom that restless, unnavigable ocean of the universal matter, motion, and space ? There are no commodities to be brought from thence serviceable to our use, nor that will better our condition. We need not be displeased that we have not knowledge enough to discover whether we have any neighbours or no in those large bulbs of matter that we see floating in the abyss, or of what kind they are, since we can never have any communication with them that might turn to our advantage. Man's mind and faculties were given him to procure him the happiness which this world is capable of ; so that had men no concernment but in this world, no apprehensions of any being after this life, they need trouble their heads with nothing but the history of nature, and an inquiry into the qualities of things, or the particular mansion of the universe which hath fallen to their lot. They need not perplex themselves about the original constitution of the universe."

Locke rises, however, out of this secularist conception of life :—

" It seems probable that there should be some better state

somewhere else to which men might arise ; since, when one
hath all that this world can afford, he is still unsatisfied.
It is certain that there is a possibility of another state when
this scene is over; and that the happiness and misery of that
depend on the ordering of ourselves in our actions in this
time of our probation here. The acknowledgment of a God
will easily lead any one to this conclusion. . . . It being
then at least probable that there is another life, wherein we
shall give an account of our past actions in this, here comes
in another, and that the main concernment of mankind—
to know what those actions are that he is to do, and what
those are he is to avoid. And in this part he is not so left
in the dark, but that he is furnished with principles of
knowledge, and faculties able to discover light enough to
guide him ;—his understanding seldom fails him in this part,
unless where his will would have it so. . . . We need no
other knowledge for the attainment of those two ends but
(1) of the effect and operation of natural bodies within our
power, and (2) of our duty in the management of our own
actions, as far as they depend on our will, and so are in our
power. Whilst, then, we have ability to improve our knowledge in experimental natural philosophy; and whilst we
want not principles wherein to establish moral rules, nor
light to distinguish good from bad actions (if we please to
make use of it),—we have no reason to complain if we meet
with difficulties in other things which confound our understanding ; for those, relating not to our happiness in any
way, are no part of our business, nor conformable to our
state or end as we find it."

The germ of the theological utilitarianism into which
Locke's ethical and political philosophy resolved itself
in the end, appears in expressions like these. He makes
the motives to right conduct depend at last upon the
fact of the Supreme Power connecting pleasures and
pains with human actions according to their kinds. We
are moved to action by an ideal of pleasure of body

or mind : the action is good or bad in proportion as the pleasure which it brings is lasting or evanescent. " That this is so, I appeal not only to the experience of all mankind, but to the best rule of this—the Scripture—which tells us that at the right hand of God are pleasures for evermore ; and that which men are condemned for is, not for seeking pleasure, but for preferring the momentary pleasures of this life to those joys which shall have no end." [1]

In these private records of his thoughts in his French retirement, while the ' Essay ' was in process of formation, Locke ever and anon expresses his profound sense of the fact that our state in this world is a state of intellectual mediocrity, dependent on probabilities ; that, in consequence, " if we were never in life to do but what is absolutely best, all our lives would go away in deliberation and distraction, and we should never come to action." " We are finite creatures, furnished with powers and faculties very well fitted to some purposes, but very disproportionate to the vast and unlimited extent of things." It is as if he had said,—" This, for us momentous fact, is as it is, and we cannot make it otherwise : things are what they are, and are not other things than they are ;—why, therefore, should one desire to be deceived ? "

" It would," he writes at Montpellier in March 1677, " be of great service to us to know how far in point of fact our faculties can reach, that some might not go about to fathom where our line is too short ; to know what things are the proper objects of our inquiries and understanding, and

---

[1] See also Lord King's ' Life,' vol. ii. pp. 161-185.

where it is we ought to stop and launch out no further, for fear of losing ourselves or our labour. This "—to which attempts to solve his new philosophical problem at last led him—" this, perhaps," he continues, " is an inquiry of as much difficulty as any we shall find in our way of know-ledge, and fit to be resolved by a man when he is come to the end of his study, and not to be proposed to one at his setting out ; it being properly the result to be expected after a long and diligent research to discover what is actually knowable, and where knowledge must stop ; not a question to be resolved by the guesses of one who has scarce yet acquainted himself with obvious truths. I shall therefore at present suspend the thoughts I have had upon this sub-ject, which ought maturely to be considered of—always re-membering that things infinite are too large for our capacity ; that the essences of substantial beings also are beyond our ken ; and the manner too how Nature, in this great machine of the world, produces the several phenomena, is what I think lies also out of the reach of our understanding. That which seems to me to be suited to the end of man, and lie level to his understanding, is (1) the improvement of natural experiments for the conveniences of this life, and (2) the way of ordering himself and his actions so as to attain happiness in the other—that is, moral philosophy, which in my sense comprehends religion too, or a man's whole duty."

Locke was pondering these things in France at a time when the intellectual revival, set agoing by Descartes, was in its strength. This was the golden age of French metaphysical philosophy. The highest spiritual expe-rience of men, rather than the transitory data of the senses, regulated the dominant philosophical conceptions. Pascal and Geulinx both died in the preceding decade ; Descartes died a few years earlier. The 'Recherche de la Vérité' of Malebranche made its appearance a few months before Locke went to Montpellier. The famous

controversy was beginning between Malebranche and
Arnauld. The 'Port Royal Logic' was in vogue, and
Nicole was issuing his 'Essais de Morale.' Three
years earlier Arnauld had been visited by Leibniz in
the course of that tour through Western Europe, in
which, after passing through London, the founder of
German philosophy went to see Spinoza at the Hague.
Spinoza himself died, and his 'Ethics' were published,
when Locke was at Montpellier.

We are not told that Locke met any of these remarkable men when he was in France, though their
names and some of their books were probably familiar
to him. Soon after his return to England he translated
the 'Essais' of Nicole, and later on he criticised Malebranche. The 'Port Royal Logic' was not without its
influence on the 'Essay' of Locke, if we may judge
from points of resemblance in structure and in doctrine.
But it was among representatives of natural science and
of medicine, not among the metaphysical philosophers,
that Locke was usually found in Paris. Bernier, the
pupil and expositor of Gassendi's mechanical philosophy,
is mentioned among his associates. His journal, and
his correspondence afterwards, imply frequent meetings
and friendly intercourse at Paris with Guenellon, the
Amsterdam physician; Nicolas Thoynard, the naturalist
and biblical critic; Justel, jurist and man of letters,
whose weekly reunions were then the fashion; Olaus
Römer, the young Danish astronomer; and Thuvenot,
the traveller, whose narratives of his wanderings grati-
fied a taste that was characteristic of Locke.

It is difficult to determine what progress had been
made with the 'Essay concerning Human Understand-

ing,' when its author returned to England in April 1679,
after these years of studious retirement in France.
Although he wrote to his friend Thoynard, a few weeks
after he got to London, that his " book was completed,"
he added, that he thought " too well of it to let it then
go out of his hands." It was held back in order that
more consideration might be given to the subject, and
the changes and additions afterwards made were the
occasion of frequent correspondence with his friends.
The extracts from his manuscripts in France already
given, express the general drift and main purpose of his
work at Montpellier and Paris. We see the intellectual
habits of the scientific physician more than the speculative philosopher in those revelations. The mind of man
is the subject of disease. Men are therefore ready to
accept empty sounds instead of ideas; to suppose that
they have ideas when they have none, or distinct ideas
when they are necessarily obscure. They are satisfied,
too, with accepting on authority what is said, without
inquiring and seeing for themselves; the human mind
is thus clouded by presuppositions which obscure the
light of facts. Attention and independent judgment
are avoided as fatiguing; and to say anything that demands reflection is putting people quite out of their way.
Empty abstractions and dogmatic assumptions afflict the
human understanding. Both seemed to Locke to be due
to oversight of the fact that " we are here in a state of
mediocrity," and that our understanding is " disproportionate " to the infinite extent of things. Men were
vainly trying to reduce the disproportion, and to ease
themselves of the pains and patience which conformity
to fact imposes, by keeping in circulation idealess words,

and by building on presuppositions that have no warrant
in experience. It is only in having ideas or meanings
in our words that we come to be in a capacity for
having any knowledge; so that the first step to knowledge is to get the mind furnished with such meanings
as it really has a capacity for. Of what sort are they?
how reached? To what extent are ideas that we can
have perfect, and in what cases must they remain obscure — so that they are in the one case avenues to
certainty, and in the other incapable of carrying us beyond faith and probability? To cure diseases of the
human understanding,—especially the two now mentioned,—with a view to its healthy exercise in life, not
to solve abstract problems of knowing and being, was
evidently the aim of Locke when his ' Essay ' was in
process of formation in France.

CHAPTER V.

ENGLISH POLITICS AND POLITICAL EXILE IN HOLLAND
(1679-89).

WHEN Locke returned to London in the spring of 1679, he found that Lord Shaftesbury had. exchanged Exeter House in the Strand for Thanet House in Aldersgate. "In spite of the attraction which had, during a long course of years anterior to 1685, gradually drawn the aristocracy westward in London, a few men of high rank," according to Lord Macaulay, "continued to dwell in the vicinity of the Exchange and of the Guildhall. Shaftesbury and Buckingham, while engaged in bitter and unscrupulous opposition to the Government, had thought that they could no longer carry on their intrigues so conveniently or so securely as under the protection of the city magistrates and the city militia. Shaftesbury therefore lived in Aldersgate, in a house which may still be easily known by pilasters and wreaths, the graceful work of Inigo Jones."[1] It was life in serene retirement in sunny France that Locke now exchanged for the clouded political atmosphere of London in the last years of Charles's reign. His life was now to be more than ever

[1] Macaulay, vol. i. p. 278.

mixed up with the history of the England that was
hastening to revolution on a troubled sea of politics.
The prospect did not attract him. "From Paris to
this place," he wrote to his friend Thoynard from
Calais on his way back, "I have been as miserable as
possible at the loss I endured in leaving you ; discontented with my journey, with Calais, with myself, and
with everything, deriving no pleasure from the prospects
of returning to my native land."

He had left England when the "pensioned Parliament," chosen in 1661, was still sitting. During his
absence Shaftesbury had been imprisoned in the Tower.
From the spring of 1675 till the spring of 1678 Lord
Danby's policy was in the ascendant. A brief crisis followed, a sort of prelude to the Revolution which was accomplished ten years later. The new Parliament, which
met in March 1679, showed a want of confidence in
the king. England was awaking to its danger on the
side of France and of Rome. The king, accordingly,
turned for a time to the popular party ; and Shaftesbury as its leader became President of the Council, a
few days before Locke returned to England. He held
office only till the following October. The succession
to the throne was becoming the great question of practical politics. The House of Commons resolved, on the
motion of Hampden, that "the Duke of York's being a
Papist, and the hopes of his coming such to the crown,
has given the greatest countenance and encouragement
to the present conspiracies and designs of the Papists
against the Protestant religion." An Exclusion Bill,
"to disable the Duke of York to inherit the crown of
England," was read a second time and supported by

Shaftesbury, who advocated the claims of Monmouth in opposition to those of the Prince of Orange, already put forward by leading politicians. The royal support was in these circumstances withdrawn from the popular leaders, who had been called to office but not really to Court favour, for a few months in 1679. Throughout this crisis Locke was at the right hand of Shaftesbury. He was overwhelmed with work at Thanet House. It was a time of plots and counter-plots, when England seemed about to plunge into another civil war. Another Parliament was called in 1680, and dissolved early in the following year, followed by one which met at Oxford in March, and was dissolved in the same month —the last of Charles's reign. In the summer of 1681 Shaftesbury was again in the Tower, charged with treason, tried in November, and acquitted. He was welcomed back with popular enthusiasm. He employed his restored liberty in support of the Duke of Monmouth for the succession, but without his former prudence. "All through the summer of 1682 he was plotting for an insurrection" with the zeal of a partisan, in spite of the advice and example of Locke and other considerate politicians. The arrest of Monmouth, in September 1682, paralysed his policy. In November, after hiding for some days at Wapping, he made his way to Harwich, disguised as a Presbyterian minister, and thence escaped to Holland. He died at Amsterdam on the 31st January 1683.

Locke's movements during this disturbed time may be thus outlined :—During the six months of Shaftesbury's administration in 1679, his hands were full at Thanet House, but not so as to forbid intercourse with old friends and a visit to Essex. In the following winter, the political change making his stay at Thanet House less important, with a return of indifferent health, the result of life in London, he made his way to his old home at Christ Church, and then to Somerset. The spring and summer of 1680 saw him much at Thanet House, or with Lord Shaftesbury at his country seat of St Giles in Dorset, indulging in hopes, which were disappointed, of a visit to Paris. In the winter of 1680-81 we can follow him to Shotover, the home of his old college friend James Tyrrell, and thence to Oxford to the meeting of the short Oxford Parliament, where he stayed till June, throughout "the dryest spring that hath been known." Of that summer he spent some weeks in London, and may have been at Thanet House in July, when Shaftesbury was arrested. Soon after he returned to Oxford, which was his headquarters for months,—though it seems he was in London in November, at the time of the trial and acquittal of his patron, and again in the following January, seeing his pupil "Mr Anthony" (the Lord Shaftesbury of the 'Characteristics'). It was then and there that the news of the first lord's death in Holland reached him; he was soon after one of the mourners at the funeral at St Giles's. His movements in 1683 are more obscure. He was now suspected and watched as the friend and adviser of the exiled lord; but there is evidence that Shaftesbury's rash policy in his last years got no encouragement from Locke's prudence and philosophic moderation, and that he had nothing to do with the later intrigues. In March 1682, Prideaux had reported from Oxford that "John Locke was living a very cunning, unintelligible life, being two days in town and three out," and that "no one knows where he goes, or when he goes, or when he returns." A year after this, the Dean of Christ Church, as visitor, in a letter to Lord Sunderland, "confidently affirms that there is not any one in the college, however familiar with him, who has heard him speak a word against, or so much as concerning the Government; and although very frequently, both in public and in private, discourses have been purposely introduced to the disparagement of his master the Earl of Shaftesbury, his party and designs, he could never be provoked to take any notice, or discover in word or look the least concern; so that I believe there is not in the world such a master of taciturnity and passion. He has here a physician's place, which frees him from the exercise of the college."

Some light now comes from the Nynehead Collection of Locke's unpublished correspondence, upon details of his history in these darkest years of Charles II.'s reign. The earliest letters in this interesting collection were written in 1681. It consists largely of friendly domestic communications between Locke and the family of his friend Edward Clarke of Chipley in Somerset, thenceforward till the close of his life. There are letters from Locke to Clarke, when Locke was visiting in Somerset, and the Clarkes were staying in London— addressed to "Edward Clarke," or "Mrs Clarke, at the Lady King's, Salisbury Court, near Fleet Street;" or, when Locke was in town, from him, at "Salisbury Court," to "Edward Clarke, Esq. of Chipley, to be left at the post-house of Taunton," when Clarke was on some

home visit about county affairs. This interchange between London and Oxford and Chipley is frequent in
1682 and the early part of 1683. The correspondence
shows a growing intimacy of Locke with the family of
Dr Ralph Cudworth, the great Cambridge Platonist and
philosophising divine of the Anglican Church in the
seventeenth century. Like Locke himself, Cudworth
was a native of Somerset, and thus intimate with the
Clarkes, with whom Mrs Cudworth was often living at
their town house in " Salisbury Court, near Fleet Street."
The letters from the Clarkes to Locke contain almost
always allusions to the Cudworths, and kindly greet-
ings; and Locke's letters end with his "humble service
to Mrs Cudworth and the rest of your good company."
The Anglican divine and philosopher himself does not
figure in the scene, and Locke's relations to him can
only be inferred. Cudworth was then in his recluse,
studious life at Cambridge. His great work, ' The Intellectual System of the Universe, or Confutation of the
Reason and Philosophy of Atheism,' had been published
in 1678, when Locke was in France. It would be interesting, and not without historical meaning, if Locke
had communication with this most learned of English
philosophers, who represented Plato and Plotinus instead
of either Bacon or Hobbes. We find instead only a
letter from Locke to Thomas Cudworth the son, then
in India, written in April 1683 (the last trace, by the
way, of Locke in London for nearly six years after it
was written). He introduced himself to the son on the
score of intimacy with the family, in a characteristic
letter, full of inquisitiveness about men and manners
in the East :—

" And now," he concludes, "having been thus free with you, 'tis vain to make apologies for it. If you allow your sister to dispose of your friendship, you will not take it amiss that I have looked upon myself as in possession of what she has bestowed upon me, or that I begin my conversation with you with a freedom and familiarity suitable to an established amity and acquaintance. If at this distance we should set out according to the forms of ceremony, our correspondence would proceed with a more grave and serene pace than the treaties of princes, and we must spend years in the preliminaries. He that in his first address should only put off his hat and make a leg, and cry, 'Your servant' to a man at the other end of the world, may, if the winds set right, and the ships come home safe, and bring back the return of his compliment—may, in two or three years perhaps, attain to something that looks like the beginning of an acquaintance, and by the next jubilee there may be hopes of some conversation between them. Sir, you see what a blunt fellow your sister has recommended to you, as far removed from the ceremonies of the Eastern people you are amongst as from their country."

Members of the Cudworth family, and in particular this "sister," reappear later on in Locke's life, and are associated with him to the end. This was the beginning of the friendship.

The story of Locke's thoughts and studies in the four years which followed his return to France is to be traced partly in his correspondence, chiefly in the journal and commonplace-books. His pursuits recall the medical years at Oxford before he met Shaftesbury, as much as that pathological investigation of human understanding which so much occupied his time in France. The Bishop of Oxford, in the letter to Lord Sunderland, referred to Locke's having "a physician's place " at Christ Church. Broken health, as well as the sudden diversion of his life to public affairs in 1667, had withdrawn him in a measure from medicine, but not entirely. Mr Fox Bourne has illustrated the continued activity of this factor in his experience after his return from France. Before he had been a month in England, and amidst the engrossments of the political crisis of that eventful summer, the journal describes medical cases in town and country; and the personal intercourse with Sydenham, interrupted by his stay abroad, was resumed.

While the intellectual habits of the physician of the body were thus sustained, they were still transferred to the diseases of the body politic and of the human understanding. Questions of social polity and the conflict of parties in England kept his attention directed to the relations of Church and State. Here is something, in a paper on "the difference between civil and ecclesiastical power,"—written, perhaps, before he went to France,—which bears traces of his Puritan education :—

"From the twofold concernment men have to attain a twofold happiness—that of this world and that of the other ; there arises these two following Societies—Civil Society or the State, and Religious Society or the Church. The end of Civil Society is the preservation of the Society and every member thereof in a free and peaceable enjoyment of all the good things of this life that belong to each of them ; but beyond the concernments of this life this Society hath nothing to do at all. The end of Religious Society is the attaining happiness after this life in another world. The terms of communion with either Society is promise of obedience to the laws of it [contract]. . . . The means to preserve obedience to the laws of Civil Society, and thereby preserve it, is force or punishment—that is, abridgment of one's share of the good things of the world, and sometimes total deprivation, as in capital punishments. The means to preserve obedience to the laws of the Religious Society or Church are the hopes and fears of happiness and misery in another world. Though the penalties annexed are of another world, yet the Society being in this world, there are means necessary for its preservation here—the expulsion of such members as obey not the laws of it. . . . The laws of a commonwealth are mutable, being made within the Society itself : the laws of the Religious Society (bating those which are only subservient to the order necessary to their execution) are immutable, not subject to the authority of the Society, but made by a lawgiver without it, and paramount to it. The proper means to procure obedience to the law of the Civil Society, and thereby attain civil happiness, is [physical] force or punishment. The proper enforcement of obedience to the laws of the Religious Society is the rewards and punishments of another world ; but not by civil punishment, which is ineffectual for that purpose, — and it is, besides, unjust that I should be despoiled of my good things of this world, where I disturb not the enjoyment of others ; for my faith or religious worship hurts not any concernment of his. . . . In all Civil Society one man's good is involved with another's ; in Religious Society every man's concerns are separate, and if he err he errs at his own private cost, only for the propagation of the truth, which every religious society believes to be its own religion ; it is equity that it should remove those evils which will hinder its propagation —disturbance within and infamy without—and the proper way to do this is to exclude and disown such members. Church membership is voluntary, and may end wherever any one pleases without any prejudice to himself; but in Civil Society it is not so."

Locke then describes various possible and actual relations between these two great organisations of mankind, —the one, as he conceived it, immediately concerned with this world, and the other with a coming world. As "almost all mankind are combined into civil societies in various forms," and as there are "very few also that have not some religion," it comes to pass that almost all are members at once of some commonwealth and of some Church; but with mutual relations that are different in different countries. Thus "in Muscovy the civil and religious societies are *coextended*, every member of the same commonwealth being also a member of the same Church. In Spain and Italy, the commonwealth, though all of one religion, is but *a part of the one Catholic religious society*. In England, on the contrary, the public established religion, not being received by all the members of the commonwealth, and the religion of the rest of the people being different from that of "the governing part of the civil society, each religious society is only *a part of the commonwealth*. As to penal laws, if any differ from the Church in faith or worship, the magistrate must punish him for it where he is fully persuaded that it will disturb the civil peace ; otherwise not. But the religious society may excommunicate him ; and this power of being judges who are fit to be of their society, the magistrate cannot deny to any religious society which is permitted within his dominions." This acute separation of the civil from the ecclesiastical society appears less in Locke's later ideas on the subject.

In 1680, Stillingfleet, then Dean of St Paul's, published a discourse on "the Mischief of Separation," in which he argued the disastrous consequences to Christianity of the separation of sects from the main body of the visible Church in any nation ; and pressed the exclusive claim of the Church of England, in virtue of

its episcopally transmitted ministerial mission, by which
visible ecclesiastical unity is sustained. Replies from
leading Nonconformists were met by Stillingfleet with
an elaborate rejoinder on 'The Unreasonableness of
Separation.' The controversy touched principles that
were settled in Locke's mind by long reflection; but
apparently for his own satisfaction he prepared a tract,
entitled 'A Defence of Non-Conformity,' which he never
published. It is a plea for compromise and toleration,
as opposed to the exclusive claim of the Church of
England, or any other religious society, to the submission of Englishmen, and above all, for the independence of individual judgment in such matters. He
writes as himself a member of the National Church,
" but from a heart truly charitable to all pious and
sincere Christians." He claims a rightful liberty for all
to choose what Church or religious society, or whether
any, each will be of, as each may find most conducive
to his personal salvation, "of which he is sole judge,
and over which the magistrate has no power." The
history of the first planting of Christianity in the
world gives no countenance, he maintains, to the exclusive claim of any National Church to determine
doctrine, ritual, and worship for all. To preserve its
comprehensive nationality, endangered in the altered
sentiment of the age by an elaborate ceremonial which
offended the Nonconformists, the Church, he argued,
should accommodate its services to the varieties of taste
and feeling.

"The taking away of as many as possible of our present
ceremonies may be as proper a way now to bring the Dissenters into the communion of our Church, as the retaining

as many of them as could be was of making converts at the Reformation. So that what was then for the enlargement, now tends to the narrowing of our Church. Since Dissenters may be gained and the Church enlarged by parting with a few things which, when the law which enjoins them is taken away, are acknowledged to be indifferent, and therefore may still be used by those that like them, I ask whether it be not a duty incumbent on those who have a care for men's souls to bring members into the union of the Church, and so to put an end to the guilt they are charged and lie under of error and schism and division, when they can do it at so cheap a rate ? "

Locke's plea for an elastic and comprehensive ritual and creed would probably have met with little sympathy from the extremes either of Church or Dissent; and his principle led him in these circumstances to stand out for the right of men to form themselves into independent religious societies, organised in any way which did not interfere with the liberties of others. In fact, visible Churches seem to have been in his view accidents of religion, and not part of its essence, which lay in personal faith and conduct, and might flourish under any ecclesiastical organisation, or even apart from all organised religious society. The revelations of his mind about this time show an indifference to questions on which theological disputants lay stress that is hardly consistent with exclusive connection with any organised body of Christians, notwithstanding a gravitation towards the Church of England, as the communion in which the freedom that he supremely loved could most easily be found.

It was thus that Locke regarded the controversies which he found raging around him in England after his return from France. But he had not forgotten his great philosophical enterprise. Thus the following significant sentences occur in his journal, in June 1681, regarding knowledge and probability, and the relation between our knowledge of things and our ideas :—

" All general knowledge is founded only upon true ideas, and so far as we have these we are capable of demonstration on certain knowledge ; for he that has the true idea of a circle or triangle, is capable of knowing any demonstration concerning these figures ; but if he have not the true idea of a scalenus, he cannot know anything concerning it, though he may have some confused or imperfect opinion, upon a confused or imperfect idea of it ; but this is belief, and not knowledge. . . . The first great step, therefore, to knowledge, is to get the mind furnished with true ideas ; and the mind being capable of thus knowing moral things as well as figures, I cannot but think morality as well as mathematics capable of demonstration, if men would employ their understanding to think more about it, and not give themselves up to the lazy traditional way of talking one after another. The knowledge of natural bodies and their operation, on the other hand, reaching little further than bare matter of fact, without our having perfect ideas of the ways and manners they are produced, nor the concurrent causes they depend on ; and also the well management of public or private affairs, depending upon the various and unknown humours, interests, and capacity of man, and not upon any settled ideas of things,—it follows that Physics, Polity, and Prudence are not capable of demonstration, but a man is principally helped in them by the history of matter of fact, and a sagacity of inquiring into probable causes and finding out an analogy in their operations and effects. Knowledge, then, depends upon right and true ideas ; opinion upon history and matter of fact. Hence it comes to pass that our knowledges of general things are *æternæ veritates,* and depend not upon the existence or accidents of thing ; for the truths of mathematics and morality are certain, whether men make true mathematical figures, or suit their actions to the rules of morality or no. For that the three angles of a triangle are equal to two right ones is infallibly true, whether there be any such figure as a triangle actually existing in the world or no. And it is true that it is every one's duty to be just, whether there be any such thing as a just man in the world or no. But whether this particular course in public or in private affairs will succeed well, whether rhubarb will purge or quinquina cure an ague, is only known by experience; and therefore is but probably grounded upon experience or analogical reasoning, but is no certain knowledge or demonstration." [1]

The 'Essay on Human Understanding' must have been well thought out by its author when these sentences, which express its main drift, were written by him. It was becoming in Locke's mind an investigation into our ideas of things; on the ground that if we have no ideas or thoughts about a thing, that thing is for us non-existent—our knowledge consisting in our having those ideas which conform (may we say?) to the ideas that are in nature; while those things of which we have imperfect ideas are only matters of belief or opinion; subsiding into doubt or even ignorance as the ideas are more obscure, or at last disappear in unconsciousness, which means absence of all ideas.

That the 'Essay' had, some time before 1683, taken, so far, the form in which it was at last published, may be inferred from what is told of Lord Shaftesbury: "One of his attendants, in his last hours in Holland, recommended to him the confession of his faith and the examination of his conscience. The Earl answered him,

[1] King, ii. p. 24.

and talked all over Arianism and Socinianism; which
notions he confessed he had imbibed from Mr Locke
and his tenth chapter of Human Understanding."
The reference is probably to the tenth chapter of the
Fourth Book of the 'Essay,' regarding the foundation
of theism, which Lord Shaftesbury must therefore have
seen in manuscript before he fled to Holland.

The 'Essay' was not the only work in which Locke
was employed amidst the troubles of these years. The
tendency of the political current, and a defence by Sir
Robert Filmer of the divine right of kings, directed his
thoughts to the first principles of government; and the
defence of the utilitarian theory of government, some
years afterwards published in the 'Treatises on Government,' was probably written in part in the interval
between his return from France and his return to the
Continent.

We trace Locke in Somerset in the summer of 1683,
but the movements are obscure. According to Lady
Masham's report, "the times now growing troublesome to those of my Lord Shaftesbury's principles,
and more especially dangerous for such as had been
intimate with him, Mr Locke with reason apprehended
himself not to be very safe in England; for though
he knew there was no just matter of accusation against
him, yet it was not unlikely, as things then were,
but that he might have come to be questioned; and
should he under any pretence have been put under
confinement, though for not very long time, yet such
was the state of his health that his life must have been
thereby much endangered." With his customary prudence, accordingly, he prepared for voluntary exile.

Among the Nynehead manuscripts there is a document entitled an " Arrangement of the affairs of John Locke of Beluton, in the parish of Stanton Drewe, Somerset; also an inventory of other property in the parishes of Stanton Drewe, St Thomas in Pensford, and Publow." This was no doubt in prospect of his leaving England, for it is dated 14th August 1683. After that he goes out of sight for a time, but in the end of that same year he suddenly reappears in Holland. Then there are letters from Holland in large numbers, the earliest dated in November, full of affection, giving the idea of a man of tender feelings, yearning for the society of his friends, on whom exile sat heavily. In these letters the little Somerset property, and the domestic affairs of his friend Clarke, are often referred to, as well as Clarke's infant child Betty, who found her way to his heart as she grew older, and of whom he thus early writes, " I love her mightily." There is also well-considered advice about the training of Clarke's son, the substance of which was afterwards given to the world in the " Thoughts concerning Education."

Holland was then the asylum in Europe for those who failed elsewhere to find religious and civil liberty. Descartes and Spinoza had meditated there some years before, and at a still earlier period it was the home of Erasmus and Grotius. In 1683 it was the refuge of Bayle, who lived at Rotterdam; and many of the English political exiles were in other parts of the Netherlands. It was Locke's sanctuary for more than five years after that gloomy autumn of 1683. He at first betook himself to Amsterdam, where he found a home and family life in the house of Dr Peter Guenellon, the friend of his old Paris days. There, too, he formed a lasting friendship with Philip von Limborch, the leader of liberal theology in Holland, successor of Episcopius as Remonstrant professor of theology, lucid and learned, the friend of Cudworth, Whichcote, and More, about his own age, with whom he corresponded largely during the remainder of his life. Their mutual influence deepened and enlarged Locke's ideas of religious liberty and liberal theology, and their names must always be associated. Limborch's society did much to soothe the pain of exile, so that Locke found in Holland that "retirement" which he had lost since he quitted France, and in which "attendance on his health" was no obstacle to the completion of the intellectual enterprise undertaken fourteen years before.

Locke was not long stationary at Amsterdam. His own curiosity, and the political suspicion which drove him from England, kept him in motion in Holland. In 1684 he made a prolonged tour of observation, and then spent some time at Leyden, so long the home of Descartes. The holiday did him good; and in November he wrote to Thoynard at Paris that he "had not for many years past felt better." Lady Masham says that in Holland, "enjoying better health than he had for a long time done in England or even in the fine air of Montpellier, he had full leisure to prosecute his thoughts on the subject of 'Human Understanding,' a work which in all probability he would never have finished had he continued in England." He betook himself to Utrecht during the winter of 1684-85, to have more leisure and better opportunities for thought and a milder climate. There he settled himself in December, "with all the

books and other luggage that I brought from England."
But he was not undisturbed even in this retirement.
The Earl of Sunderland, the Secretary of State, on the
6th of November 1684, wrote to Fell, Bishop of Oxford,
then Dean of Christ Church, that Charles II. " being
given to understand that one Mr Locke, who belonged to
the Earl of Shaftesbury, and has upon several occasions
behaved himself very factiously and undutifully to the
Government, is a Student of Christ Church, his Majesty
commands me to signify to your lordship that he would
have him removed from being a Student." In a few
days the Bishop replied, that "His Majesty's command
for the expulsion of Mr Locke from the college was fully
executed." He was thus suddenly and without a trial
deprived of what had been an Oxford home for thirty-
two years, and of the emoluments which belonged to it.
It cannot, indeed, be said that he was expelled from the
university, but only that Bishop Fell, in obedience to the
king's command, withdrew from him his Studentship at
Christ Church. Lady Masham mentions that she had
herself heard a friend of the Bishop say that "nothing
had ever happened which had troubled him more than
what he had been obliged to do against Mr Locke, for
whom he ever had a sincere respect, and whom he believed to be of as irreproachable manners and inoffensive
conversation as was in the world." Mr Locke, she adds,
had not been gone abroad "above a year, when he was
accused of having writ some libellous pamphlets which
were supposed to have come over from Holland, but have
since been known to have been writ by others. This
was the only reason that I have ever heard assigned of
his Majesty sending to Dr Fell, the Bishop of Oxford

and Dean of Christ Church, to expel Mr Locke that house immediately." Not even to this extent had he as yet given his thoughts on any subject to the world. "It is a very odd thing," he writes to Lord Pembroke in December 1684, "that I did get the reputation of no small writer without having done anything for it; for I think two or three copies of verses of mine, published without my name to them, have not gained me that reputation. Bating these, I do solemnly protest in the presence of God that I am not the author, not only of any libel, but not any pamphlet or treatise whatever, good, bad, or indifferent." [1]

His loss of the Studentship, which left him with only the little Somerset property and his annuity from Shaftesbury, was not the only inconvenience which Locke suffered from the political troubles of the time. The death of Charles II. led to the Duke of Monmouth's insurrection, and that to his execution, after his defeat at Sedgemoor, in July 1685. The suspicion that Locke was somehow concerned in this insurrection brought him at once into danger of arrest. His name was put in a list of eighty-four dangerous Englishmen in Holland, alleged to be plotting against the life of King James, whose persons were demanded to be given up to the English Government. For weeks he was in hiding at Amsterdam, in that summer, in the house of Veen, Guenellon's father-in-law, and his correspon-

---

[1] This reference is to two copies of verses contributed by Locke to a volume of poems in praise of Cromwell, brought out by Dr Owen so early as 1654, in which many members of the university shared. It is curious that Locke's first appearance in print should have been as a writer of verses, and the verses, as might be expected, contain little poetry.

dence with his friends in England was for a time maintained in cipher. In September he went for more secure concealment to his Continental home of twenty years before, at Cleve, to return soon to his former retreat at Amsterdam, where, for concealment, he took for a time the name of "Dr Van der Linden." With the year 1685 the danger passed away.

At Cleve we find him working at the 'Essay.' "I wish," he wrote to Limborch in October, "that the book I am preparing were in such a language that you might correct its faults; you would find plenty of matter in it to criticise." About this time he was also writing the Latin letter to Limborch on "the mutual toleration of Christians in their different professions of religion," which made its appearance in print four years later.

That winter introduced a new friend to Locke, whose influence was memorable, as through him he first appeared as an author. This was Le Clerc, then the youthful representative of letters and philosophy in Limborch's College, who had, a year or two before, escaped from his birthplace at Geneva, and from Calvinism, into the milder ecclesiastical atmosphere of Holland. The 'Bibliotheque Universelle,' commenced under Le Clerc's management in 1686, soon became the chief literary organ in Europe. Locke was early associated with him in the work, and contributed several articles in that and the following year. Though he was now fifty-four years of age, and afterwards author of so many bulky volumes, these three or four anonymous articles were his first prose performances in print. This tardiness means much. It agrees with the prudent and

cautious temper, massive common-sense, and repressed
enthusiasm which belong to his character—in contrast
to the eager impetuosity which hurried Spinoza or
Berkeley or Hume to produce their bolder and more
subtle speculations in the morning of life. Locke was
almost sixty before the world received the thoughts
which long observation of men and affairs, and much
patient consideration, had been gradually forming in his
mind. The occasional articles in Le Clerc's journal prepared the way. The last of these was an epitome in
French of the forthcoming 'Essay concerning Human
Understanding,' contained in the 'Bibliotheque' of January 1688.

Locke had meantime removed to Rotterdam, where
he lived for more than a year in the family of a Quaker
friend, the wealthy Dutch merchant and book-collector,
Benjamin Furley, whose friendship he owed to Edward
Clarke of Chipley. The course of English politics was
now opening a way for his return to his native country.
At Rotterdam he was the cautious confidant of other
English political exiles, especially Burnet, afterwards
Bishop of Salisbury, and Mordaunt, in the end the
renowned Earl of Peterborough, and even William of
Orange himself. The scene suddenly changes. William
landed in England in November 1688; Locke followed
in February 1689, in the fleet which carried the Princess to Greenwich. In that month the Prince and
Princess were proclaimed joint sovereigns, and the political struggle which had been going on for half a
century was consummated in the Revolution, of which
Locke was to be the philosophical defender, and, though
as yet unknown to popular fame, the intellectual repre-

sentative. The England in which he found himself in the spring of 1689 was politically a very different England from the one he left under Charles II., in the gloomy autumn of 1683. He returned to play his part in philosophical authorship, with London for a time as the stage of operations.

SECOND PART.

THE PHILOSOPHY: EXPOSITION AND CRITICISM
(1689-91).

CHAPTER I.

LONDON : PUBLICATION.

"Mr Locke," says Lady Masham, "continued for more than two years after the Revolution much in London, enjoying no doubt all the pleasure there that any one can find, who, after being long in a manner banished from his country, unexpectedly returning to it, was himself more generally esteemed and respected than ever he was before. If he had any dissatisfaction in this time, it could only be, I suppose, from the ill success now and then of our public affairs; for his private circumstances were as happy, I believe, as he wished them, and all people of worth had that value for him that I think I may say he might have what friends he pleased. But of all the contentments that he then received, there was none greater than that of spending one day every week with my Lord Pembroke, in a conversation undisturbed by such as could not bear a part in the best entertainments of rational minds— free discourse concerning useful truths. His old enemy, the town air, did indeed sometimes make war upon his lungs ; but the kindness of the now Earl of Peterborough and his lady, who both of them always expressed much esteem and friendship for Mr Locke, afforded him so pleasing an accommodation on those occasions at a house of theirs near the town (at Parson's Green), advantaged with a delightful garden, 'which was what Mr Locke always took pleasure in, that he had scarce cause to regret the necessity he was there under of a short absence from London."

It was during these two years that Locke, late in life, suddenly emerged through authorship into European fame. On his return from Holland in February 1689, he went to live in hired apartments in the house of Mrs Smithsby, Dorset Court, Channel Row, Westminster. This was his headquarters till the beginning of 1691. "Dorset Court," from which the 'Essay concerning Human Understanding' is dated, has long since disappeared ; but "Channel Row" probably corresponds to what is now called Cannon Row. It was near the centre of affairs, and within easy reach of his political friends. It was a stirring time in English politics. During the last year of his stay in Holland, he had been an unobtrusive but influential agent in the preparations for the Revolution. Accordingly, within a few days after his return to London, the high office of ambassador to Frederick, the new Elector of Brandenburg, and founder of the future kingdom of Prussia, was offered to him by King William. The obligation to decline this offer, he says in a letter to Lord Mordaunt, was "the most touching displeasure I have ever received from that weak and broken constitution of my health which has so long threatened my life, and which now affords me not a body suitable to my mind in so desirable an occasion of serving his Majesty in—the post one of the busiest and most important in Europe — at a season when there is not a moment of time lost without endangering the Protestant and English interest throughout Europe, all which makes me dread the thought that my weak constitution should in so considerable a post clog his Majesty's affairs. If I have reason to apprehend the cold air of the country, there is yet another thing that is as inconsistent with my constitution, and that is their warm drinking. Obstinate refusal in that would be but to take more care of my own health than of the king's business. The knowing what others are doing would be at least one half of my business; and I know no such rack in the world to draw out men's thoughts as a well-managed bottle. If there be anything wherein I may flatter myself I have attained any degree of capacity to serve his Majesty, it is in some little knowledge I may have in the constitution of my country, the temper of my countrymen, and the divisions among them, whereby I persuade myself I may be more useful to him at home." At home, accordingly, he remained. In May, three months after his return from Holland, he accepted instead of the Embassy a Commissionership of Appeals, "a place," as Lady Masham explains, "honourable enough for any gentleman, though of no greater value than £200 per annum, and suitable to Mr Locke on account that it required but little attendance." So

we have him settled at Mrs Smithsby's, immersed in the
work of the press and in politics, with this modest
addition to the little patrimony in Somerset and the
Shaftesbury pension.

The "divisions" among his countrymen which then
perplexed home politics occupied much of Locke's time
for at least a year after his return. "I have hardly had
a moment of leisure since I arrived," he wrote to Limborch in March, "in the worry I have had in hunting
up and collecting my scattered goods for immediate use,
and in the many claims that have been made upon me
by the urgent pressure of public business." The matters
in practical politics which chiefly interested him then
and afterwards are thus mentioned: "In Parliament
the question of Toleration has begun to be discussed
under two designations—Comprehension and Indulgence.
By the first is meant a wide expansion of the Church, so
as, by abolishing a number of obnoxious ceremonies, to
induce a great many Dissenters to conform. By the
other is meant the allowance of civil rights to all who,
in spite of the broadening of the National Church, are
still unwilling or unable to become members of it."

These two objects had already engaged Locke much in
early and middle life. They continued to determine his
course of thought and his public action as long as he
lived. But the press, rather than direct influence over
legislation, was now to be his chief instrument in bringing
public opinion to favour social toleration of the exercise
and expression of individual judgment.

The Toleration Act of 1690 fell short of his ideal
of the liberty due by the State to those who dissent
from the National Church. The Comprehension Bill, in-

tended to enable the Establishment to absorb dissent, was withdrawn; partly on account of the exclusive claims of the Church, and the inability of ecclesiastics to see the unique position which the Church of England might come to occupy in Christendom by a generous and comprehensive statesmanship.

It was in the course of these two transition years in Dorset Court that Locke offered to the world in books the results of his study of human understanding, and of those principles of religious liberty and social polity which successful search for truth by the finite mind of man presupposes. His philosophy—political and intellectual, the political rooted in the intellectual—is contained in three books which had been prepared chiefly in France and Holland, but also amidst the interruptions to study in England in the years immediately before his exile. They were all given to the world in 1689 and 1690, when he was living in London.

The first to appear was the 'Epistola de Tolerantia,' written in Latin in 1685, and addressed to his Dutch friend Limborch. It had been published anonymously at Gouda in Holland, a few weeks after its author returned to London, as a philosophical argument for the religious liberty of the individual. The substance of the argument had been in his mind, and found its way into his manuscripts, in the long-past days in Oxford, even before he had become associated with Shaftesbury in their common warfare with the foes of freedom. The characteristic title-page ingeniously conceals and yet reveals the author. It runs thus:—'Epistola de Tolerantia; ad Clarissimum Virum T. A. R. P. T. O. L. A.

scripta a P. A. P. O. I. L. A." The first series of
these mystical letters stands for — "Theologiæ apud
Remonstrantes Professorem, Tyrannidis Osorem, Lim-
burgium, Amstelodamensem," to whom the 'Epistola'
was addressed ; while the second series represents its
author — " Pacis Amico, Persecutionis Osore, Joanne
Lockio, Anglo." Locke's prudential caution, sometimes,
perhaps, approaching to timidity, made him anxious to
preserve the secret of authorship, which was known to
Limborch alone when the little volume was published
early in 1689. The secret intrusted by Locke to his
friend was the occasion of a characteristic incident.
Limborch, in a moment of weakness, was induced to
discover the secret to Guenellon, and also to Dr Veen,
Guenellon's father-in-law, in whose house at Amsterdam
the 'Epistola' was written. He confessed his weakness
in one of his letters to Locke, who was less easily propi-
tiated than his friend had expected, for this revelation
produced a strong remonstrance and a transitory coolness.
It was only in his last Will that Locke himself acknowledged the authorship.

The 'Epistola de Tolerantia' soon attracted attention.
It was translated into English by William Popple—a
Unitarian merchant, author of the 'National Catechism'
—in the year in which it was published at Gouda ;
and the translation appeared in London in 1689, and
again "corrected" in 1690. Excepting his contributions to Le Clerc's 'Bibliothèque' when he was in Holland, it was the earliest published of Locke's prose writings. The argument could not at that time escape hostile
criticism, although its own influence has now made its
paradoxical teaching commonplace. A few weeks after

Popple's translation was published in London, a tract issued from Oxford, entitled, ' The Argument of the Letter concerning Toleration briefly Considered and Answered.' According to Anthony Wood, its author was Jonas Proast, of Queen's College, elsewhere mentioned as an archdeacon. This attack at once involved Locke in controversy. He published a second anonymous 'Letter on Toleration' as a rejoinder, towards the end of 1689. Another critique of the 'Epistola,' by a certain Thomas Long, soon followed, entitled, ' The Letter for Toleration decyphered, and the Absurdity and Impiety of an Absolute Toleration demonstrated, by the judgment of Presbyterians, Independents, and by Mr Calvin, Mr Baxter, and the Parliament of 1662.'

Within a year after his return to London, Locke presented to the world a philosophical defence of the English Revolution, under the title of 'Two Treatises on Government.' In one of them the "false principles and foundations" of Sir Robert Filmer's arguments for the divine right of kings are analysed and redargued; the other is an examination of the true nature, origin, and end of civil government. Like the 'Letter on Toleration,' this too was anonymous, and also, like the 'Letter,' it was a vindication, in another relation, of the freedom and rights of the individual. The 'Letter' vindicates individualism in religious opinion as against legislative obstructions; and the 'Treatises' vindicate individualism in civil affairs, and the rights of majorities to govern the State. The author seems to have carried the manuscript of the 'First Treatise' to and from Holland; it was probably prepared in England, during the troubles which followed the downfall of Shaftes-

bury's last Administration. In the preface he describes
the 'Two Treatises' as only "the beginning and the
end" of a "projected Discourse" concerning government, "fate having otherwise disposed of the papers
that should have filled in the middle, and which were
more than all the rest." But the fragments which he
offered at last were, he hoped, "sufficient to establish
the throne of our great Restorer, King William, to make
good his title in the consent of the people, the only one
of all lawful governments."

The 'Essay concerning Human Understanding' was
delivered to the world almost simultaneously with the
'Two Treatises on Government.' It expressed the
philosophy that was latent in the 'Treatises' and in
the 'Epistola.' It was Locke's long-considered answer
to the pregnant question which he had proposed to his
friends at their memorable meeting nearly twenty years
before. Part of it must have been sent to the printers
soon after he arrived in London. The "Epistle dedica-
tory" to the Earl of Pembroke is dated from Dorset
Court in May 1689. All that year his letters and journals
show that his time was much given to superintending
the press. In August he tells Limborch that all are so
busy about politics that there is a "dearth of books,"
but that he is submitting his "treatise 'De Intellectu'
to the criticism of those friends who are weak enough
to read it :" adding that already he had sent the first of
the four books into which it was divided, in proof to
Le Clerc. On the 3d of December he hoped that the
last sheet of the 'Essay' would that day be in type.
"If it comes to be translated into Latin, I fear you will
find many faults in it. I sent Mr Le Clerc the second

and third books as well as I can recollect in September. I shall send him the rest very soon. As soon as I receive the proof of the table of contents, I shall write to him."

A few months after this, in March 1690, the long-looked-for 'Essay' was in circulation, with the author's name appended to the dedication. It was his first public acknowledgment of authorship. He received £30 for the copyright, about the same sum as Kant received, ninety-one years after, for his 'Kritik of Pure Reason,'—the philosophical complement to the 'Essay.' These two great works are the fountains of the philosophy of our epoch, the one dominating philosophical thought in the eighteenth, and the other, partly by reaction, in the nineteenth century.

CHAPTER II.

THE PHILOSOPHY IN THE 'EPISTOLA' AND IN THE 'TWO TREATISES'—RELIGIOUS AND CIVIL LIBERTY.

THE three books in which Locke's philosophy was published, within a year after his return from Holland to London, were in intention practical more than speculative. They were meant to help men to right conduct, especially intellectual conduct,—not to satisfy abstract metaphysical curiosity. Like all that he published, they were books for the times, weapons constructed for defending the free action of reason in men, in an age in which their persons were in danger of persecution through pressure of ecclesiastical or civil government. Moreover, to those then becoming intellectually awake, man's power of understanding the world in which he lived seemed to have been too long wasted in empty verbal reasonings, and his liberty of thinking to be still crushed by inherited traditions. Locke's three books, produced in these two London years, after much consideration and varied experience of life, agreed in encouraging resistance to "masters or teachers who take men off the use of their own judgment, and put them upon believing and taking upon trust without further examination."

That each man should be *himself* intellectually, and be
able to see things as things are, with the eyes of his
own mind, and not merely through the eyes of others,
is the principle on which he invariably falls back in
all of them. The sense of human individuality, developed in Locke in even extreme reaction against the
pressure of the past, and along with this his ruling idea
of the rightful supremacy of reasonableness in everything,
made it the chief duty of his life to show what constitutes reasonableness. This is the key to his defence
of free toleration for the expression of individual belief,
and to his whole conception of civil government. His
lessons of religious and civil liberty are sustained
philosophically by what he found in the course of a
prolonged analysis of the ideas of a human understanding, and the limits of our knowledge. The 'Epistola
de Tolerantia' is an argumentative defence of the religious liberty of the individual. The book on 'Government' is a vindication of the rights of individuals, as
members of the body politic, to govern the State of
which they are members in the way most fitted to
secure individual happiness. And the 'Essay concerning the Human Understanding' may be interpreted as
the intellectual philosophy that is presupposed in human
liberty,—in the form of a logical analysis of the complex
and abstract ideas which man is capable of having ; the
source and extent of the knowledge or certainties that
he can reach within the sphere of his ideas ; and the
nature and grounds of those presumptions of probability
by which, in lack of absolute certainty, our conduct has
to be regulated. The arguments and views of life which
run through these treatises were urgent in a generation

which was above all engaged in the great modern
struggle against verbalism and the dead weight of dogmatic authority.　The 'Essay' expressed the intellectual
groundwork of the whole.　All the three illustrate, each
in its own way, the strong English common‑sense of
a considerate politician, who sought, by their means, to
resist encroachments upon private judgment, out of love
for truth, which is "the seed-plot of all the virtues," according to their author.

The 'Epistola de Tolerantia' has been called the most
original of all Locke's works.　This opinion may appear
doubtful now, when its own success has made its arguments and conclusions commonplace.　What when Locke
wrote was a paradox, which had to work its way into
the minds of men through innumerable obstructions, is
the very intellectual air we breathe, so that the super-
abundant argument and irony of this famous plea for
liberty is apt to weary those who now try to follow its
ramifications.

Yet the "toleration" for which Locke argued,—the
idea which was the mainspring of his life from youth
onwards,—then implied a complete revolution in the
previously received view of human knowledge and
belief.　It carried in it elements of revulsion from the
dogmatic or absolute point of view that was characteristic of medievalism, while it was in harmony with the
critical and relative point of view that, even when
Locke lived, was becoming the distinctive mark of
the modern spirit, — represented by Luther and the
Protestants in religious life, and by Montaigne and
Descartes, Campanella and Bacon, in speculative philosophy.　Free toleration implied a protest against those

who, in theological and other inquiries, demand absolute certainty in questions where balanced probability alone is within reach of a human intelligence. The practice of universal toleration amidst increasing religious differences, in the room which it gives for the exercise of understanding by each person, free from everything except the reasonable restraints of experience, was perhaps at the time the most important practical application of that answer to his own memorable question, about the extent of man's knowledge of the universe, which had been forming in Locke's mind amidst the busy political life of the twenty years before he returned from Holland.

The freedom of religious opinion from political restraints, which Locke argued for, was not entirely a novelty. It had been already defended, upon various grounds, in the seventeenth century. The idea was then entering into the air. Chillingworth, Jeremy Taylor, Glanville, and other philosophical divines of the Church of England, argued for a large toleration by the State, as well as for a generous comprehension on the part of the National Church; on the ground of the natural limits and inevitable weakness of the profoundest merely human understanding of the universe, especially when men's attempts to interpret things carry them into the region of religious thought. Puritans like Owen and Goodwin, on the other hand, whose idea of ecclesiastical comprehension was narrow and dogmatic, defended liberty of different religions within the same nation; while they objected, on grounds of orthodoxy, and as members of separatist communities, to a wide comprehension within their respective sects.

The ideal of liberal Anglican Churchmen was that of
one Church, coextensive at least with the nation, if
not even with Christendom.   Locke himself, exclusively
attached on principle to no one religious organisation,
while desirous to be in charitable sympathy with all
who loved truth and lived for righteousness in each,—
who had for his ideal the simple or practical Christianity
of the synoptic gospels, and the ecclesiastical liberty of
the apostolic age, as he interpreted it,—brought the test
of a sagacious and experienced intelligence to a question
which had been largely one either of academic discussion
or of sectarian controversy.   The intellectual freedom
of each person, under whatever civil or ecclesiastical
institutions, was his ideal, rather than the collective
liberty of societies ; for he saw that societies, whether
Churches or States, often use their collective liberty to
crush persons and their independent judgment.   The
idea of the State, however, which Locke favoured in
some of his earlier unpublished writings, was not the
Aristotelian, or that which has for its end the education
of the entire man by one social organism.   It was rather
that of the Puritans, which divides the entire man and
a. full human life, between the State on the one hand
and the Church on the other.   In Locke's sober utilitarian imagination and severely argumentative mind, it
must be confessed, too, that the idea of toleration lost
some of the poetic beauty or philosophic grandeur which
it received from Jeremy Taylor and Milton.   But it was
Locke who first adapted it to the wants of practical
statesmen, and by his luminous reasonings carried it
into the convictions of the modern world.

A deep and abiding conviction of the narrow limits

of man's understanding in the sphere of religion was at the bottom of Locke's argument. While some of his abstract reasonings lead towards a mutual exclusion of the spheres of Church and State, and thus towards the dissolution of that connection between them which has been maintained in one form or another since Europe was conquered by Christianity, he was ready to accept the fact of their union in European civilisation. He only pleaded that it should rest upon a basis comprehensive enough to embrace all whose conduct was in conformity with the spirit of Christ ; so that the National Church should be really the Christian nation organised to promote goodness, not to protect the verbal subtleties by which professional theologians have spoiled the simplicity of Christianity in its transmission through the ages. The recall of the national Christianity of England to early simplicity, and so from elaborate dogmas to virtuous life, would, he hoped, render nonconformity or sectarian separation unnecessary, as few would then seek to remain outside the National Church, and thus need toleration. In this respect he receded from the Puritan conception, and approached the Aristotelian and that of Hooker. In this more comprehensive conception of the Church, its functions and that of the State are inseparably blended.

Locke had found all parties and sects, as well as the Church, disposed to persecution. Government had been partial in matters of religion ; and yet those who suffered from its partiality had vindicated their rights upon narrow principles, confined in their regard to the immediate interests of their own sects. He felt the need for more generous remedies than had yet been applied.

"Absolute liberty, just and true liberty, equal and impartial liberty, is the thing that we stand in need of." A mutual toleration of Christians by Christians, Locke regards as "the chief characteristical mark of the true Church." Sacerdotal succession and external ritual, with that orthodoxy in which each assumes his own orthodoxy, are marks of men striving for power and empire over one another. Let one have ever so true a claim to all these things, yet, if he be destitute of charity, meekness, and goodwill towards all mankind, even to those who are not called Christians, he is still short of being a true Christian himself. He who denies not anything that the Holy Scripture teaches, cannot, he thought, be either a heretic or a schismatic. Religion is not a matter of inheritance. No person is born a member of any Church, which is a free and voluntary society. In each of the many forms of organisation which it adopts, it is only a mean to an end, and a useful mean so far as it expresses and sustains individual religion. But this may be sustained under any of its organical forms; or, in the case of some, independently of all ecclesiastical organisation. Religion lies in the individual, not in any outward organs. This was the spirit of Locke.

The harmlessness to society of most persecuted beliefs is another point insisted on in his argument for toleration by the State, as distinct from comprehension by the Church. "No man," he maintains, " is hurt because his neighbour is of a different religion from his own; and no civil society is hurt because its members are of different religions from one another." On the contrary, when we take into account the necessarily narrow extent of attainable certainties, and still more of those actually attained by each man, we see that even an encouragement of variety in individual opinion, and of the relative freedom of inquiry, may be advantageous to society, because it tends to develop the intellectual resources of mankind, and thus adds to the security for the discovery of truth. The independent activity of each mind makes it probable that a truer and deeper insight of what the lover of truth is in quest of may thus be gradually gained, and added to the previous heritage of the race. Anyhow, physical punishment, and ecclesiastical ostracism or excommunication, are, in Locke's view, unjust and even immoral means for presenting the light of truth to individual minds. Persecution merely transforms the man whom it overawes into a hypocrite. Genuine belief and insight of truth can be attained only according to those methods which are founded on the ways in which knowledge grows in a human mind; consistently with its necessary limits; and on grounds of reasonable probability. As long as a man is out of sight of good and sufficient evidence, he cannot determine his beliefs reasonably; for one cannot, without subsiding into unreasonableness, settle arbitrarily, as a matter of taste or desire, not on evidence, what opinions he should hold. Thus all Locke's pleas for universal toleration at last resolved themselves into his philosophical conclusions as to the origin and limits of the insight into realities that is within the reach of a human being of limited ideas.

But even Locke does not teach the duty of an unlimited toleration by the State. He argues for the forcible suppression of opinions that operate to the

dissolution of society, or which subvert those moral rules
that are necessary to the preservation of order.   He even
applies this principle so as to exclude from toleration all
who are themselves intolerant, and who will not own and
teach the duty of tolerating all other men in matters
of religion—"who themselves only ask to be tolerated
by the magistrate until they find that they are strong
enough to seize the government, and possess themselves
of the estates and fortunes of their fellow-subjects."
The tyranny of the sects, which had so much scandalised
Locke in his youth, was probably here in his view.
The political part which, since the Restoration, Cathol-
icism had played in Europe, and especially in England,
with the recent Exclusion Bill debates, moved him also
to refuse toleration to "a Church constituted upon such
a bottom that all who enter into it do thereby deliver
themselves up to the protection and service of another
prince."   He saw in the position of the Roman Church
at that time, a political force, which, on grounds of public
policy, it was necessary to restrain as dangerous to the
newly reconstituted State.   Locke also refused toleration
to "all who deny the being of God."   Atheism, as understood by him, means practically rejection of the principle of order or reason in the universe.   "The taking
away of God, though but even in thought, dissolves all."
If atheism means a practical denial that reason is at
the root of things, or thus immanent in the universe in
which we, through our experience, participate; and that,
while we seem to be living in a cosmos, we are really
living in chaos,—then indeed the atheist "dissolves all";
for this atheism is universal scepticism, bound in consistency to surrender the physical and natural sciences,

and even common experience, along with the ordinary
rules of prudential conduct and expectation, thus making citizenship and society impossible. Thus understood,
it would indeed be irreconcilable with the sanity of those
who yielded to it.

Locke's 'Treatises on Government' unfold his political philosophy, while they too presuppose his philosophical conception of human understanding. Hobbes
had taught that the State originates in the virtual consent of those formed into its society. For the sake of
their individual happiness they have agreed, unconsciously in fact if not consciously in form, to a partial surrender
of their otherwise complete personal freedom. The absolute power of their king is in this way rested ultimately upon the selfish regard of the people for their
own interests, not on abstract divine right. Locke's
'First Treatise' is a laboured argument against a
divine right of kings to rule independently of popular
consent, which was asserted by Sir Robert Filmer in his
'Patriarcha.' It was probably written by Locke before
he went to Holland. The main position maintained in
the 'Patriarcha' was, that men are not naturally free ;
and on this his theory of absolute monarchy rests. It
was already an anachronism, and so, too, was Locke's
rejoinder. Locke's 'Second Treatise' is an expansion
of the conception of Hobbes ; for it goes beyond
Hobbes, in maintaining the right of each civil society to resist the ruler to whom they had, for a self-
regarding reason, surrendered part of their natural liberty
as individuals. Kings, in virtue of this origin of their
power, are therefore always responsible to the society

which they rule, when it deliberately expresses its will through its representative assemblies. So that civil liberty implies the right and duty of the individual to resist and expel a ruler whose acts are not sanctioned by a majority of the assembly which represents the implied consent of the community to be governed at all. The State, according to Locke's idea, is the artificial result of a potential contract on the part of the persons who compose it—not a natural organism evolved, unconsciously to the individual, under a universal law of social development. The terms of the implied original contract, he further argued,—in this going beyond Hobbes,—might and should be modified from time to time by the sovereign society into a reasonable accordance with their ever-changing circumstances. He saw clearly that if we are living in a potential cosmos, it is one in which, nevertheless, things and society are in an actual flux; so that a return to chaos, not a realisation of cosmos, must be the issue of attempts to remain always under the power of the past, and to follow custom when "reason," in the changed circumstances, "has left the custom." The essentially democratic idea which determines Locke's reasonings does not, of course, imply that only a republican form of government can receive the consent of a self-governed society. It only means that each society has the right to make itself happy by organising itself under that form of government which a majority of those who compose it consider most expedient for their common weal. This in one society may be a pure monarchy, in another a pure republic, in a third a mixture, with a balance of forces, as in the British constitution, at least as it was in Locke's time. It also means that the self-governing society, whether it has surrendered its executive in one of these ways, or in any other way, is bound to permit the overt expression by individuals of any opinion, religious or other, that is not inconsistent with the permanence and safety of the social organism itself; and further, that the State so constituted is bound to protect individuals in the property, in land and otherwise, which each has conquered for himself, out of what originally belonged to mankind in common, but which they thus appropriate in order that the common stock may be of use to each individual. Locke's theory involves the surrender by its members to the democratic State of their liberty, property, and life, to be disposed of in the way that seems to the State most expedient for the general happiness. No form of government is absolutely good or bad; each is to be judged according to the circumstances of society at the time. Such is the essence of Locke's political philosophy.

Locke, it has been said, was the political philosopher of England in the latter part of the seventeenth, as Hegel was the political philosopher of Germany in the early part of the nineteenth century. In their political ideas each was the converse of the other. Locke, in resting the organisation of society in the State,—if not also by implication in the family,—upon the advantage of an implied contract among individuals unsupported by history as a fact, disavows the organic rational necessity of civil government in this empirical idea of social development. His teaching, regarded as an abstract theory, found its logical outcome in French revolutionary convulsions. Hegel's conception, on the contrary, when taken exclusively, tends to the absorption of the individual in the unity of the State, and thus, with its defective idea of human personality, is a reaction from the individualism characteristic of political science in the eighteenth century. But neither the individual nor the universal is sufficient, in abstraction from the other : the individual needs the social organism, and this again is vital only through the vitality of the individuals comprehended in it. The complete truth as regards society, civil or ecclesiastical, may be sought in the conciliation of the two.

The English Revolution, of which Locke was the philosophical advocate and expositor, was in principle a struggle between those, on the one side, who invested inherited monarchy with the sacredness of divinity—thus securing its independence of utilitarian criticism; and those, on the other, who regarded monarchy and every other form of government only as a means to the happiness of the governed, to be judged in each case by its experimentally proved efficacy in securing this end. Those who opposed the Revolution guarded the succession to the monarchy on *a priori* grounds of right which put expediency out of court. Now the drift of Locke's political reasoning was to substitute considerations of expediency, and to determine questions in politics by constant reference to contingencies. Like his doctrine of toleration, with its relative or individual theory of knowledge, it was a transfer of political philosophy from the absolute to a relative foundation. It tended to exclude all *a priori* presuppositions in the struggle of politics, and to press the proved expediency of leaving the individual to dispose of himself, and leaving each civil society to govern itself, according to its own ideas and desires, delivered through its majorities. "Innate principles" in politics found no favour with Locke, in his sense of innateness.

The Revolution of which Locke was the intellectual exponent was the speculatively incoherent issue of compromise, in the truly English spirit of "give and take" carried further than Locke approved;—notwithstanding his strong common-sense conviction of the need for compromise in political conduct, and his regard for the *via media* in human action and speculation. It was brought about by the prudent moderation of men of all parties and opinions, with a conservative regard for the historical constitution. The peaceful and lasting settlement of the great conflict of the seventeenth century was found in the mixed government of 1689, which reconciled 1640 and 1660.

Locke's work on Civil Government contains incidental arguments, subordinate to its philosophical principles, some of which are of great merit. It contains the earliest recognition of the true sources of wealth and value. Locke was among the first to see distinctly that gold and silver are not real wealth; that a State unprovided with either, if well supplied with food and other useful articles, would be wealthy; while it must perish, however abundant its supply of the precious metals, so long as it could not exchange them for the means of subsistence. He enlarges upon the dependence of wealth on labour, and of human labour on individual freedom, and touches principles which are at the root of modern socialism. "If," he says, "we will rightly consider things as they come to our use, and cast up what in them is purely owing to nature and what to labour, we shall find that in most of them ninety-nine hundredths are wholly to be put on the account of labour. 'Tis labour that puts the greatest part of the value on land, without which it would scarcely be worth anything. 'Tis to that we owe the greatest part of all useful products ; for all that the straw, bran, bread of an acre of wheat is more worth than the product of an acre of good land that lies waste is all the effect of labour." A man's right of property in his own person, and thus in his own expenditure of labour, is "the great foundation of individual property, and able to overbalance the community of land." Locke, according to an eminent economist, "has all but completely established the fundamental principle which lies at the bottom of the science of wealth. He has given a far more distinct and comprehensive statement of the fundamental principle, that labour is the grand source of value, and consequently of wealth, than is to be found even in the 'Wealth of Nations.' It was but little attended to by his contemporaries or by subsequent inquirers. He was not himself aware of the vast importance of the principle he had developed ; and three-quarters of a century elapsed before it began to be generally perceived that an inquiry into the means by which labour might be rendered most efficient was the object of that portion of political economy which treats of the production of wealth." [1]

Locke's appeals to ethical principles in the 'Treatise

[1] See M'Culloch's 'Literature of Political Economy.'

on Government' usually presuppose that they are founded in the reason or nature of things, independently of utilitarian considerations, although he is always ready to reinforce moral rules by considerations of pleasure and pain as the motive to action. In treating of natural law he is some points in advance of Grotius and Puffendorf.

CHAPTER III.

IN the 'Essay concerning Human Understanding' one finds a philosophical defence of that modest estimate of man's intellect which is presupposed throughout Locke's reasoning on behalf of national toleration of different religious beliefs, and for a largely utilitarian theory of civil government. The 'Essay,' like the 'Epistola de Tolerantia' and the 'Treatises on Government,' is a plea for the free exercise of reason under the conditions which reason itself imposes—but here in its most comprehensive form. In pleading for toleration, he had argued for the right of each man to form and express his own opinions without let or hindrance on the part of society; and his theory of government is founded on the right of individuals, when associated in civil society, to adopt at first, and then to change, their form of government and their governors, according to their own views of what is most expedient for their happiness. The 'Essay' goes

---

[1] See 'Essay concerning Human Understanding,' Book I., in connection with this chapter.

deeper. It is a plea for the intellectual freedom of the individual mind from whatever is found by experience to obstruct the light of truth; and it constantly recognises the fact that one chief obstruction is, man's habitual oversight that, as finite or individual, he is in a state of intellectual mediocrity,—endowed with intellectual powers that may be adapted to all truly human ends, but which are very disproportionate to the infinite reality. This oversight often leads men to proceed upon assumptions for which there is no reasonable warrant, and then to draw conclusions from them; and it leads them, too, to suppose that they have got ideas of things when they are only employing idealess or empty words. Intellectual freedom consists in practical reasonableness; bondage to dogmas, and to empty or ambiguous phrases, contradicts reasonableness, and deadens individual insight of truth.

The main design and motive of the 'Essay' is accordingly practical; not indulgence of speculative curiosity. It is directed against those forces which Locke had found by experience to be most at variance with a life of reasonableness in all things, and adverse to the attainment by each man of the knowledge that is consistent with an inevitable state of intellectual mediocrity. The foregoing history of Locke's early life, and of the working of his mind, has brought into prominence the two adverse forces which were chiefly in his view when he was preparing the 'Essay.' The bondage of unproved assumptions, accepted indolently on authority, under pressure from the past, incapable of verification by "experience," but defended as "innate," or independent of experience—this was one of them.

The other was the bondage of empty words—phrases necessarily meaningless, because they pretend to express what really transcends human understanding and experience, or at least the individual understanding and experience of those who at the time employ them. The idealess words were vindicated, on the ground that they represented a knowledge got independently of individual activity, and which therefore did not require, nor even admit, of experimental verification. These two antagonistic forces Locke thought he found in an aggravated form in the medieval scholasticism against the remains of which it was his mission to struggle.

In accordance with this motive, the 'Essay' attempts, for the first time and on a comprehensive scale, to show, in "historical, plain"[1] matter-of-fact fashion, what the questions are as to which man is in a condition to reach certainty—the things which he finds cannot be doubted ; what those are in which he can attain only some degree of probability ; and in what other questions he is consigned, by the "disproportionateness" of his understanding to the infinite reality, to irremediable doubt, or even absolute ignorance. This intellectual enterprise seemed to promise the best practical settlement of questions, often unanswerable by a human mind, which some men are fond of raising ; and to give the best prospect of relief from bondage to unreasoned traditions, and to empty words and phrases, which had come to supersede genuine knowledge, or reasonable submission to probability when certainty was out of reach.

This key-note is found in the Introduction to the 'Essay.'[2] The ill-fortune of men in their endeavours

[1] 'Essay,' Book I., chap. i. s. 2.   [2] Ibid., Book I., chap. i.

to comprehend themselves and their surroundings, and their slavery to prejudices and idealess phraseology, are there attributed mainly to an unrestrained disposition to extend their inquiries into matters beyond any man's intellectual reach; whereas, "were the capacities of our understandings well considered, the extent of our knowledge once discovered, and the horizon found which sets the bounds between the enlightened and the dark parts of things, between what is and what is not comprehensible by us, men would perhaps with less scruple acquiesce in the avowed ignorance of the one, and employ their thoughts and discourse with more advantage and satisfaction on the other." Accordingly, the design of the 'Essay' takes the form of an inquiry into the "origin, certainty, and extent of human knowledge; together with the grounds and degrees of belief, opinion, and assent." Locke wanted to make a faithful report, based upon what he found when following what he calls the "historical plain method" of accepting facts as they are presented in mental experience. These show how far human beings *can* attain certainty, and in what matters they can only judge and guess on grounds of greater or less probability. Although he might have to report that the sphere of human certainties is narrow, and far short of "a universal and perfect comprehension of whatsoever is," he might also, he hoped, be able to show that our intellectual sphere is for us "sufficient," because "suited to our individual state." At any rate, we must take whatever we find to be real in this inquiry. Things are what they are, and are not other things; why, therefore, should we desire to be deceived? If, on the other hand, we will disbelieve everything, and so go to the opposite

extreme of scepticism, because we find that we cannot
certainly know all things, " we shall do much as wisely
as he who would not use his legs but sit still and perish,
because he had no wings to fly."—The "physical consideration of the mind" is expressly shut out from the
scope of the inquiry, which is confined to what intro-
spection can discover,—to the exclusion of the phenomena of the human organism, in itself and in its causal
relation to the extra-organic world.[1]—A theory of knowledge in its most abstract form, and of the abstract conditions of the intelligibility of experience, would have
been still more foreign to Locke's purpose, and perhaps
even to his power of philosophical apprehension. To go
in quest of it even, would have seemed to him "a letting
loose of his thoughts into the vast ocean of being." He
was contented to take for granted that, in dealing with
the sense-given data of the universe, human understanding is dealing with what *is* fit to be reasoned
about. So he made his investigation only an investigation as to the extent to which a conscious being, working under human conditions and in the circumstances
of man, can attain to a reasonable insight of the practical
meaning of his surroundings.

The 'Essay' opens in a tone of moderation and
homely cheerfulness. It suggests a hope that, if it
should turn out—after due investigation, conducted in
this "historical plain method" of appeal to the facts of
the case—that the understanding of man cannot fully
solve the mysteries of the universe, men may nevertheless attain some sort of reasonable satisfaction, that
at no stage of their individual existence are they the

[1] Book I., chap. i. s. 2; Book II., chap. xxi. s. 73.

sport of chance or unreason ; that there are ways enough in which to secure their final wellbeing, if they will only make use of the certainties and probabilities that lie within their reach, and not peremptorily or intemperately demand certainty where probability only is to be had, "which is sufficient to govern all our requirements."

Although discovery of the nature and extent of the few certainties that are within the scope of human understanding, and of the ground and office of probability, is announced as the aim of the 'Essay,' it is curious that only the last of the four books into which it is divided is directly concerned with this subject. Dugald Stewart suggests that this book may have been prepared earlier than the other three, especially as it contains few references to them, and as it could have been published separately without being less intelligible than it is. The fourth book treats of human certainties and probabilities. The second and third books investigate our "ideas" of things, apart from their truth and falsehood, and thus embrace more abstract inquiries. They urge the lesson that knowledge or certainties, and our probable presumptions too, necessarily presuppose ideas or conceptions ; that in an entire absence of ideas things must be unintelligible, and (to us) as though they did not exist ; while, on the other hand, our ideas may be out of conformity to what is real, or (to use other language than Locke would have employed) inconsistent with the divine ideas that are latent in experience and that constitute reality.

That without "ideas" there can be no absolute certainties, beliefs, opinions, doubts, or even errors, no use

for words even ; while there may be erroneous ideas
that are out of relation to reality ; and also that there
may be realities of which man can have no ideas—are
implied postulates of the 'Essay.' Another is that all
men have ideas; for without ideas there could be no
consciousness. "Every one is actually conscious of
having ideas in himself, and man's words and actions
will satisfy him that they are in others." To "have
ideas" is virtually, in Locke's language, to be intelligent ; ideas and conscious intelligence are inseparable.
Now one cannot doubt that he is conscious, though he
may doubt whether the stream of his individual consciousnesses or perceptions is in harmony with the reality that is independent of him.

Accordingly, the human and practical questions, about
certainties, more or less probable opinions, and errors,
which Locke wanted to settle, all seemed to him to
lead back to previous abstract questions "about ideas."
Mere "ideas" are not certain knowledge, nor probable
opinions, nor even errors—when they are looked at, as by
Locke, in abstraction from what they profess to be ideas
of, and from the criteria of certainty. "In themselves,"
Locke warns us, "ideas are neither true nor false, being
nothing but bare appearances"—"simple apprehensions,"
in the language of the old logicians,—abstracted from the
judgments into which they may enter as subjects or as
predicates. Actual truth and falsehood belong only to
judgments, not to mere ideas, simple or complex, nor
until the mere ideas are affirmed or denied of our ideas
of things. Till we assert or deny, there is nothing of
which truth or falsehood can be predicated. "The mere
idea of a centaur has no more falsehood in it when it

appears in our minds (*i.e.*, when it has been logically abstracted from all judgments of reality), than the name centaur has falsehood in it when it is pronounced by our mouths or written on paper."

"Idea" thus comes to be the word of all others of commonest occurrence in the 'Essay'; with Locke's idea of what an idea is, this could not be otherwise. But he offers no *theory* of what ideas are that I can find, any more than a nineteenth-century psychologist offers a theory of what "consciousnesses" are. Ideas are ideas, or consciousnesses are consciousnesses; both alike unique, incapable of being defined. We may call them "objects" of which we are conscious or percipient, or consciousnesses, or perceptions, or conceptions, or states of mind, or modifications of mind. In doing so we are only putting one term in place of another; not explaining what any of the terms mean. It is enough to say, that without ideas or conceptions of things—that is to say, in the absence of all conscious intelligence—there cannot be knowledge, opinion, or even doubt; realities would be, for those who were *idealess*, as if they were not. It is darkness: the light of intelligence comes through ideas, is in ideas. Locke insists that although he uses the word idea so often, his so-called "new way of knowledge through ideas" is just another way of saying that a man should use no words but such as can be made signs of meanings. "The new way of *ideas* and the old way of *speaking intelligibly* was always and ever will be the same." [1]

[1] Compare the valuable observations of the Duke of Argyll on the need for analysis of the meaning of words, in 'What is Truth?' (1889), in connection with Locke's design to analyse our "ideas" in his 'Essay.'

The four chapters in the first book, and not merely its first chapter, may all be regarded as introductory. That even self-evident truths (which Locke recognises as facts of mind) are not "innate," is the position argued for. In the epitome of the 'Essay,' which was translated into French by Le Clerc, and first published in the 'Bibliothèque Universelle' a year before Locke left Holland, this book is omitted. "In the thoughts I have had concerning the understanding," so the epitome opens, "I have endeavoured to prove that the mind is at first _rasa tabula._ But that being done only to remove prejudice that lies in some men's minds, I think it best in this short view I design here of my principles, to pass by all that preliminary debate which makes the first book; since I pretend to show in what follows, the true original from whence, and the ways whereby, we receive all the ideas our understandings are employed about in knowledge." If in the sequel it should appear that even the most complex and abstract ideas a man can have, when they are logically analysed, do not afford ground for supposing that any of _them_ are innate, or independent of some contingent data of experience,—that of itself," Locke thought, "would be a refutation of the hypothesis that any of our knowledge is innate—I suppose on the principle 'entia non sunt multiplicanda præter necessitatem.'"

This refutation was the watchword of the 'Essay,' which became in Locke's hands a defence of intellectual freedom, as opposed to bondage to the two despots his philosophy was directed against — idealess words and unreasoned assumptions. Locke saw them both lurking in what _he_ intended by innateness of knowledge, and therefore of ideas. The really moral purpose of his persistent war against innateness must be kept constantly in view in our interpretation of the whole ' Essay.' The drift of this famous argument has been overlooked by critics. It has been read as if it were an abstract discussion as to universality and necessity in knowledge, like that now at issue between empiricism and intellectualism. It has indeed, in the course of historical evolution, led on to this discussion; but abstract epistomology and ontology was not in Locke's design, which was more directly practical, and concerned with the conduct of a human understanding. The argument against innate principles and ideas is expressly put by him as a protest of reason against the tyranny of traditional assumptions and empty words shielded by their assumed innateness from the need for verification by our mental experience. Locke's war against the "innate" is in its spirit human understanding in revolt against the despotism of dogmas which disdain to be verified by facts; and against words and phrases for which there are no corresponding ideas or meanings. Locke believed that by insisting upon a recognition of "experienced" ideas and principles only, he was helping to put self-evidence and demonstration and well-calculated probabilities in the room of blind repose upon authority; and that he was thus (to use his own words) "not pulling up the foundations of knowledge, but laying those foundations surer." Truth, or correspondence of *our* ideas of things with the universal system of things,—with the objective reason that is in nature, if we like so to express it,—truth presupposes consciousness of this correspondence, as well as some criterion of

its having been attained. But when men were required
to accept some general propositions, without this criterion
being applied to them, " it was a short and easy way of
defending them to assume that they were 'innate,'" and
to act as if perception of their truth, or even of their
meaning, was therefore unnecessary; whereas " every one
ought very carefully to beware what he admits for a
principle, to examine it strictly, and see whether he
certainly knows it to be true of itself by its own self-
evidence or otherwise." The supposed opinion that
part of human knowledge, and this the most important
part, exists from the first, ready-made consciously in
our minds, independently of experience and prior to
experience, " eased the lazy from the pains of search,
and stopped the inquiry of the doubtful concerning
all that was once styled innate." Dogma was in this
way sheltered from criticism of its reasonableness. A
blind prejudice that their assumptions were "innate "
was enough "to take men off the use of their own
reason and judgment, and to put them upon believing
and taking upon trust without further examination.
Nor is it a small power it gives a man over another to
have the authority to make a man swallow that for an
innate principle which may serve his purpose who
teacheth him." [1] Those who have in this way imbibed
wrong principles are not to be moved by the most con-
vincing probabilities, till they do so much justice to
their own understanding as to examine the meaning
and reasonableness of what they blindly accept only
because called "innate." Thus the negative conclusion
defended in the first book, meant to clear the way for

[1] Book I., chap. iv.

the analytic and constructive part of the 'Essay,' is simply a philosophical defence of that plea for personal insight, as against blind dependence on authority, which was contained in the 'Epistola de Tolerantia.'

In arguing against innateness of principles and ideas, Locke explains that he does not mean to deny that some truths come to be seen by human understanding as demonstrably necessary, and that others as self-evidently true. On the contrary, he reports, as a fact found by reflection, that in some cases the intellect becomes able to perceive a truth "as the eye doth light, only by being directed to it by bare intuition, which kind of know-ledge is the clearest and most certain that human frailty is capable of. This part of knowledge is irresistible, and, like bright sunshine, forces itself immediately to be perceived as soon as ever the mind turns its view that way, and leaves no room for hesitation, doubt, or examination, but the mind is presently filled with the clear light of it. It is on this intuition depends all the certainty and evidence of all our knowledge; which certainty every one in such cases finds to be so great that he cannot imagine and therefore cannot require a greater. Thus we see in this light of reason that three are more than two, and equal to one and two."[1] He further reports the fact that reason leads us on from those self-evident intuitions into "demonstrative" reason-ings, in which each step has intuition or self-evident certainty. He argues in the first book against the "innateness" of our ideas and knowledge of God and of morality, while in the fourth book he reports, in his own "historical, plain," matter-of-fact way, that the

[1] 'Essay,' Book IV., chap. ii.

existence of God is a " demonstrable " conclusion, in
which each step is intuitively certain; and that, if we
exert our minds, we can see a like demonstrable necessity in the truths of pure mathematics, and even of
abstract ethics. The "innate principles" against which
the 'Essay' wages war are not the assumptions which
are thus (by degrees) seen by growing reason to be either
self-evident or demonstrable. His aim was to get men in
all cases to try whether their assumptions are either.
Then, if found to be self-evident, or demonstrable, let
them be accepted; not as "innate," but as rationally
intuited, and thus with an experienced perception that
they cannot be doubted. But if the so-called "innate
principles" are not able on trial to stand this or any
other experimental test, we are under an intellectual
obligation to reject them as bondage to the understanding, as meaningless phrases, or at any rate as not proved.
Locke wants us all, by submitting to the fatigue of this
sort of mental experiment, to find for ourselves whether
what had been blindly taken for granted, under the
character of "innate," really is perceived truth, "which
like bright sunshine forces itself to be perceived" as
soon as the eye of intelligence is open to perceive it.
Thus, even amidst the negative arguments of the first
book, he appeals to intuitive reason,—under the name
of "common-sense,"—on behalf of the self-evidence of
one of the very "principles" against the "innateness"
of which he was arguing. "He would be thought
void of common - sense who asked, on the one side,
or who, on the other, went to give a reason, why
it is 'impossible' for the same thing to be and not
to be. It carries its own light of evidence with it,

and needs no other proof; he that understands the terms, at once assents to it for its own sake, or else nothing else will ever be able to prevail with him to do it."[1]

The truth is, that neither Locke nor those who advocated innate elements in human knowledge expressed their meaning definitely enough. When the controversy is a speculative one about the philosophical constitution of knowledge, and not, as with Locke, the occasion of a polemic against blind prejudices and empty idealess phrases, the argument of the first book is seen to be inadequate, in the light of a deeper conception of what should be meant by an innate idea and principle than Locke intended. It is difficult to find any philosopher, then or since, who would deny what Locke maintains; nor is it easy to determine whom he had in view in this celebrated augmentative assault. Lord Herbert alone is named as the advocate of innateness.[1] Locke was perhaps too little read in the literature of philosophy to do full justice to those who, from Plato onwards, have recognised, with increasing distinctness, the presuppositions of reason, and the activity of the often latent faculties of intellect and moral judgment, to be involved in the very constitution of a developing physical and spiritual experience. "Innate," as his pupil the third Lord Shaftesbury afterwards remarked—"innate is a word Mr Locke poorly plays on" —that is, if his argument is to be taken as directed against those who allege the presence, latent if not patent, of elements in experience deeper than the con-

[1] 'Essay,' Book I., chap. iii. s. 4.
[2] Ibid., Book I., chap. iii. ss. 15-19.

tingent and ever - changing phenomena which enter into experience. "The right word, though less used," Shaftesbury adds, "is connatural. For what has birth or the progress of the fœtus to do in this case?" The question of ultimate philosophical interest is not as to the time when individual men first become conscious or intellectually percipient of self-evident or of demonstrable truths. The true question about innateness is, as Shaftesbury himself puts it, "whether the constitution of man be such that, being adult and grown up, the ideas of order and administration of a God will not infallibly and necessarily spring up in consciousness." Now Locke himself does not deny this. "That there are certain propositions," we find him saying, "which, though the soul from the beginning, when a man is born, does not (consciously) know, yet, by assistance from the outward senses and the help of some previous cultivation, it may afterwards come self-evidently, or with a demonstrable necessity, to know the truth of, is no more than what I have affirmed in my first book." He had no intention to deny the fact that we can rise to self-evident truths which neither need nor admit of proof; for innateness with him means a man's original possession of such truths consciously.

By "innate" Locke means consciously realised in the mind, or, as he metaphorically expresses this, "stamped" upon the consciousness which the individual soul has in its first being, and brought into the world with it; truths possessed independently of all experience and individual activity,—in the way that all truth may be supposed to be always present to the divine mind, without any need of experience either for its acquisition or for its evolution into consciousness. A *consciousness* of the ideas is inseparable from all Locke's "ideas." This appears in his argument, at the beginning of the second book, against the soul "always thinking" or being conscious—*e.g.*, during sleep.[1] "Whatever idea is *in* the mind, the mind must be conscious of." To say that an idea or principle is in the mind and yet not actually perceived by the mind in which it is, is, according to Locke, the same as to say that at once it is and is not in the mind, which is self-contradictory. Whatever is thus innate must be therefore in the consciousness of all men, savages, infants, even idiots. Of course it was not difficult for Locke to show that men have no principles, or ideas either, which answer this description. Even the self-evident principles, that "whatever is, is," and that "it is impossible for the same thing to be and not to be," do not answer it; for they are not consciously realised by idiots, infants, or savages; and indeed only in educated minds do they ever rise into full consciousness. Therefore, even they are not, in Locke's sense, innate; and if they are not, *a fortiori*, none others can be so. To reply that they are nevertheless present "potentially" in the mind of the unconscious individual, either means nothing at all, Locke would say, or it means, what he does not deny, that the mind has latent faculty for knowing them to be intuitively true. But what this "faculty" implies, what is presupposed in mind having power to know intuitively, or, still more,

[1] 'Essay' Book II., chap. i. ss. 9-19.

in the possibility of its having real intelligible experience—was a question which Locke did not entertain, and which, if it had been put before him, he would perhaps have thought too speculative to lie within the scope of his inquiries. It was reserved for Kant and his successors. The *æternæ veritates,* — the abstract presuppositions regarding the universe in space and time, which intellect implies independently of the universe being actually known—with the theory of knowing and being therein involved,—were all foreign to Locke; and, if he could have entertained them, would all have been treated as subordinate to his main design,—of determining the limits of the variable data of experience ; of keeping our words in contact with concrete meanings; and of testing our assumed principles by obviously verifiable evidence. He announced, as the fundamental thesis of the 'Essay,' that the human mind "has all the materials of its knowledge from EXPERIENCE, that in that all our knowledge is founded, and from that it all ultimately derives itself." He failed to see that innate knowledge and experienced knowledge are not contradictory, but are really two different ways of regarding *all* knowledge. Yet this is surely the true *via media.* But he was biassed by his unwarranted assumption that "nothing can be in the mind of which the mind is not conscious,"—that mental activity is identical with consciousness of it,— and so he overlooked the now acknowledged fact that a man's individual consciousness may include only a small part of what he potentially knows. Locke's habit of physical experiment led him to look at knowledge, and also at the universe, on the natural rather than on the metaphysical or supernatural side,—as a succession of caused causes, rather than in their constant originating cause,—from the point of view of natural science, in short, rather than from that of the philosopher. He failed to show that the supernatural or metaphysical is continuously immanent in nature and in natural law.

CHAPTER IV.

LOGICAL AND PSYCHOLOGICAL — ANALYSIS OF OUR IDEAS, ESPECIALLY OUR METAPHYSICAL IDEAS.[1]

LOCKE takes for granted that without ideas there can be no knowledge, belief, or even doubt about anything; and also that we may have ideas without having knowledge. Knowledge presupposes "ideas," but ideas do not presuppose knowledge, since our ideas may be erroneous. And error as well as truth presupposes ideas. Things and persons are virtually non-existent for those who have no ideas—in other words, for those who are unconscious. To think or judge without ideas would be to think without thought, which is a contradiction in terms. Judgments presuppose ideas : innate knowledge would presuppose innate ideas. Accordingly, nearly half of the 'Essay' is a logical analysis of the complex, especially the metaphysical, ideas that men are conscious of, into their simple concrete elements. The question of the truth or falsehood of ideas, and the criteria of their truth and falsehood, are reserved for examination in the fourth book. The second and third books treat

[1] See 'Essay,' Books II. III., which may be compared with the 'Port Royal Logic,' part i.

of ideas in abstraction from realities, and in their relations
to their verbal signs, thus kept apart altogether from the
judgments which express their real or supposed relations,
and from their relations as true or false. As logicians
might say, these two books are concerned with the "apprehensions" of the mind, simple and complex; the
fourth book, besides more about ideas, treats especially
of judgments and reasonings, for it is in these alone,
and not in mere ideas, that knowledge, probability, and
error are to be found. By ideas, — simple and complex,—Locke means whatever can be signified by the
subject or the predicate of a proposition—not what is
signified by the proposition itself—not knowledge, or
probability, or error, but an element in each, which by
abstraction may be separately considered. It is that in
a proposition without which the proposition would be
unintelligible, as of course all propositions when deprived
of their subjects and predicates would necessarily become.
Without "ideas" our judgments are empty; with judgments our mere ideas are blind.

It is for this reason that the "new way of ideas,"
which Locke was charged by his critics with "invent-
ing," is, and ever will be, he says, "the same with the
old way of speaking intelligibly." For it means that
the only words which can be employed in propositions
must be significant and not idealess. Meaningless words
are empty sounds, which have no relation to any understanding, human or other. It is only by keeping the
words which one uses charged with meanings that one
can preserve himself from jargon—whether he pleases
to call meanings by the name of ideas or by any other
name. To have ideas is to realise consciously what we

say; whether our conscious meaning corresponds or does not correspond to objective reality. Moreover, ideas can be, in Locke's view, ideas only when there is consciousness of them. As he says, "ideas" are "nothing but actual perceptions in the mind, which cease to be anything when there is no perception of them;" and he adds that, when we speak of "keeping them in our memories" while we are not conscious of them, this is just a metaphorical way of saying that "the mind has a power to revive perceptions or ideas which it had once had." [1] "Whatever idea was never *perceived* by the mind was never *in* the mind." Whatever idea is "in the mind" is either an actual perception, or else, having formerly been an actual perception, is "so in the mind that by the memory it can be made an actual perception again." Wherever there is the actual perception of an idea without memory, the idea then appears perfectly new and unknown before to the understanding." [2] "The scene of ideas that makes up one man's thoughts cannot be laid open to the immediate view of another man," [3] and is in this respect private or individual; but we may reasonably assume that the microcosm of meanings which makes up one man's collection of ideas of the universe so far corresponds to that of another man, as that a logical analysis of human ideas which shall refer them all to their elementary sources is possible. And if possible, it would, if it were made, be a safeguard against the employment of the meaningless words and phrases which discredited the schools; and it would also help in determining the limits within which human

[1] Book II., chap. x.   [2] Book I., chap. iv. s. 20.
[3] Book IV., chap. 21.

judgments, certain and probable, are possible. When a proposition, as to which we are in doubt whether it has any meaning, is put before us for our assent, we should, by this analysis, have a criterion for determining the doubt, and for making sure that, whether true or not, it is at least in some degree intelligible. It was in this spirit that Hume afterwards dealt with *his* ideas. He asked for their corresponding " impressions," which are his equivalent to Locke's " simple " ideas, assuming that if a corresponding impression does not exist, the words which pretend to express meaning are only empty sounds. Hume's " impressions " may be an inadequate criterion of the possible meanings of our words, but the principle of a verification of our mere ideas is illustrated by this example. When we run over libraries, demanding " impressions " as antetypes of the ideas or meanings which the books profess to contain, what havoc, Hume suggests, would be made among them! "If we take in hand any volume of divinity or school metaphysics, for instance, let us ask, ¿Does it contain any abstract reasoning concerning quantity or number?' No. 'Does it contain any experimental reasoning concerning matter or fact or existence?' No. 'Commit it then to the flames; for it can contain nothing but sophistry and illusion.'"[1] Hume of course presupposes that, in his philosophy, all human ideas must be either those involved in abstract judgments about quantity, or those involved in empirical judgments about impressions of sense.

It was Locke who first employed logical analysis of our ideas on a comprehensive scale, as a step to the

[1] See Hume's ' Inquiry concerning Human Understanding,' sec. 12.

settlement of the limits of the knowledge or absolute certainty that is within man's reach ; and also to the settlement of the grounds and gradations of our reasonable probabilities. In arguing against "innate" ideas at the outset, he had argued against what I suppose no philosopher ever articulately maintained—that each man always had, like God, knowledge ready made or conscious, independently of the slow growth of experience, and therefore prior to any experience. But thus, he thought, he was clearing his way "to those foundations" in experience which are "the only true ones whereon to establish the notions we can have," so as "to erect a philosophical edifice uniform and consistent with itself."

Let us now see how he finds by analysis the actual constituents of our most complex and abstract ideas of the universe, after he had by argument banished the "prejudice" that some of them were "innate," or consciously present in the original constitution of each mind.

For one thing, he finds that the "scene of ideas," which "makes up each one's thoughts about things," is complex or analysable ; and that it can be analysed into ideas which are called simple because found to be incapable of analysis. The main point, therefore, must be to ascertain what those unanalysable data are of which all ideas or meanings, even the most elaborate and sublime, are composed ; for when this is found, we have a test for determining whether any alleged example of an idea is genuine meaning or not. This investigation might be otherwise described as an attempt to fix the source and limits of the connotations of the words that can be used intelligently by human beings. Further, complex ideas of things — so Locke finds — are often "made for us" and presented to us by nature, as well as "made by us" in our own subjective and arbitrary constructions. In fact, the complex ideas which *we make*, correspond, he might have said, to the complex ideas which are *made for us*, in the universal order and constitution of things, in all those cases in which our complex ideas are really true. For when the mind has once got a store of simple ideas, it is not confined barely to those complex ideas which have been "made for it" in external nature. " It can by its own power put together those ideas it has, and make new complex ones, which it never received so united, and which never are so united." [1]

Man's "complex ideas" of things, according to Locke, are of three sorts, "though their number in each sort be infinite, and their variety endless, wherewith they fill and entertain the thoughts of men." They are either (1) ideas of *modes* or *qualities*, which "contain not in them the idea of their subsisting by themselves, but only the idea that they are dependent on, or affections of, individual substances ;" or they are (2) ideas of *substances* —that is to say, of "distinct particular things subsisting independently or by themselves ;" or they are (3) ideas of "*relations* between substances." In short, "the scene of ideas," which gives intelligibility to the words that human beings use, consists of complex ideas of possible *modes* of things, abstracted from individual things or substances ; of individual *substances ;* and of *relations* among substances.[2] What the simple or unanalysable ideas are, out of which all this complexity and abstractness

[1] Book II., chap. xii.   [2] Ibid.

in the meanings of words arises, is the inquiry pursued throughout the second and third books, and in parts of the fourth book. [1]

It is surely a defect in the 'Essay' that it offers no reason for this threefold, and presumably exhaustive, arrangement of the complex thoughts about things that men have. It is stated dogmatically, not defended in a reasoned criticism, — presumably as the issue of what Locke had found, in his "historical, plain," matter-of-fact investigation of the contents of a human understanding.

Modes, substances, and relations of individual substances, are Locke's in short three uncriticised categories, subject to which our thoughts of things have to be elaborated by us, and according to which (so he appears to intend) things themselves are already elaborated for us in nature, as in the case of the individual substances we perceive, which are complex ideas ready made.

Some of Locke's critics have accused him of meaning that at the beginning of life each human being is conscious only of simple ideas in their simplicity—that is to say, of isolated sensations only—out of which he gradually elaborates, by association and generalisation, the complex and abstract ideas of the adult; and they

[1] "Simple ideas," "complex ideas," "simple modes," "mixed modes," &c., are part of Locke's small stock of technical terms, which through him gained currency in last century in England. "Simple ideas" are the unanalysable phenomena contained, in manifold modes, in the complexity of individual substances, material and spiritual, and in substances as related. A rose is a complex idea; its colour, fragrance, odour, softness, &c., are each simple ideas.

have also complained that he offers no adequate ex-
planation· of why and how they become complex and
abstract.

"It is not true," says Cousin,[1] "that each· of us starts in
life with a consciousness only of ideas that are simple and
isolated, as Locke alleges, and that we afterwards become
conscious of those that are complex.   Rather we begin with
very complex ideas ; afterwards, by abstraction from these,
we advance to those which are simple : so that the history
of the individual mind, in its acquisition of its ideas or
thoughts about things, is the very reverse of that described
by Locke.   Our earliest ideas are, without exception, complex ; for the plain reason that our faculties to a great
extent act simultaneously.   The simultaneous activity of
the senses affords us at once several simple ideas in the
unity of an individual substance.   All our primitive ideas
are complex, particular, and concrete."

Now I do not find that Locke is open to this charge.
The second book of the 'Essay' admits, I think, of
being interpreted, in fact if not in form, as a logical
analysis of the complex ideas of things which are
either "made for us" or "made by us," and of which
our intellectual life consists.   "Simple ideas," he says,
"are *found to exist in several combinations united together*, but the mind has power to consider them separately."   "The qualities that affect our senses," he says
again, "are, in the things themselves, so united and
blended that there is no separation between them ; yet
it is plain the ideas they produce in the mind enter by
the senses simple and unmixed.   For though the sight
and touch often take in from the same object, *and at*

[1] 'Cours de l'Histoire de la Philosophie· Moderne.   System de
Locke.'

P.—XV.   I

the same time, different ideas—as a man sees *at once* motion and colour, or the hands feel softness and warmth at once in the same piece of wax; yet the simple ideas (motion and colour, softness and heat), thus *perceived as united* in the same object, are as perfectly distinct as those that come in by different senses; and each, in itself uncompounded, contains in it nothing but the uniform appearance or conception in the mind, and is not distinguishable into different ideas." In short, Locke recognises, with psychologists of all schools, what has been called "abstraction by the senses"; by which, in the presence of things, intellect operative in each sense "abstracts" colours (*i.e.,* "simple ideas" of colour) by the eye, sounds by the ear, &c. But this need not mean that we are at first percipient of simple ideas only in their simplicity; or that we do not, implicitly at least, always refer them as qualities to things or individual substances, of the existence of which Locke finds in the fourth book that we have an intuitive knowledge, and our ideas of which are of course necessarily complex.

Locke has also been charged by Mr Green and others with mixing together throughout the 'Essay,' in chaotic contradiction, two irreconcilable theories about ideas, and about the origin of knowledge. It is alleged that in some parts of the 'Essay' he describes our knowledge as beginning with simple and unrelated ideas—isolated sensations—and as somehow advancing from those to the complex and related. But in other parts, especially when treating of general terms, they say that he makes our knowledge begin with individual substances manifested in their qualities—that is to say, with complex ideas, from which it advances by an arbitrary and unreal abstraction towards the simple.

Is not this charge of confusion between two contradictory theories due in the critics to oversight of what Locke is doing in those parts of the 'Essay' in which he seems to say that knowledge begins in unrelated sensations, and in those other parts of the 'Essay' in which he makes complex ideas of individual things the starting-point? For in fact, any "knowledge" of the unrelated is impossible, consistently with Locke's own definition of knowledge, and with his often reiterated principle, that it necessarily involves perception of relation among ideas.[1] In one of those two sets of passages which are supposed by the critics to be contradictory, he is, is he not, offering a true logical analysis of the matter, or phenomenal constituents, of already formed complex and abstract ideas signified in words; in the other set, is he not describing as a psychologist that ascent from the complex individual presentations of sense phenomena, or "sense ideas," to the generalisations of the understanding which marks the growth of our knowledge?

The central position of the second book, on which all its facts and discussions converge, is, that all concepts of which a human mind can be conscious, however complex, and whatever their logical comprehension and extension may happen to be, must be resolvable into either "qualities of external things," or "operations of our own minds." What words pretend to mean neither of these, cannot contain positive meaning for a human mind, and must be empty sounds. And neither of

[1] Book IV., chap. i.

these kinds of ideas can be innate, but must appear in the course of our experience; neither, too, can be due to our voluntary acting, for we cannot help having the experience. So that, in this sense, we are "passive" in our consciousness of them. "The objects of our senses obtrude their particular ideas *whether we will or no;* and the operations of our minds *will not let us* be without, at least, some obscure notions of them. . . . As the bodies that surround us do diversely affect our organs, the mind is *forced* to receive the impressions, and cannot (by any act of will) avoid the perceptions or ideas that are annexed to them." [1] Thus the sensible qualities of external things, and the mind's own operations, are two sources in experience to one or other of which, Locke proposes to show, all the meanings of all the terms men can make use of with any significance must be referred.

" These, when we have taken a full survey of them and of their several modes, combinations, and relations, we shall find to contain all our whole stock of ideas. Let any one examine his own thoughts, and thoroughly search into his understanding; and then let him tell me whether all the original ideas he has there are any other than of objects of his senses or of operations of his mind; and how great a mass of knowledge soever he imagines to be lodged there, he will, upon taking a strict view, see that he has not any idea in his mind but what one of these two have imprinted (*i.e.*, presented) — though perhaps with infinite variety compounded and enlarged by the understanding. . . . Even the most abstruse ideas, how remote soever they may seem from (simple ideas of) the external senses, or from (simple ideas of) the operations of our own minds, are yet . . . no other than what the mind, by the ordinary use of its

---

[1] Book II., chap. i. s. 25.

own faculties, employed about ideas received from objects of sense, or from the operations it obtains in itself about them, may and does attain to."

One lesson taught in all this is,—that man is not wise and knowing originally, or by his nature, like God. He *becomes* wise and knowing, gradually and imperfectly, under conditions of experience. The omniscience of God, on the contrary, is supposed to be eternally present in the constitution of Deity, all and always therein contained. This fact about man, Locke would say, is the fact of facts in human understanding; and we must take it as it is, for we cannot alter it. Man's knowledge and wisdom is of a sort that begins with qualities of individual substances, and thus with ideas already complex, although by abstraction they may be analysed into their simple constituents. It is at first narrow and for the present hour: we find it expanding in space and time and under other complex relations, in proportion as the individual elaborates what is presented, till at last he rises to comprehensive thoughts in theology and philosophy.

That some of our ideas are not innate,—in Locke's sense of having no dependence on a gradual experience, —might be illustrated by their evident dependence on data which are presented to the senses. Thus it would be absurd to suppose ideas of colours innate or inexperienced when we find that God has given us a power to perceive those qualities by the eye. No less unreasonable would it be to attribute any of the meanings which our minds can put into words, to mysterious consciousness that is independent of and prior to mental experience; especially if we can show that, without "external

senses" and without "reflection upon its own operations," the mind would be a blank, all language meaningless, and the supposed innate knowledge as if it
were not. We find that it is by degrees that all meanings rise into our consciousness and take possession of our
words ; and, although the conditions under which we
live are such that we cannot help having some consciousness or ideas, yet their dependence on contingencies of
experience may be proved by the possibility of *shutting
off* many of them from an individual mind. This is
especially the case with the ideas of the qualities of
external things.

"All that are born into the world being surrounded with
bodies that perpetually and diversely affect their organs of
sense, some variety of ideas, whatever care we might take to
prevent it, *must* arise in the minds of all. Yet if a child
were kept in a place where he never saw any other but *black*
and *white* objects till he were a man, he would have no more
ideas of *scarlet* and *green* than he that from his childhood
never tasted an oyster or a pine-apple has of these particular
relishes. I would have any one try to fancy any taste
which had never affected his palate ; or frame the idea
of a scent he had never smelt ; and when he can do this,
I will also conclude that a (born) blind man hath ideas of
colours, and a (born) deaf man notions of sounds. It is not
possible for man to imagine (*i.e.*, have ideas of) any other
qualities in bodies besides sounds, tastes, smells, visible and
tangible qualities. And had mankind been made with
' four senses,' the qualities then which are the object of the
fifth sense had been as far from our imagination or conception (*i.e.*, from our limited world of possible meanings) as
now any belonging to a sixth, seventh, or eighth sense can
possibly be ; which, whether some other creatures in some
other parts of this vast and stupendous universe may not
have, will be a great presumption to deny."

It is thus that Locke argues, that the microcosm of ideas, or conscious thoughts, true or false, about things, of which each human mind is the theatre, has been the gradual formation of an experience, entire arrest of which from the first would have left the mind from which it was withdrawn a blank unconsciousness —actually if not potentially a *tabula rasa*. But although the awakening of each individual mind into consciousness, perception, or idea is in this way dependent on contingencies of individual experience, Locke hardly recognised the other truth, that such dependence is not inconsistent with the latent presence of reason, immanent or innate in all the knowledge or experience into which we awake.

Much has been said about Locke's "theory of perception." After all, I do not find in the 'Essay' any theory proposed to explain either man's perception of the qualities of matter, or his consciousness of the operations of mind. Our original knowledge of *both* (or *neither*) is "representative," according to Locke's way of putting it, in the passages in which he lays stress upon the dependence of our knowledge upon our ideas, which may mean that each one's own mind is the only mind he has for knowing either about things or about spiritual acts. The subtleties of sense-perception "theories" were foreign to his practical design. It was sufficient for Locke that in point of fact men do have complex and abstract ideas of things in "the storehouse of the mind ;" and that what those are depends on contingencies in the individual organism and its surroundings,— without determining either *how* qualities of matter are also ideas of mind, or *how* the mind is able to be conscious, in the ways it is conscious, of its own operations. The main truth for Locke's purpose was,—that without ideas or meanings referable to "things of sense," the things themselves are to us non-existent; and that without ideas or meanings referable to "operations of mind," they too would be as if they were not. All language would then be meaningless, in lack of material about which to think. In his way of it, our knowledge of matter and of mind is equally dependent on our having ideas of their phenomena. Perception of external things and self-consciousness are equally and alike presentative or representative. We perceive external things *in having ideas of them;* we are conscious of our mental operations *in also having ideas of them.* Deeper than this Locke does not care to go—in this direction; unless it be that, as regards external things, he recognises that the fact of our now having ideas of their qualities in our memories and imaginations is somehow made by God to depend upon our having had certain "organic impressions or motions" made, by extra-organic things or otherwise, in "some parts of our bodies;"—which motions are the constant antecedents of the ideas, but in no manner of way to be identified with the ideas in consciousness, nor to be regarded as their ultimate cause. This is just to say that without duly affected organs we cannot be sense conscious, in the way of seeing, or touching, or hearing, or tasting, or smelling.

The 'Essay' argues throughout that the ideas which men are able to have are by no means confined to the qualities of external things, together with the various modes, substances, and relations of substances into which *they* are "made for us" in nature, or "made by us" in our

own arbitrary elaborations. If our store of possible meanings were limited to those which relate to matter and
its qualities, then those words or phrases which pretend
to express spiritual meanings would necessarily be empty.
Now men *do* find meanings in such words as perception, thinking, willing, remembering, knowing, believing,
God, immortality, &c. Those words must be meaningless, unless we get ideas of spirit, in addition to those
which arise under the organic conditions of the five
senses. As Locke expresses it, " reflection " as well as
" sensation " contributes to that stock of unanalysable
ideas out of which all the matters we can think about
are composed. The " operations " of each man's spirit
enable him, if he chooses to attend to them, to throw
meaning or connotation into a class of words which
without " reflection " would be empty.

One of the questions that has been most disputed
in the exegesis of the 'Essay' is, what Locke intended
by " reflection." Sometimes he describes it as if he
had in view only data accidentally contributed by an
inner experience, in the manner of an internal sense.
" This source of ideas," he says, " each man has in himself ; and though it be not sense, as having nothing
to do with external objects, *yet it is very like it, and
might properly enough be called internal sense.*" Does
this mean that, alike through sense commonly so called,
and through reflection, we become aware only of fluctuating phenomena, which appear and disappear, so that
the only element in conscious life is this " contingent "
one ? Does it exclude from experience anything deeper
than this ? Or, on the contrary, does Locke recognise
in reflected " operations " ideas which *explain* experi-

ence ; forming one side of it in all its varieties, external
and internal ; so that, in virtue of having them, the ideas
of sense themselves become connected in intelligible
relations ?   In short, is the intellectual philosophy of
the ' Essay ' empiricism, or is it not ?   Does its analysis
of our complex and abstract ideas in the second and
third books reveal a constitution of knowledge other
than mere observation could supply ?

By some critics Locke has been understood to mean
that all complex and abstract ideas that can rise in
human consciousness must, when brought to their state
of ultimate decomposition, resolve into mental pictures
of qualities of sense ; and that, since all that rises in
consciousness consists only of pictures of accidentally
presented data of sense, all significant language must
have its meaning analysable into those empirical data ;
so that it shall be a fundamental rule in the conduct of
the understanding that every verbal expression which
cannot find a sensible object to which it can claim
affinity, must be a meaningless expression ?   This is the
interpretation put upon the ' Essay ' by Condillac and
other French empiricists of last century, who believed
that they were teaching what Locke taught when they
asserted that all human ideas are compounded of sensations which happen to occur in external or internal
sense, so that ideas in their most elaborate state may
be described as only naturally "transformed " sensations.
Even Sir W. Hamilton, in opposition to Dugald Stewart,
sometimes accepts this interpretation of Locke.

" The French philosophers," he says, " are, in my opinion,
fully justified in their interpretation of Locke's philosophy ;
and Condillac must, I think, be viewed as having simplified

the doctrine of his master without doing the smallest violence
to its spirit. I cannot concur with Mr Stewart in allowing
any weight to. Locke's distinction of reflection or self-consciousness as a source of knowledge. Such a source of experience no sensualist ever denied, because no sensualist ever
denied that sense was cognisant of itself. [Can *mere* sense
be cognisant of itself, or of anything?] It is a matter of
no importance, that we do not call self-consciousness by the
name of sense, if we allow that it is only conversant about
the contingent. Now no interpretation of Locke can ever
pretend to find in his reflection a revelation of aught native
or necessary to the mind."[1]

Yet elsewhere we find him saying that "had Descartes
and Locke expressed themselves on the subject of innate
ideas and principles with due precision, both would have
been found in harmony with each other and with truth."[2]

Locke's meaning is not to be got from the ambiguous
language in which it is expressed in such statements as
that all our ideas must be ideas of what has been experienced in external or in internal *sense*. The term
"sense" has many meanings. Thus Reid's "common
sense" expresses the analogy of reason, in its *direct* insight of the intelligible, to sense in its relation to the
phenomenal. "Experience," as used by Locke, may or
may not be meant to connote its own rational implicates,
as well as its contingent or variable data. Probably this
distinction was outside Locke's calculations. We can
best reach his implied opinion by looking at his actual
analysis of our metaphysical ideas, in the second
book, and at the 'Essay' as a whole. In fact he does
not attempt criticism of pure reason. He would probably have said with Cardinal Newman, that he was

[1] 'Lectures on Metaphysics,' vol. ii. p. 199.   [2] Reid, p. 785.

"unequal to antecedent reasoning in the instance of a matter of fact," and not disposed to follow "those who feel obliged, in order to vindicate the certainty of our knowledge, to have recourse to the hypothesis of intellectual forms, and the like, which are supposed to belong to us by nature, and are considered to elevate our experiences into something more than they are in themselves."[1] He thinks it enough to appeal to the common voice of mankind in proof of the reality of knowledge. For him the matter of fact that certitude *is* "discerned" is sufficient.

But questions about "knowledge" or "certainty" belong to the fourth book; they are not immediately involved in that logical analysis of our ideas, irrespective of the certainty of judgments in which the ideas may be contained, which occupies the preceding part of the 'Essay.' The problem, especially of the second book, is the verification, by analysis of crucial instances, of the position which at the outset Locke proposed to prove—that no concrete meanings can enter into the subjects or predicates of judgments which are not in their elements dependent either on external sense or on reflection; and yet that within these bounds there is room even for "the capacious mind of man to expatiate in; which takes its flight further than the stars and cannot be confined by the limits of this world; that extends its thoughts often even beyond the utmost expansion of matter, and makes excursions into that incomprehensible inane."[2] He challenges any one to assign a single complex idea we can be conscious of, which may not be analysed into the result of perception of the qualities of

[1] 'Grammar of Assent.'   [2] Book II., chap. vii.

sensible things, or consciousness of our own spiritual operations. "Nor will it be so strange to think these few simple ideas sufficient to furnish the materials of all that various knowledge and more variable fancies and opinions of all mankind, if we consider how many words may be made out of the various composition of twenty-four letters; or if we will but reflect on the variety of combinations that may be made with barely one of the above-mentioned ideas,—number, whose stock is inexhaustible and truly infinite, and what an immense field extension alone doth afford the mathematicians."[1]

Locke sees each man starting with perceptions of qualities of external things of which he becomes aware in his five senses, and then gradually awakening to a consciousness of his own spiritual operations — his memory charged with ideas thus mysteriously received —reason occupied with the innumerable combinations which these its materials assume in nature, or in our minds through man's own (often mistaken) operations of synthesis and analysis. He sees in all this, concrete examples of what the second book professes to analyse logically. He asks for proof that this collective product, in any part or instance, includes *more material* than can be resolved into qualities of things, and "operations" of spirit.

Locke's matter-of-fact way of proceeding to a settlement of this question is,—to show that even those complex ideas we have that seem to be composed of phenomena the most unlike those apprehended through our senses or by reflection—our sublimest ideas, in short —may all be analysed into modes, or substances, or

[1] Book II., chap. vii.

relations of substances, made up of sensible qualities or of spiritual operations. Take some crucial instances, he seems to be saying, from the thirteenth
chapter of the second book onwards. Take our ideas of
the Infinite in extension, or in time, or in number, or
abstract infinitude; or take the idea of Substance—
either in matter or in spirit—to which we refer "qualities" and "operations," and cognate the idea of personal
Identity; or take our ideas of causal connection and
Power; or our ideas of Morality. Some of these look
very unlike either qualities of things, or operations of
mind. But if even those metaphysical ideas admit of
being analysed into data of sense or reflection, we may
pretty safely conclude, *a fortiori*, that we have no other
ideas which would resist this analysis, or which might
claim, on this ground, to be ours by nature, and not to
have *become* ours consciously only in and after experience. The ideas above named supply what Bacon would
call "crucial" instances for testing the truth of Locke's
proposed logical analysis even of our most sublime and
mysterious ideas, proving that they are all syntheses of
qualities of matter or of operations of spirit. And this
testing process is virtually what is going on in the
thirteenth and most of the remaining chapters of the
second book, which thus bring us face to face with the
metaphysical mysteries of thought.

For one thing, it might seem,—if men's ideas can
really all be resolved into what they perceive under the
conditions of sense, and the operations of which they
are conscious in themselves,—that we can think only of
what is finite; and that "infinite and eternal realities"
must be meaningless words. Whatever we see, touch,

hear, taste, or smell, is narrow, rounded, transitory, finite. The "operations" of which we are conscious are also fluctuating, and therefore finite. Yet we do have, and indeed are obliged by something in our minds to have, an idea of a surrounding Immensity that is without bounds, infinite, eternal; we do have, and are obliged by something in our minds to form, the idea of Time unbeginning and unending; we do have, and are obliged by something in our minds to have, the idea of innumerable Number. Then, too, the unanalysable phenomena of sense rise into consciousness in perception as complex ideas or qualities contained in individual Substances, and in this their substantiation there must be some meaning, unless the term "substance" is "jargon." Again, every change makes us think of its causes, its causes when found make us think of another cause, and so on in an infinite regress; of all which we must be supposed to have idea, unless the term Cause is a meaningless word. Do all *those* terms, the critic may ask, contain nothing that is not significant either of qualities of visible things, or of operations of invisible mind or spirit?

Locke's answer to this question consists in analysis of metaphysical ideas, which helps to explain "ideas of reflection."

Take the actual Immensity within which our bodies are conceived continually to exist, and the unbeginning and unending Duration within which our little lives, between birth and death, are conceived to be contained. The terms Immensity and Eternity are not idealess. We are on the way to what Immensity means, when we see or touch any object, and then mentally realise its finite extension; each transitory change giving rise to a consciousness of its finite duration. The one idea begins to form when we begin to use our senses of sight and touch; the other is "suggested" by every change in qualities of which we are percipient in sense, and by every "operation" which "passes" through our minds. Now the "modes" of which these initial ideas are susceptible are, Locke reports, "inexhaustible and truly infinite." In his own patient judicial way, he finds curious analogies between what we mean by extension and immensity, and what we mean by succession or change and eternity. Neither is limited to concrete things or concrete persons, for by abstraction we can suppose a space empty of bodies, and a time empty both of bodies and spirits. Particular places and periods are of course relative to what is individual and finite; but Immensity and Eternity mean what is irrelative and independent of the concrete individual. Space is trinal, while succession has only one dimension. No two individual things can exist in idea in the same space; all things can be conceived to exist at the same time. The parts of extension cannot be imagined as successive; the parts of succession cannot be imagined to coexist. All these are somehow intellectual necessities; they include what we can never see; for infinite space or immensity is invisible, and infinite duration cannot be found in any consciousness we have of a transitory mental "operation." Yet we are able to throw meaning into the words "immensity" and "eternity." Whether what we mean by unoccupied space and unoccupied time is substance or quality, Locke says that he is not obliged to explain; at least till those that ask the question put some clear and distinct meaning into the term substance and into the term quality. But the metaphysical mystery which he reports in the ideas that we find (actually or potentially) constituting the meaning of the words " space " and " time " is,—that something in our minds hinders us from thinking any limit to either. We find, when we try, that we are *obliged* somehow to lose our positive idea or mental picture of a finite space—however extensive—in the *negative* idea of Immensity ; and our positive idea of the longest succession in the *negative* idea of Eternity. Now we have never seen or touched Immensity ; nor is any succession of which we can have experience an unbeginning and unending succession. Immensity and Eternity are outside and beyond all merely finite presentations or representations. Yet Locke suggests that if we reflect we are sure to have the ideas through an operation of mind which forces us to think of space as being boundless, and of time as unbeginning and unending. " I would fain meet with any thinking man that *can* in his thoughts set any bounds to space more than he can to duration." Thus, by implication at least, he acknowledges, in the meaning of the terms Immensity and Eternity, something which cannot be exemplified in finite mental images, something in which all finite spaces and times are lost or transformed. This is virtually to acknowledge that we are intellectually obliged to *add* to the concrete extensions and times of external and internal sense. The addition, and the mental obligation to add, are neither of them fully accounted for by our perceptions of the finite phenomena of things and of persons. Locke virtually makes it come under the head of

" mental operations " of which, when our intelligence is sufficiently educated, we are obliged to be conscious,— thus recognising in " reflection " more than an empirical internal sense. His own reports about the meaning of Immensity and the meaning of Eternity imply (whether he saw this or not) that those terms connote something that is *put upon us* by intrinsic necessity of reason, not *accidentally presented to us* in the finite data of sense. The terms Immensity and Eternity, he insists, are not empty idealess sounds. They express ideas in which (if I may so put it) finite spaces and times are lost, and make way for unimaginable ideas, which last neverthe- less are not meaningless but carry a negative significa- tion—individual finitude in contrast with the Infinity which transcends it—so that

> " Our weakness somehow shapes
> The shadow time."

Locke, with characteristic honesty, reports this mental fact, and does not appear to find in it disproof of his main proposition—that all human ideas may be analysed into meanings we acquire in the use of our senses, and meanings we acquire through reflection. He does not ask, indeed, *why* the mind is obliged to add without limit, and to divide without limit, when it is dealing with spaces and times. He simply reports, as a fact of human understanding, that Immensity and Eternity are inevitable negative ideas; and that the infinite divisi- bility of spaces and times is also an inevitable negative idea. Every mental endeavour to exemplify the mean- ings expressed by these terms, in positive or imaginable examples, ends, he would have to allow, in the contra-

dictory attempt to represent as a quantity, and therefore as finite, what is outside the category of quantity.
The idea of *the unquantifiable* is "suggested" by the
positive ideas of spaces and times which we have
had in our sense experience. For when we try to
"ideate" the infinite in space, or in duration, we at
first usually form some large idea (imaginable *as a quantity* by beings whose imagination is powerful enough),
as of millions of miles, or of years multiplied millions of
times. But this sort of mental exercise does not explain
the mental obligation always to go further; nor the
conviction we have that, after going ever so far, we are
as remote from the unquantifiable Infinite on which we
are being precipitated, as we were at the beginning of
the process. It only describes the initial steps which
lead to the unique issue of what Locke calls "an idea
which lies in obscurity, and has all the indeterminate
confusion of a negative idea." The finite ideas of particular spaces or times, however vast, only lead us on to
this; but they are not themselves this, nor can they, as
finite, account for what they thus lead us into. Locke,
with all his dislike to "obscure ideas," and consequent
desire to reduce all ideas to finite distinctness in imagination, was too faithful to facts to pass by these inevitable mysterious ideas. This appears in his way of
making the thoughts of Immensity and Eternity crucial
tests of the sufficiency of his logical analysis of human
ideas.[1]

Another crucial test is found in the intractable idea
of Substance, contained in complex ideas of concrete or

[1] See Book II., chaps. xiii.-xvii.

individual things, and in the complex idea of our own individuality that is presupposed in all ideas "given to us" in experience. He tries, indeed, to phenomenalise Substance into sense or imagination, as he had tried to phenomenalise Immensity and Eternity; but he finds that it, as little as they, *can* be positively phenomenalised, and yet that none of them can be got rid of, or, bereft of their unimaginable meanings, be dismissed as empty sounds. For the complex idea of an *unsubstantiated* aggregate of sensible qualities, or of a like aggregate of self-conscious operations, without a centre of unity to which they may be "attributed," is, he finds, unthinkable. An adjective without a corresponding substantive is meaningless till a substantive is assumed to be understood. To say that all adjectives necessarily presuppose substantives in their meaning, is to express in another way this obligation to *substantiate* our simple ideas. Locke feels this; but he complains that the meaning of substantiation is "obscure," and that we neither have it, nor can have it, directly from external or internal sense; although the data of the senses lead up to it, or give occasion for it,—just as finite spaces and times lead up to, or give occasion for, obscure negative ideas of Immensity and Eternity. He concludes that the idea of Substance must be a complex and abstract idea, made up of the general idea of "something" (not a meaningless word, although he does not analyse its meaning), along with the idea of a support (also a significant term) to qualities of which we become aware in sense or in reflection. Abstract "substance" is an unreal "creature of the understanding," which our minds form. "Substance" is not a meaningless word, therefore ; although the only meaning Locke can put into it at last is the negative one of " an uncertain supposition of we know not what." [1] Any attempt to phenomenalise, and form an idea-image or example of, substance, material or mental, apart from the sense phenomena or spiritual phenomena in which actual substances are manifested, would thus be as impossible as it would be to form an idea-image of Immensity or of Eternity. It is another sort of idea than a mental image that we have when we put meaning into the term. When we try to embody the meaning in a finite image, we are baffled by an endless incomprehensible regress. If one asks *what* the "substance" is to which this colour or that odour belongs, and is told that it is the solid and extended particles of which the coloured and odorous mass consists, this indeed gives a substance that is picturable, as such particles are ; but then it is inadequate to the genuine idea of substance—for one finds that one is mentally obliged to ask in turn what *their* substance is, and having got in reply only something else that is picturable, he has to repeat the question for ever, as long as he gets nothing which transcends imagination. " He is," says Locke, " in a difficulty like that of the Indian, who, after explaining that the world rested on an elephant, which in its turn was supported by a broad-backed tortoise, could at last only suppose the tortoise to rest on 'something'—I know not what." We can neither (in one sense) think, nor (in another sense) refrain from thinking, the meaning that is connoted by the term substance. The only positive part of this complex idea is the aggregate of

[1] Book I., chap. iv. s. 18.

simple ideas or qualities in which abstract substance is exemplified. Apart from these, we cannot have any idea-image of that which manifests them, *per se;* whether what we are trying to think about is a sensible thing, or a finite spirit, or the Divine Being. The only way in which we can have any positive idea of God, for example, is through our power of supposing ideas or qualities given in reflection enlarged without limit—*i.e.,* without regard to the category of quantity. *Why* we are in this strange mental predicament, of neither being able to image substance, nor to refrain from thinking this its negative unphenomenalisable meaning, Locke does not ask. Curiously, it does not seem to have occurred to him that this mental inability to refrain from thinking more than we can mentally picture, needs itself to be explained; and that it cannot be explained by the contingent advent of a miscellaneous crowd of idea-images in external and internal sense.

Locke's perplexity about Substance partly arises from the tendency of his philosophic thought to isolate it from all its phenomena or qualities, and then try to find meaning in a term which pretends to express what is thus meaningless because isolated. "Taking notice," he says, "that a certain number of simple ideas go together, and not imagining how they can subsist of themselves, we accustom ourselves to suppose some substratum wherein they do subsist, and from whence they do result." Of this "substratum" our only idea would be the impossible one of something without qualities. This, accordingly, would be Locke's general idea of "reality," which, curiously, he did not otherwise include among what I have called his crucial instances.

ʌowing the phenomenal data, he seems to imply
ʍe know nothing of the substantial reality, which
ʌus concealed instead of being revealed by its own
ʌnomena.   The substantial reality with Locke seems
be something that exists without making any revela-
ʌon of what it is; not a something that is continually
ʀevealing itself in its qualities, which are its various
ways of acting, in which it is concreted while they in
turn are concreted in it.   He complains that we have
an obscure notion, or indeed cannot know at all, a substance thus stripped of all qualities, and existing in its
empty "reality."   If this is pure or absolute Being, it
is indeed shut out of all relation to knowledge, for it
needs its phenomena to make it known or manifest.[1]

Locke's reluctance to admit as meaning in a term
anything which cannot be analysed into what is imaginable, is further illustrated in his somewhat incoherent
treatment of the meaning of the personal pronoun "I,"
in the chapter on "Personal Identity."   He is at a loss
to find *continued* personality in the absence of continued
conscious manifestation and memory of the same ; although, in another part of the 'Essay,'—when leaning
to the conclusion that we are all at intervals unconscious
—*e.g.*, in dreamless sleep,—he argues that such breaks or
intervals in conscious life are not inconsistent with the
permanence of the spiritual substance. He distinguishes,
too, between sameness of spiritual substance and sameness of person, using the latter in its forensic meaning.[2]

[1] Book II., chap. xxiii.; also Book I., chap. iv. s. 18.
[2] Book II., chap. xxvii.

And he does not analyse the meaning of the ambiguous
term " same."

The report which Locke gives of our ideas of Causality and Power presented in their concrete or individual
examples, as we have it in the twenty-sixth and twenty-
first chapters of the second book, deserves special attention, inasmuch as these are (above all) metaphysical
ideas or meanings.   Moreover, his account of our knowledge of two of the three ontological realities, in the
fourth book,[1] is an application of the idea of causality.
The intellectual demand for a " cause " of an event, is
what we find a matured mind cannot help, making,
whenever a change is observed.   Yet it is a demand
for something which, when we try to analyse our meaning, we find it difficult to explain.   So that " cause " and
" power " have become endowed with various connota-.
tions, and are eminently ambiguous terms.   The idea
of " power " perplexed Locke more than any other
idea.   This appears in the transformations which the
twenty-first chapter, in which it is analysed, underwent in the successive editions of the ' Essay.'   His
perplexity is not so obvious in the twenty-sixth chapter,
in which he may be said merely to describe the occasions
on which the relational idea of " cause and effect " arises,
and in which it is exemplified.   We think a cause, he
tells us, whenever we see or hear or otherwise become
aware of a change ; because we constantly " observe "
that " qualities " and " finite substances *begin* to exist ; "
and also that they " *receive* their existence " from other
beings which " produce " them.   Seeing, for example,

[1] Book IV., chaps. x., xi.

that in the substance which we call wax the change
which we call fluidity is constantly produced by the
application of a certain degree of heat, we in consequence, somehow (he does not explain how), come to
think of heat as its cause (whatever cause may mean)
and fluidity as the effect. This is merely to report (a
part of) what happens in our minds when we observe
a particular instance of customary sequence, and are
thus led by habit to connect the change with something else. It leaves what is peculiar in this sort
of mental experience unexplained and even unstated,
under cover of question - begging terms, such as " receive existence from," " produced by," &c., which *mean
more* than merely causal succession, however frequent
or " customary." How do we come to throw their
peculiar meaning into such terms, and what is the
peculiar meaning that we throw into them ? What is
meant by a " cause " of heat ? We can image mentally
what we mean by heat; but can we, in like manner,
image mentally all that we mean by its " cause"; or can
all that meaning be resolved into " observation " of
phenomena followed by other phenomena ;—including
even the inherited observations of our ancestors, of
which Locke, by the way, takes no account ? Is there
not—in the genuine meaning of the term " cause," when
it is fully analysed, and made to include the intellectual
obligation we are somehow under to think it,—is there
not something which no " observations," however constant — individual or inherited — of such sequences as
fluidity " issuing " from the application of fire to wax,
can explain ? What is the *need*, in the reason, order, or
nature of things, for the causal expectation ; or *what*

do we look for when we "expect" and try to find a cause? Do we not find that the obligation at last resolves into one that is imposed by the Reason that is immanent in the nature of things (yet in which men share), to think the universe as an orderly system,—as a system in which this reason *is* immanent,—a system essentially and ultimately teleological; or, in theological language, constantly created, or constantly sustained, by the reason and purpose that are supreme in it? For does not all merely physical or natural causality, at last, presuppose power—power to produce and sustain laws in nature—evolutionary or any other laws— of mere succession? Is not the idea of "power," acaccording to even Locke's account of it, a meaning really got "through consciousness of our own voluntary agency, and therefore through reflection."[1] As far as *mere* "observation" can give rise to the causal idea or meaning, anything might *a priori* be supposed the cause of anything. No observable or finite number of examples of sequence can guarantee the *universal* constancy of *such* sequences; nor can it even introduce into the meaning of the ambiguous term "cause" what is meant by "production," or by "giving existence to." Locke himself seems to allow that no "succession"— however constant — of sensible phenomena can present ultimate originative agency,—this being an idea which cannot be phenomenalised, especially in external sense. In changes among bodies and their atoms, neither an individual, nor successive generations of men could "observe" origination—*i.e.*, creation. Only partial and temporary phenomenal order—order, the existence of

[1] Book II., chap. xxi.

which itself needs originating cause—can be observed; only phenomena, which *may* be significant and therefore interpretable, but which must receive their significance from Supreme Reason immanent in them.

Our ideas of the " production " of changes, or of the outcome of changes from sufficient " causes " into which they may be refunded, is obscurely referred by Locke to reflection upon what we are morally conscious of when we exert will; because (he might have added) this consciousness involves obligation to acknowledge personal responsibility for the voluntary exertion, thus revealing voluntary agents as creative causes of their own responsible acts. But his account of this personal power or agency is obscure and vacillating. Although the chapter in which it occurs was almost rewritten in the course of the four editions of the 'Essay' which appeared before his death, he remained at the end dissatisfied with his own report in it about the meaning of the term "power." He made no attempt to explain the transformation of the idea of *ourselves* as free or creative authors of our own actions—for which, in consequence of the " freedom " from *natural* causality, we recognise responsibility — into the *universal* rational principle of causality which he afterwards proceeds upon in the fourth book, when he is explaining our metaphysical knowledge of the real existence of God, and of the real existence of sensible things.[1] His language sometimes seems to *imply* that this transformation,— which connects the principle of a Divine cause of all merely natural causation with a metaphysical necessity involved in the constitution of intelligence,—is the

[1] Book IV., chap. x., xi.

issue of an inexplicable instinct; while, in other passages,
he seems to refer it to custom, or to inductive generalisation.   Now instinct is only a verbal cover for our ignorance of why causality is imposed on things and on our
minds ; and custom, as well as inductive generalisation,
presuppose, and are themselves explained by, causal connection and dependence, instead of being the explanation
of causality.   The postulate of the rationality of nature
is surely at the root of all possible reasoning about
what is given in experience.   The mere *fact* that I
and other persons find ourselves "free" causes of our
own actions, does not of itself justify the universal proposition, that *all* changes in the universe *must* be referred to a Power like this creative power of which
we are conscious in ourselves when we recognise our
moral responsibility ; with the implicate that *we* have
created the acts for which we are responsible, and that
they are thus in us supernatural acts.   That we are
somehow induced to conceive caused or "phenomenal"
causes in nature, and at last free uncaused or supernatural power in God and in man, is a fact vaguely proceeded upon in the 'Essay'; but without an explanation of its origin, as involved in the rationality, first of
physical experience, and then of the moral experience
to which the physical is subordinate, so as to leave those
who reject it the prey of universal scepticism.   Locke
only describes the circumstances in which the idea arises
in an individual mind—the idea, too, embodied in particular examples.   But one still puts the previous question,—*Why* the human mind is obliged, or induced, to
refund all perceived changes into sufficient causes of
which they are the issues ; and why each set of ante-

cedent phenomena into which we refund in thought new phenomena, themselves give rise to a fresh demand for yet preceding phenomena, on which they in turn depend—while at the end of the longest causal regress the mind is still conscious of dissatisfaction, until it finds rest in a truly originative cause, that is to say, in uncaused or final Reason, which stops the regress.

It was too, *a priori*, a speculation for Locke to show that without natural causality in the succession of phenomena there could be no rationality in nature, and therefore no reasoning on the part of man, either demonstrative or probable, about natural sequences and coexistences ; and that if free, or phenomenally uncaused, power—" final cause "—was not a constituent of our experience, those words in language which express moral government and responsibility could have no meaning or idea in them. This reduction to the absurd of every virtually empirical analysis of the meaning of the terms " cause " and " power," we find no trace of in the ' Essay on Human Understanding.' Its author's aversion to whatever had an appearance of mysticism, made him pass slightly over the metaphysical mysteries that are wrapped up in an experience like ours ;—which is conditioned by ideas of place that are at last lost in the unimaginable idea of Immensity ; of time, at last lost in the unimaginable idea of Endlessness ; and of changes among phenomena at last lost in the unimaginable ideas of Substance, continuous Personality, and physical backed and explained by originative Causation.

Locke next analyses our complex ideas of Morality.[1]

[1] Book II., chap. xxviii.

In ethics he had to face questions which he hardly helps us to appreciate. What is the meaning of " ought " ; and can that meaning be resolved into " is,"—consistently with the implicates of our moral experience ? Are not " ought " and " is " different in idea ? Is Duty only prudential ? Does it not presuppose something distinctive that is latent in all our judgments of ourselves and others, as persons responsible for our acts ? The metaphysic of our ethical ideas is more meagre in the ' Essay ' than its metaphysic of our ideas of nature. But enough has been said to illustrate Locke's crucial instances in verification of his thesis,—that our ideas are dependent on the activities of experience.

The ideas of good and evil, according to Locke, are in the last analysis ideas of pleasure and pain. " Moral good and evil is only the conformity or disagreement of our voluntary actions to some law whereby good or evil is drawn on us from the will and power of the Lawmaker, which good or evil, pleasure or pain, is that we call reward or punishment." The foreseen pleasures and pains which follow actions are our motives to the performance of them, and in this Locke is at one with utilitarian moralists. On the other hand, he finds that our knowledge of the principles of right conduct is due to a perception or intuition of their obligation, which is thus self-evident. But it is not innate ; for in individual minds it may lie undeveloped into idea or consciousness. Locke's rejection, in the first book of the ' Essay,' of the innateness of moral ideas led to the misunderstanding which imputed to him also rejection of self-evidence in moral judgments.

Throughout Locke's logical analysis of our metaphysical and moral ideas, we find a constant aversion to regard them independently of the concrete experience in which they are embodied,—independently, that is, of their actual realisation in consciousness and in individual examples. Exemplified space, time, number, substance, causality, and morality, depend upon experience, which supplies the examples. The underlying necessities of reason which pervade the concrete experience in those cases, with its implied ideas and judgments that are independent of examples, together with the explanation of those abstract "necessities,"—all involved considerations too remote for Locke, and foreign to the investigation of facts that alone fell within the design of the 'Essay,' which sought to settle what *is* exemplified in experience, not what *must be* in *a priori* independence of the actual.

CHAPTER V.

METAPHYSICAL : HUMAN KNOWLEDGE AND ITS LIMITS— THE THREE ONTOLOGICAL CERTAINTIES.[1]

LOCKE's logical and psychological analysis of our ideas, contained chiefly in the second and third books of the 'Essay,' does not comprehend his main design. At the end of this long and patient analysis, he saw that his reader might be apt to complain that he had been all the while only amused by "a castle in the air," and ready to ask "what the purpose is of all this stir about mere ideas." Mere ideas, he might say, even the most complex and abstract, do not carry us beyond ourselves into real certainties about God and the external Universe. Our ideas themselves are neither God nor the Universe. They may be true and conformable to reality—whatever reality means,—but they may also be false, for aught that they themselves show. We may take for granted, if we please, that we have a real knowledge of whatever we have an idea of; or we may take for granted that we know nothing at all, whatever our ideas may be. If our consciousness may only reach to "simple apprehensions," the visions of

[1] See 'Essay,' Book IV., chap. i.-xiii.

an enthusiast and the reasonings of a sober man will be equally certain, or equally uncertain. The supreme question remains : Are all or any of our ideas true—that is to say, conformable to the reason that must be presupposed in nature ; and if so, on what ground in reason may one feel certain of this ? Can my claim to be certain, or even to presume probability, be vindicated ; and if so, how, and what is the extent of the absolute certainty, or even reasonable probability, which man can vindicate for himself ?

Answers to these questions are given in the fourth book. To find them was the design of the ' Essay.' And its fourth book, in treating of certainty and probability, treats by implication of the ideas signified by those and like terms, which were omitted in the foregoing logical analysis of ideas. In introducing simple ideas of reflection in the second book, Locke had proposed in the sequel to analyse some of their modes, such as "reasoning, judging, knowledge, belief, opinion, and faith."[1] He does this in treating of knowledge or certainty and of probability, when he has to make what is virtually an analysis of these complex ideas of reflection.

Locke assumes that neither certainties nor probabilities can carry men beyond their own ideas—in other words, make them independent of intelligence. Whatever they know, if they know anything, must be related to their conscious life ; for things out of all relation to consciousness or idea they can neither know nor believe in. And the only consciousness into which each man can immediately enter must be his own. Men cannot think other ideas, or think with other faculties,

[1] Book II., chap. v.

L

than their own. Their certainties and their presumptions of probability must be their discernments of the relations of their own ideas or meanings. The propositions in which these find expression must all contain significant, not idealess, terms — singular or common. The realist element was, by abstraction, left out of account, in the book about ideas, which were there of set purpose treated irrespectively of their truth or falsehood. Till assertion or denial enters in, our mere ideas are not looked at in the light of being either true or false : they are so looked at only when account is taken of the element of reality with which they may be charged. Knowledge involves more than ideas. It involves " perception," or rational intuition, Locke goes on to explain —" discernment of agreements, or disagreements "—in a word, of the relations—of our simple or complex ideas.[1] This needs a proposition to express what it involves. To say that certainty and probability are concerned with relations among our ideas, and that ideas are involved in all our judgments, is only another way of saying, that the subjects and predicates of propositions must each contain meaning ; that meaningless terms in any proposition cannot become certainties or even probabilities, for their propositions do not affirm or deny anything. No idea, no meaning : nothing for us to know, or as to which we can even be in error. If we are certain, for instance, that " matter exists," or that " God exists," there must be some idea or meaning in the terms " matter," " God," and " existence " in order to our having this knowledge. Otherwise the words are empty sound—jargon—abracadabra.

[1] Book IV., chap. i. s. 2.

By Knowledge Locke means absolute certainty, or rational perception of necessary relations between ideas or meanings ; and by Probability, assent induced on more or less probable presumption, that the ideas are related according to what we presume. To such presumptions Locke, by a peculiar usage of his own, confines the term "judgment."[1] Now, all the "perceptions," or rational intuitions, which constitute knowledge, and the "presumptions" which constitute probability, are concerned with relations. Each is articulately expressed by a proposition, in which the ideas or meanings compared are signified by the subject and predicate ;—an "idea" being whatever can be signified by the subject or predicate of a proposition. Further, both intellectual certainty and probability, he would say, may be either (1) in regard to relations between any ideas ; or (2) between an idea and the idea of reality—*i.e.*, between any idea and what we mean by the word "real." The second, which Locke calls real certainty or knowledge, contains a faith or assurance which is wanting in the former. "Where we perceive the agreement or disagreement of any of our ideas, there is *certain knowledge ;* and wherever *we are sure* that these ideas agree with [what we mean by] the *reality* of things, there is *real knowledge.*"[2] But when we presume agreement (or disagreement) between an idea and what we mean by reality, "before this relation certainly appears"—*i.e.*, when it is not perceived by intuitive reason—then there is only probability, with correlative "assent" or "opinion," —"judgment," in Locke's peculiar meaning of that word. And he reiterates, as the fact of chief human

[1] Book IV., chap. xiv. s. 4.   [2] Book IV., chap. iv. s. 18.

interest, that a great deal of what is commonly supposed to be knowledge, or absolute certainty, is not really such — being only more or less probable presumption, in which the clear rational intuition of absolute certainty is wanting.

Locke's matter-of-fact report about our rational certainties — that is, our "perceptions" or intuitions of the necessary relations that are discerned in all self-evident and demonstrated propositions — is contained within the first thirteen chapters of the fourth book. The remainder of the book reports, in the same matter-of-fact way, what he found in examining the "assent" which we are moved to give, on grounds of more or less probable presumption, and in giving which most of our erroneous beliefs arise. On those presumptions of probability, nevertheless, human life really turns, as Locke and Butler are fond of reminding transcendental philosophers.

"Perception," in the second book, was usually a synonym for mere idea. In the ninth chapter of that book it is limited to "the first faculty of the mind exercised about ideas," or "the first and simplest idea we have from reflection;"—in which "the mind is for the most part only passive," because what it perceives it cannot, by an act of will, perceive otherwise than it does. But in the chapters on knowledge, in the fourth book—in which absolute certainty is treated of, and contrasted with merely presumed probability — "perception" is equivalent to intellectual intuition. Examples occur when we see intellectually that "this is not that;" that "two and three are five;" or that "an object, the qualities of which are present to our senses, actually exists." "It is on *intuition* that depends all the certainty and evidence of all our knowledge ; which certainty every one finds so great that he cannot imagine, and therefore not require, a greater." [1] On the other hand, where this distinct rational insight is wanting, as in our expectation of some future event, there is only a "presumption." "Mr Locke," Reid says, "has pointed out the extent and limits of human knowledge, in his fourth book, with more accuracy than any philosopher had done before ; but he has not confined it to 'agreements and disagreements of ideas,' as his definition of it would require. And I cannot help thinking that a great part of the fourth book is a refutation of the principles laid down in the first chapter." But if Locke means by knowledge consisting in "perception of agreement or disagreement of ideas," that it is perceived relation between significant (*i.e.*, not idealess) subjects and predicates of propositions, this alleged inconsistency between the definition and the subsequent treatment of the subject disappears. In fact, the term " perception " is expressly used in three different meanings in the 'Essay': (1) Sense phenomena and acts of mind as simply apprehended ; (2) perception of the signification of signs ; and (3) perception or rational intuition (immediate or mediate) of relations between ideas or meanings,—which last alone is Locke's "knowledge." [2]

The first question discussed about human knowledge, or the indubitable judgments that arise in human consciousness, relates to the *sorts* of relations which reason thus perceives, a question which also concerns our pre-

[1] Book IV., chap. ii. s. 1.   [2] See Book II., chap. xxi. s. 5.

sumptions of probability. Here Locke finds that all the certainties and probabilities man can have must regard one or other of *four* sorts of relations; and also that in only one of these four is there included that "common sense" assurance of agreement of any idea with the idea of reality which constitutes *real* knowledge,—by which he here seems to mean, knowledge of what exists independently of the person who knows it.

According to Locke's report of the mental facts, all that we can be certain of must be either—(1) that the ideas compared in our judgments[1] are or are not identical,—as when we know that "blue cannot be yellow"; or (2) that they are in a necessary relation to one another,—as when one sees that "two triangles upon equal bases between two parallels must be equal"; or (3) that one idea or phenomenon coexists (as a quality) with certain other ideas or phenomena in the same substance; also (as implied in this) that this idea or phenomenon invariably precedes or follows that other in succession—orderly companionships of coexistence or of succession, in short, among the phenomena of the material and spiritual universe,—as when we judge that "iron is susceptible of magnetical impressions"; or (4) that one of our ideas corresponds to the idea of reality—to which term "reality" we must be able to attach *some* meaning, otherwise it could not enter into our judgments at all. All possible certainties, he assumes, must be found among one or other of those four sorts of relation.

But Locke does not find the absolute certainty of "knowledge" within *man's* reach alike in all the four.

[1] Book IV., chap. i. Judgment is *not* here used in its narrow Lockian meaning.

Indeed he finds it wanting in regard to what ordinary men might regard as practically the most important of the four relations—those of physical coexistence
and sequence, that make up our experience of what
happens in time, which form the third class. The
absolute certainty of knowledge, on Locke's report of
the mental facts, is found only in the other three kinds ;
—with this important difference, that, as regards the
first and second sorts of relation, we may reach universal truths that are certain as well as particular facts,
while our certainties about real existence are necessarily
limited to certainties about individuals ; for only individuals really exist, he assumes with the Nominalists,
universals being unreal products of abstraction.[1]

But while examples of absolute certainty, about particulars if not about universals, may be found among
the first, second, and fourth relations, man seeks for it
in vain in the practically all-important judgments about
coexistence or succession among phenomena. Here the
element of change enters ; and whatever is changeable is
subject to conditions of which we can have only obscure
ideas, for we know too little of the powers that are at
work to be able to anticipate their operation with certainty. Relations of coexistence and succession may
enter into presumptions, but they cannot, on account of
the obscurity of the conditions on which they depend,
be either self-evident or demonstrable to us. Now, as
these are the relations which men are trying to find in
all their experimental researches in quest of "laws of
nature," and as they are involved in all our scientific
expectations, it follows—so Locke argues—that man

[1] Book IV., chap. vii. s. 16.

can never reach the certainty of absolute knowledge in
any physical or inductive science; which thus, properly
speaking, is not science at all, if we mean by science
the absolute certainty of intuitive or demonstrated
reason. Conclusions reached by men in any of the
physical and natural "sciences" can be only subjective
presumptions or probabilities, at the root of which there
is obscurity to *our* eye of reason; man has always to
make a "leap in the dark," when he passes from the
now and here present, to the past, the distant, the
future, the general law.[1]

The account given in the 'Essay' of probabilities,
which thus belong to the third of the four sorts of
relation between the subjects and predicates of our propositions, may meanwhile be put aside, that we may
first consider Locke's report about human knowledge,
or our absolute certainties, as we have it chiefly in the
first thirteen chapters of the fourth book.

Locke reports, for one thing, regarding the certainties contained in mental experience, that he finds
differences in the way in which the "perceptions"
of necessary relations are arrived at. In some cases the
perception of the relation is immediate; that is, the
relation is self‑evident, so that we only need to be
distinctly conscious of the meanings expressed in the
subjects or predicates of the corresponding propositions
to become certain of it. It is so when we judge that a
"circle is not a triangle," or that "three is more than
two, and equal to one and two." In instances like
these, the intellectual obligation to make the judgment
is at once felt and perceived, without room for reason-

[1] See Book IV., chap. iii. ss. 9-17.

ing, or evidence external to what is contained within the terms of the proposition itself. But in a number of other cases the "perception," or rational intuition, is gained through the medium of some other certainty already reached intuitively. It is so, for instance, in the series of conclusions to which we are gradually led in chains of mathematical reasoning. There each step is taken with a rational perception of its self-evidence; but then we need to take several steps. This is what is called "demonstration," which is thus more difficult than intuition of self-evidence, so that in it we are in some degree liable to error, through want of memory, or from confusion of thought.

"In every step reason makes in demonstrative knowledge," to use Locke's own weighty words, "there is an intuitive knowledge of that agreement or disagreement it seeks with the next intermediate idea which it uses as proof; for if it were not so, that yet would need a proof, since without the perception of such agreement or disagreement there is no certainty of knowledge produced. If it be perceived by itself, it is intuitive knowledge; if it cannot be perceived by itself, there is need of some intervening idea, as a common measure, to show the agreement or disagreement. By which it is plain that every step in reasoning that produces knowledge [not mere presumption of probability] has itself intuitive certainty; which when the mind perceives there is no more required but to remember it, to make the agreement or disagreement of the ideas concerning which we inquire visible and certain. . . . So that this intuitive perception of the agreement or disagreement of the intermediate ideas in each step and progression of the demonstration, must be carried exactly in the mind; which, because in long deductions and the use of many proofs, the memory does not always so readily and exactly retain, therefore it comes to pass, that demonstration is more imperfect than [immediately] intuitive knowledge, and that men often embrace error for demonstration." [1]

To immediate perception of the self-evident, or to mediate perception of the demonstrated, as in all abstract mathematical and abstract ethical demonstrations, Locke reports that whatever in strictness can be called "knowledge" is confined, at least, in the processes of a human understanding. He can find examples of propositions from which the intellectual obscurity of "probable presumption" is excluded, only among those seen to be self-evident, or those which, with considerable help from memory, are seen to be demonstrated. The known with certainty, as distinguished from the merely presumed, is all either immediately or mediately self-evident to reason.

Yet he also finds among the facts of human understanding, when examined in the "historical, plain, matter-of-fact" method, notable examples of a sort of certainty that is neither immediately nor mediately self-evident in the light of its rational necessity, while nevertheless it *is* certain. Sense-perceptions, in which men mentally affirm the real existence of things that are actually present to one or more of their senses at the time, involve judgments which contain more than mere presumption of probability; nevertheless, they want some marks of the certainty we have in self-evident knowledge, and in mathematical or other demonstrations.[2] For there is nothing contradictory to what is self-evident, or to the demonstrated "perceptions" of reason, in the supposition that our sense-perceptions may all be illusions. We could have our sense ideas or perceptions

[1] Book IV., chap. ii. s. 7.   [2] Book IV., chap. ii. s. 14.

exactly as we now have them, and at the same time exclude all assurance of reason that the objects perceived were " real "; on the other hand, we cannot suppose that self-evident propositions, or abstract conclusions reached by demonstration, are other than, in their self-evidence, or by demonstration, they are seen to be.   When I see with the eye of sense a man or a tree, I *may* suppose that I dream, and that the "sight" is part of a prolonged dream.   But when I see intellectually that "a whole is greater than its part," I *cannot* even suppose that the reality is other than I see it to be. Nevertheless, one can distinguish in another way between a dream and an actual perception of sense-given reality.   For one cannot consistently with sanity identify "looking on the sun by day, and only imagining a sun at night."   So Locke recognises among the certainties, and not merely among the probabilities, all sense perceptions of the real existence of things now and here present.   He finds in sense more than isolated individual sensations, from which no external conclusions can be drawn, because no perception of reason is involved in them.   We must therefore separate him from those who consider sense-perception as only a passive capacity for isolated sensations.   Locke sees an obscure presence of intuitive reason in the operations of the senses.

On the whole, according to Locke's report, there is in human understanding an intellectual " perception,"— mediate or immediate,—of abstract mathematical and abstract moral relations; and there is also immediate sense " perception " of the real existence of things visible and tangible while they are actually present to sense —inasmuch as every sane man judges that qualities

sensibly perceived are qualities of things that would
exist whether *he* had ideas of them or not. In all
this, however, there is one important difference. The
rational "perceptions," in which pure mathematical and
moral knowledge consists, are abstract, and therefore
may be universal. Sense "perceptions," on the contrary, are concrete, matter of fact, and only of this,
that, or the other individual thing. What we know in
complete abstraction from concrete reality *may* be seen
to be universally necessary, although its knowing subject is only a human understanding. But knowledge
which involves actual existence is limited, in a human
understanding, to individuals only, and cannot become
universal. In this sphere of earthly life, when we rise
above the individual, we enter the realm of probability.
Except in abstract truth, no human judgments about
finite things and persons can rise higher than presumption. Such is Locke's report.

What is meant by "reality" or "real existence"—
that is to say, what our "idea" of it is—Locke curiously
left unexplained in his logical analysis of our metaphysical ideas. Unless in the case of certain qualities
of matter, it hardly occurs to him that, as with Berkeley, ideas themselves *may* be the real things—or at least
one side of reality, true or false according as *they* fulfil
certain conditions,—that an idea and a thing may be
two phases of what is essentially the same. Locke's
"mere ideas" are logically abstracted from knowledge
and reality.

But things of sense that are now and here present
are not the only *individual* realities which Locke re-

ports that he finds on reflection to be contained in human knowledge. We can be certain of more individual reality than this. Indeed, knowledge is presupposed in the more certainties of sense. Locke reports three ontological certainties. For, — besides existing things presently around him,—each man is, at least potentially, if not with distinct consciousness, certain of the reality of his own existence as a conscious being ; and he is also certain of the real existence of God, although not quite in the same way as he is of his own self-conscious existence. Take these two last.

1. That each man has an intuitively certain knowledge of his individual existence as a conscious being, Locke shows after the fashion of Descartes :—

" We perceive this fact," he says, " so plainly and so certainly by intuition, that it neither needs nor is capable of any proof. I think, I reason, I feel pleasure and pain : can any of these be more evident to me than my own existence is ? If I doubt of all other things, that very doubt makes me perceive my own existence, and will not suffer me to doubt of that. If I know I feel pain, it is evident that I have *as* certain perception of my own existence as I have of the pain that I feel ; or if I doubt, I have *as* certain perception of the thing doubting as of that thought which I call doubt. Experience [reflection] thus shows us that we have an intuitive knowledge of our own existence, and an internal infallible perception that we are. In every act of sensation, reasoning, or thinking, we are conscious of our own being, and, in this matter, come not short of the highest degree of certainty." [1]

Such is Locke's report about our knowledge or certainty of our own existence. It is that we find ourselves

[1] Book IV., chap. ix.

obliged to predicate what is meant by the term "real existence" of that which is signified by the personal pronoun "I." Yet in the parts of the 'Essay' in which our ideas were logically analysed, he had not helped us much to understand the meaning or idea intended by "real existence." He reports, indeed, that he finds what we mean by "existence" to be an idea that is suggested by all the "simple ideas" of sensation and reflection.[1] Now all knowledge is concerned about ideas, for whatever we know must have some sort of meaning. What then is the idea or meaning that we have when we are conscious of our individual existence and continued identity? As Berkeley remarks, with a reference to Locke, "the words 'real,' 'existence,' &c., are often in our mouths when little that is clear or determined answers them in our understandings." Indeed, in this very instance, Berkeley distinguishes what we have a *notion* of from what we have merely an *idea* of, as it "seems improper and liable to difficulties to make a person an idea, and ourselves ideas."[2] He would say that we have a "notion" rather than an idea of our own existence, when "our own existence" is distinguished from the changing operations in which it is manifested. Hume assumed that no idea of self (or notion either) other than that of successive consciousnesses could be found, and so he became bound to banish personal pronouns as empty sound.[3]

---

[1] Book IV., chap. vii. s. 7.

[2] *I.e.*, a sensuous presentation or representation (*Vorstellung*), in Berkeley's use of "idea."

[3] Locke in one passage seems to say that neither idea nor notion (for he regarded them as synonyms) is necessary in the case of the personal pronoun. "Since the things the mind contemplates are

But the fact of our own continuous existence as self-conscious persons is assumed by Locke as one of the individual facts which do not need proof because they are self-evident,—although not innate, *in his meaning of innateness.* My own existence means more than the existence of a series of separate conscious states. It implies their continuity in a permanent substance. We cannot know the states apart from the Ego manifested in them, nor can we know the Ego except as manifested in its changing acts and other conscious states. Consciousness necessarily involves the conviction of its own permanence, and this conviction is awakened in each conscious state, so that without it the state could not arise. This implication, however, is not expressed by Locke.

2. The existence of God, or the One Infinite Mind, is another of Locke's absolute certainties.[1] It is not innate knowledge ; but neither does he regard " perception " of our own existence as innate ; both depend on the individual man rising up unto the mental experience which contains the evidence. The certainty that God exists is not, like our knowledge of our own existence, self-evident : it is one of those demonstrable truths that are reached by a succession of steps, each of which has intuitive certainty, but which depend on memory and distinct thought for their recognition. It is thus only gradually that each man comes to see the intellectual necessity for One Supreme Reason and Will, in seeing

none of them *besides itself* present to the understanding, it is necessary that something else, as a representation of the thing it considers, should be present to it when it is considering them ;—and these are ideas."—Book IV., chap. xxi. s. 4. Elsewhere his language is different.

[1] Book IV., chap. x.

the necessary connection of this with the empirical fact that his individual conscious existence had a beginning.

"Though God," says Locke, "has given us no innate ideas or knowledge of Himself, though He has stamped no original characters on our minds wherein [at first, and before we began to have any experience] we might read His Being; yet, having furnished us with those [innate] faculties our minds are endowed with, He hath not left Himself without a witness. . . . We cannot want a clear proof of Him as long as we carry *ourselves* about with us. . . . Though the existence of God be the most obvious truth that reason discovers to us; and though its evidence be, if I mistake not, equal to mathematical certainty; yet to see it requires thought and attention, and the [individual] mind must apply itself to a regular deduction of it from some part of its intuitive knowledge."

In fact, neither this, nor indeed any part of "our intuitive knowledge," is innate, in Locke's meaning of innateness. "Demonstration," on which he makes the knowledge of God depend, is, on the contrary, a bit by bit application of what is assumed (at least in the fourth book) to be implied in universal ideas of causality and power. But justification of universality is hardly found in the previous analysis in the second book of the meaning of causality and power. The eternal existence of Supreme Active Mind is, in the fourth book, a concrete expression of the abstract necessity for uncaused Intelligence in a universe that is changing, of which we become aware with a certainty equal to that of mathematics, when we realise that our own self-conscious existence had a beginning. Each of us has a "perception" of his own existence now; each is also obliged to believe that *he* has not existed always. Men are also absolutely certain (Locke does not show how or why), that "nothing can no more produce any real being than it can be equal to two right angles." By this reasoning, each step seen by rational intuition to be absolutely certain, he lands in the conclusion, that there must ever be one most powerful and most knowing Being ; in whom, as the origin of all, must be contained all the perfections that exist, or that can exist, and whence can issue causally only what is therein potentially contained. In the instance of my self-conscious existence, "mind" *has* "come out of" this Power ; so that, in order to be *adequate*, the Power must itself be "what we mean by mind." Intellect, this argument assumes, can alone explain intellect ; and therefore, if "sufficient" causality and power to explain the empirical fact that I began to exist is a necessity involved in the reason of things, there *must* be One Supreme Mind. As to what "mind" means when predicated of the Supreme Power, Locke is not so clear. In a letter written a few weeks before his death to Anthony Collins, referring to what we are entitled to mean by "mind" when we apply the term to the Supreme Being —the "idea" of Infinite Mind, in short— he says · "Though I call the thinking faculty in *man* 'mind,' yet I cannot, because of this name, equal it in anything to that infinite and incomprehensible Being, which, for want of right and distinct conceptions (ideas), is *called* Mind also, or the Eternal Mind."

The existence of One Supreme "Mind," or God, is Locke's unique example of a matter-of-fact reality that is seen, through demonstration, to be eternally necessary —at least on the supposition that the reasoner himself

P.—XV.   M

now exists and began to exist. It is the one exception to the contingency of all the other real beings whose existence we know or presume. For the certainties we can rise into in mathematics are certainties only when they are abstracted from real things. The real existence of God is the *one* necessity in concrete existence that comes within the range of a human understanding—the one ultimate necessity that is more than an abstraction. My own existence, though I cannot doubt its present reality, is not thus universally and absolutely necessary; still less the real existence of things presently existing around me.

As I have just said, it is not easy to reconcile Locke's account of the mathematical certainty of the real existence of One Supreme Mind with his previous analysis of the meanings of the principal terms contained in the "demonstration." His meagre analysis of the meaning of "cause," in the twenty-sixth chapter of the second book, even when supplemented by the hesitating account of the idea or meaning of "power," in the twenty-first chapter, fails to show how either term can contain the meaning needed to justify conclusions which involve the eternally necessary connection required by his argument. The idea signified by the term "cause" he had analysed into the meaning which rises in consciousness when we observe customary successions of phenomena; and when we observe that the substances to which the phenomena are referred "begin to exist," and judge that they "receive their existence" from the "operation of some other being." Though we may "observe" that they begin to exist, one asks how we can *observe* that they *receive their existence* from some other being, in merely

seeing that their existence *follows* its presence ? A
sequence may be observed ; but that one of the terms
is producer and the other the product is not observable.
At any rate the intellectual necessity, universality, and
eternity implied in this theistic argument are not " observable." Locke might call them negative "modes"
of simple ideas, which we are obliged to elaborate out
of the unanalysable data of external and internal
sense ; and which, having elaborated, we are obliged
to charge with the "*assurance*" that they agree with
reality. This is perhaps what he intended, in recognising as mental fact a demonstrably evident certainty of
the existence of God. He had to assume that the
relations of the ideas or meanings connoted by the subjects and predicates of the propositions contained in the
"demonstration" somehow carry this common - sense
assurance of the reality of what is asserted at each
step, and thus of the ultimate conclusion. But this
argument implies universality and necessity in other
propositions than those concerned with abstract truth ;
for Locke treats the conclusion that God exists as one
of individual fact and yet as eternally true. It is as
certain, he says, that God exists as any mathematical
conclusion can be. A "probable God" is inconsistent
with Locke's argument.[1]

The complex meaning that corresponds to the term
" God," when the Divine attributes as well as bare
" existence " are included, Locke had analysed inci-
dentally in the second book, in arguing that the term
expresses a meaning that is intelligible by man. He

[1] Compare with this of Locke, Clarke's ' Demonstration of the Existence and Attributes of God,' published fifteen years after.

makes it out to be a complex idea, composed of the complex idea of a finite spirit, modified by the negative idea of infinity.

"There is nothing," he remarks, "that can be included in the meaning of the word God, bating the negative meaning which alone we can attach to 'infinity,' that is not also a part of our complex ideas of other [individual] spirits. . . . For if we examine the idea we have of the incomprehensible Supreme Being, we shall find that we come by it in the same way as we come by the complex ideas we have of ourselves and other finite spirits; and that the complex ideas we have both of God and separate spirits are made up of the simple ideas we receive from reflection. That is, we having, from what we experiment in ourselves, got the ideas of existence and duration; of knowledge and power; of pleasure and happiness, and of several other qualities and powers which it is better to have than to be without;—when we would frame an idea the most suitable we can for the Supreme Being, *we enlarge every one of these with our idea of infinity*, and so putting them (thus enlarged) together make our complex idea of God. For that the mind has the power of enlarging (to infinity) some of its ideas received from sensation and reflection has been already shown. . . . In His essence we do not know God, not knowing either the real essence of a pebble or of a fly, or of our own selves. We can have no other idea of Him but a complex one of existence, knowledge, power, happiness, &c., infinite and eternal; . . . all which being, as has been shown, originally got from sensation and reflection [*i.e.*, not independent of them], go to make up the complex idea or notion we have of God."[1]

The basis of Locke's theism is a modification of what has been called the cosmological argument, for it turns upon the contingent nature of his own existence as a self-conscious being. Because an intelligent person

[1] Book II., chap. xxiii. ss. 33-35.

now exists and began to exist, it is eternally necessary that an intellectual Being should exist and be supreme. As Locke puts it, the argument leads to the individual existence of a Supreme Mind,—one among many yet Supreme—rather than to recognition of the constantly necessary immanence of Active Reason, so implicated in the experienced universe, that it might be truly said that we all live and move and have our being in a reasonably constituted and morally governed system. Locke's argument, on the contrary, leans to the deistic conception of a God apart,—inferred from the contingent appearance of sensible things, or rather of intelligent persons,—not to the idea of pervading order, or ever-active reason, in nature, subordinate to moral reason and ever-active moral government of persons, as necessary presuppositions in our experience of things and persons. His is the theological idea that was characteristic of the eighteenth century ; not the theological idea which harmonises with the conceptions of dialectical and physical evolution which govern thought in the nineteenth century ; nor with a due sense of the inadequacy of a conception of God as an individual among individuals, rather than as the constant, all-pervading, yet transcendent presence of Supreme Order and Goodness, with what this implies,—necessarily presupposed at the root of all that happens—the rational implicate of a complete human experience.

3. Return now to Locke's account of our knowledge of the real existence of the universe of " things around us."

This—according to his account of what he found in human understanding—we can have " only by sensation." That there is " no *necessary* connection of rea-

son that any other real being (except God) has with the
real existence of any particular man and his or its
existence," was what Locke assumed in arguing for
God's existence ;—so that our knowledge of the existence of " things around us " had still to be vindicated.
No man can know the real existence of any other particular being than himself,—except that of God,—save
only when, and as long as, by actually operating upon
his organism, the thing makes itself perceived by him.[1]
" For the mere having an idea of anything in our mind,
or picturing its meaning, no more proves the real existence of that thing, than the picture of a man evidences
his being in the world, or than the visions of a dream
make up a true history." Merely knowing what the
words " real existence " mean, does not prove that
something is really existing,—unless there is embedded
in this idea of the thing that *inevitable assurance* of
the " reality " of its existence, which Locke assumes
that we do have in the knowledge of our own existence and our knowledge of the existence of God.
What, then, makes the difference between " only having ideas of " surrounding things, or being able to picture mentally what the words that signify them mean,
and an absolute certainty that they really exist ?
How can my ideas, which, so far as they are only
mine, can have no existence except when I am conscious of them—one perception going out of my consciousness before the next begins, — how can these
transitory operations reveal to me a real—that is, a

---

[1] This " operating " refers to the organic conditions which are
occasions rather than proper causes of sense-perception, as Locke
elsewhere explains.

permanent—external world? Instead of a reasoned theory of perception like that, for instance, of Malebranche, or that afterwards offered by Kant, Locke suggests a practical answer to this question in this fashion :—

"It is the *actual receiving* of ideas from without [what 're-ceiving' means he does not explain, for he offers no theory of sense-perception] that gives us notice of the real existence of other things [including other persons]; and makes us *know* that *something* doth exist at that time without us which causes [occasions] that idea in us—though perhaps we neither know nor consider *how* it does it. For it takes not from the certainty of our senses, and the ideas we receive by them, that we know not the manner in which they are produced. For example, whilst I write this, I have, by the paper affecting my eyes, that idea produced [*i.e.*, that perception called forth] in my mind which I call white ; by which I know that that quality . . . doth then really exist, and hath a being without me. And this, the greatest assurance I can possibly have, . . . is the testimony of my eyes, which are the proper and sole judges of this thing ; whose testimony I have reason to rely on as so certain, that I can no more doubt, whilst I write this, that I see white and black, and that something [extra-organic] really exists that causes [regularly precedes or accompanies] that sensation in me, than [I can doubt] that [within my organism] I write or move my hand,—which is a certainty [regarding what is extra-organic] as great as human nature is capable of concerning the real existence of anything—except a man's self alone, and God."

The " perception " we thus have, conditioned by our sense-organism, of the existence of things " without us " (extra-organic things), though it be not altogether so certain as our intuitive and demonstrated knowledge of our own existence and that of God ; or as the deductions of reason about clear abstract concepts of our own minds, in pure mathematics and in abstract ethics, yet involves, Locke maintains, " an assurance that deserves the name of knowledge or certainty." [1] When we have the inevitable assurance that our sense-faculty informs us aright concerning the real existence of things that naturally affect it (as when an appropriate extra-organic object affects our organ of sight), this—

"Cannot," Locke thinks, "pass for an ill-grounded confidence; for nobody can, in earnest, be so sceptical as to be uncertain of the real existence of those things which he is actually seeing and feeling. At least, he that can doubt so far, whatever he may have with his own thoughts, will never have any controversy with me—since he can never be sure I say anything contrary to his own opinion. . . . We cannot talk of knowledge itself but by the help of those faculties which are fitted to apprehend what the word means [*i.e.*, which give us the 'idea' of knowledge]. . . . But if, after all this, any one will be so sceptical as to distrust his senses, and to affirm that all we see and hear, feel and taste, during our whole being, is but the series and deluding appearances of a long dream, wherein there is no reality, and will therefore question the existence of things, or our knowledge of anything, I must ask him to consider, that, if all be a dream, then he doth but dream that he makes the question, and so it is not much matter that a waking man should answer him. . . . The testimony of our senses for this reality is not only as great as our frame can attain to, but as our condition needs. For he that sees a candle burning, and hath experimented the force of its flame by putting his finger in it, will little doubt that this is something which puts him to great pain; which assurance is enough, when a man requires no greater certainty to govern his actions by than what is *as certain as his actions themselves.* The evidence

[1] Book IV., chap. ii.

that this is something more than bare imagination is as great as we can desire,—being as certain to us as our pleasure and pain ; beyond which we have no concernment, either of knowing or being, . . . as this is sufficient to direct us in the attaining the good and avoiding the evil."

But with Locke each man's knowledge of the real existence of a sensible thing is confined to the moments in which he is actually sentient; together with the knowledge of its past existence which is afforded by his memory of his own previous sense-perceptions of it. This important qualification which he attaches to his practical refutation of scepticism concerning the things of sense, reduces human certainty of their real exist-ence or permanence to very narrow limits, if it does not, indeed, dissolve it altogether. " The certainty of this knowledge extends,"—so he explains,—" only as far as the present testimony of our senses employed about the particular objects that do thus affect them, and no fur-ther. When our senses do actually convey into our understandings any idea, we cannot but be satisfied that there doth something really exist without us at the time which doth actually produce (give occasion to) that idea which we then perceive; and we cannot so far distrust their testimony as to doubt that such col-lections of simple ideas (*i.e.*, complex ideas) as we have observed by our senses to be united together, do really exist together." That is to say, when we have the actual perception we cannot doubt the real exist-ence of what we perceive—as long, but only as long, as it is sensibly perceived.

But whenever we pass from present and remembered data of sense to expectations, or judgments about absent things, sense-knowledge gives place, Locke finds, to presumptions of probability. Our judgments of the real existence of sensible things that are not now, or have not been, present to our senses, are exclusively judgments of probability, not perception or knowledge.

"For, if I saw such a collection of simple ideas [*i.e.*, such a complex idea of an individual substance] as is wont to be called [*i.e.*, as is meant by the term] ' man,' existing together [coexistence of ideas] one minute since, and if I am now alone, I cannot be *certain* that the same man exists now. For there is no *necessary connection* of his existence a minute since with his existence now : by a thousand ways he may cease to be, since I had the testimony of my senses to his existence. And therefore, though it be highly probable that millions of men do now exist [unperceived by me], yet, whilst I am alone writing this, I have not that certainty of it which we strictly call knowledge ; though the great likelihood of it puts me past [practical] doubt ; and though it be reasonable for me to do several things upon the confidence that there are men now in the world [although my senses are not at the time informing me of this,—*i.e*, actually presenting the relative sense-phenomena to me]. But this is only probability, not knowledge " [*i.e.*, not immediate sense-perception, because its object is absent].

Locke thus reduces the entire certain knowledge of sensible things that man is capable of to one's present data of sense, and one's memory of past data—to what is, and what has been, presented to one's senses ; and transfers from the sphere of certainties to the sphere of probable presumptions, our assurance of the existence of any *absent* reality that is not remembered by us as having existed. There is no "necessary natural connection," that Locke can see, binding together "simple ideas of sense " in *continuous* coexistence in one subject, of which they would thus be qualities. A power by us incalculable may at any time interfere to alter the previously perceived appearance. Accordingly, in physical investigations *man* can go no further in the way of knowledge, or discernment of connection, than the immediate perception of the moment, or the mediate perception of memory, informs him. " We can have no certain knowledge of *universal* truths concerning natural bodies." The certain knowledge of them does not extend beyond the time when we are, or were, actually having the sensations in which they are, or were, perceived.

Locke seems hardly to apprehend the depth of the problem here suggested, and raised when the sceptic asks, how in reason we can in that case get at all beyond the narrow range of our immediate sense-perceptions? This is the problem which Hume afterwards made the main subject of *his* 'Inquiry.' " It may therefore," so Hume there puts it, " be a subject worthy of curiosity to inquire, What is the nature of that evidence which assures us of any real existence and matter of fact *beyond* the *present* testimony of our senses, or the records of *our memory.* This part of philosophy," he adds, " has been little cultivated either by the ancients or the moderns." [1]

Hume's question, by implication, asks the meaning and ultimate ground of all inductive beliefs; and in his answer he argues that induction must be an unreasoning act. According to him, it involves a step for which no adequate reason can be given by man; it must therefore be referred to blind instinct, or

[1] See his ' Inquiry concerning Human Understanding,' sect. 4.

some automatic process which we share with the lower animals. It does not occur either to Hume or Locke that it may be a process objectively rational, but often only *unconsciously* rational in the individual mind—developed under the influence of custom, but of a custom that is by implication reason; and that, so far as the inductive beliefs of the individual correspond to laws in nature, they must be at least unconsciously rational, and the laws may be said to express the action of supreme Reason. Even in the world of the senses we are unconsciously, if not consciously, living and moving and having our being in the Infinite Mind.

If the present and the remembered qualities of a thing constitute all the absolute certainty we can have about the thing, how can we be said to know "things of sense" at all? We know the sense-phenomenon while it is perceived; but to know the thing means more than this. Such knowledge implies more than is present in sense, or represented in memory. Even when I see another *man* (*i.e.*, his body), to take Locke's own example, more than *visible* qualities must be included in the present "sight." Otherwise it is not a *man* that I see, but only an aggregate of extended colours; which may justify the presumption that they signify a man. But this, *per se*, is not intellectual perception of the man. The sense-object, when *only* seen, is not a human body; for its *invisible* qualities (hardness, temperature, odour, taste, &c.) are as little "actual present sensations" as if the man's body was out of the range of our senses altogether. Now, what constitutes the objectivity and reality of that "collection of simple ideas," belonging to various senses, which in seeing an object we "observe by our faculties of sense"? What is meant by (*i.e.*, what constitutes the idea of) their reality or substantiality ? Locke did not raise, and of course did not answer, this question, either in treating of sense-knowledge, or when he analysed the complex idea of a substance, material or spiritual, in the second book.

It leads to a question which, as I have already said, Locke forgot in his logical and psychological analysis of our metaphysical ideas. What is meant by—what is our "idea" of — "reality" or "real existence"; and especially what is meant by "matter" and its "real existence"? It was left to Berkeley to suggest this ontological question. The need to include it in a philosophical analysis of our ideas is thus put by him :— "Nothing seems of more importance towards erecting a firm system of sound and real knowledge, which may be proof against the assaults of scepticism, than to lay the beginning in a distinct explication of what is meant by THING, REALITY, EXISTENCE ; for in vain shall we dispute concerning the ' real existence ' of ' things,' or pretend to any knowledge thereof, as long as we have not fixed the meaning of those words."[1] Thus Locke led to Berkeley.

Is the real existence of things necessarily dependent on a consciousness, perception, or idea? Is idea truly the opposite of a really existing thing? Can things be ideas and yet be also what we mean by real things? Are related ideas and things ultimately identical; at least when the ideas are those presented in sense, and therefore connected by the necessary and universal relations which constitute the divine reason that is at the root of

[1] Principles of Human Knowledge, sect. 89.

nature ? May not ideas thus endowed with validity be themselves the reality ; while ideas not thus in agreement with the divine reason, or the synthetic intelligence immanent in nature, must be false or fictitious ? May not real knowledge and reality be the same,— looked at on different sides ? Knowledge looked at objectively, and immanent in the rational nature of things, would then *be* reality ; real existence looked at subjectively, or in its process of acquirement and formation, as the conscious possession of an individual, would be knowledge or experience only. The world would thus be a unity in which reason and reality are inextricably fused together.

Idealistic questions of this sort were foreign to Locke, although in course of time they arose out of the problem which he suggested in his account of our certainties about sensible things. His only solution consists in showing that human knowledge depends for its materials upon the qualities and spiritual acts of which we can become aware, and that it is essentially a rational intuition or perception of the relations of those presented materials. Perception or discernment of relations, either immediately in their self-evidence, or mediately through demonstration, is of the essence of Locke's "knowledge." As to its limits, we find that we *may* have this "perception" as to abstract mathematical and abstract moral truths ; also as regards our own existence as self-conscious individuals, the existence of God or Supreme Mind, and the existence of individual substances with their sensible. qualities, as given in perception at the time when they are perceived. But the "perceptions" of reason on which this limited amount of knowledge ultimately depends are not "innate," when innate means, as it does with Locke, having them before we have had any sense-experiences or exercise of our innate faculties. On the contrary, "perceptions," physical or moral, potentially ours, may, and do in many individual men, remain unconscious through life. "If," he says, "by innate moral principles is meant only a faculty to find out in time the moral difference of actions (besides that this is an improper way of speaking to call a power a principle), I never denied such a power to be innate; what I denied was that any ideas [of which we were conscious] or any perception of connection of ideas, was innate. If they were innate they would be from the first *consciously* in all men. I think nobody who reads my book could doubt that I spoke only of *innate ideas* [of which there must be consciousness], and not of *innate powers*. Natural [innate] powers may be improved by exercise, and afterwards weakened by neglect, and so all knowledge must be got by the exercise of these powers. But innate ideas or propositions [consciously] imprinted on the mind, I do not see how they can be improved or effaced." [1] It is thus that Locke explains his account of knowledge, in reply to hostile criticism.

---

[1] Comment in Locke's handwriting on the margin of his copy of Burnet's "Remarks" on the 'Essay.' See 'Yale Review' for July 1887.

CHAPTER VI.

PROBABILITIES : PHILOSOPHY OF PHYSICAL INDUCTION AND EVOLUTION.[1]

ACCORDING to the 'Essay on Human Understanding,' the only absolute certainty which a man can have about the things of sense is, that they are, or that they have been, present in his own experience. He can neither have the intuitive nor the demonstrable certainty, in which knowledge properly consists, as to any absent things; for when things are absent there is nothing presented in such a way as to keep him certain of their continued existence, still less of their condition ;—which is always subject to change from the operation of (by us) unknown or incalculable powers. This is just another way of saying that all expectations about anything, and inductive interpretations, can be only presumed probabilities, void of that absolute certainty of reason which makes knowledge. The philosophical conception, that the invariable coexistences and successions of natural phenomena are the sensible expression of divine reason, immanent both in them and in man's common rational sense—in *them* independently of our consciousness, in *us* consciously, in proportion as our intelligence develops

[1] See 'Essay,' Book IV., chaps. xiii.-xxi.

—the conception of nature as in this way capable of being reasoned about, and so having the thought that is immanent in *its* changes translated by our intellectual efforts into *our* thoughts,—was too subtle and speculative for Locke. The idea, too, of human history as the record of a gradual intellectual progress towards complete agreement between the thought or reason that is immanent in nature and the individual thoughts of men, was not less foreign to his mind. In his view, the vast region of the Real that lies beyond one's consciousness of one's own individual existence; the existence of the Supreme Spirit; and the present, or the remembered, sense-perceptions of the individual,—all realities beyond those present and past ones—are matters of probable presumption, in its degrees from practical certainty down to doubtful opinion; or else they lie wholly within that veil which for ever conceals what is behind it from human understanding. On Locke's philosophy, it is unphilosophical for a human understanding to assert absolute certainty of more than abstract mathematical, and perhaps abstract moral, truths; and, in what is concrete, of more than one's own existence as far back as memory goes; the existence of supreme active Mind; and the present existence of finite things that are, or past things while they were, perceived in sense. For all the rest, a man can at the most rise into subjective " presumptions " of probability ; which are, he thinks, enough for all the purposes of human life. And herein lies the difference between probability and certainty, faith and knowledge,—that in all the parts of knowledge there is either rational or sense intuition. Each step has a visibly necessary, or at least inevitable connection with the next. In beliefs, however probable, this is not so. That which makes me believe is something extraneous to the thing I believe, and so it does not manifest necessary agreement or disagreement of the qualities involved. It does not put me under an intellectual obligation to affirm or to deny what is signified in the subject and predicate of the judgment I then make. Judgments or presumptions of probability are the commonest of all the relations of a human understanding to reality. The only reality which is other than a probability,—besides our own existence and that of present things of sense,—is the existence of the Infinite Mind ; it being, according to Locke, " as certain that there is a God as that the opposite angles made by the intersection of two straight lines are equal,"—demonstrable in virtue of the principle of causality, which is used universally in the demonstration, although it is a fact and not an abstraction that is demonstrated. With this exception, it is only in abstract truth that he finds any universal proposition rising higher than probability. The entertainment which the mind gives to probable propositions—called by Locke "judgment," belief, assent, opinion—is described as "admitting or receiving any proposition for true, upon arguments or proofs that are found to persuade us to receive it as true, without certain knowledge that it is so." It is upon judgments of this sort that the lives of men turn; for probability, not intuitive certainty, is the guide of human life.

It is indeed the main outcome of the ' Essay ' that probability and not absolute certainty is the sort of insight to which beings of limited understanding like men are confined, in their intellectual intercourse with the *changing* universe that is presented to them in their experience. The sphere of probability is that in which objections to various conclusions have to be carefully balanced, and in which demands are made upon wisdom more than upon subtlety. It is the sphere of the intellectually intermediate ;—for, on the one hand, mere sense cannot even calculate probabilities ; on the other hand, divine or perfect insight, which always sees all in each, leaves no room for probabilities. But man, through his participation in Sense, cannot dispense with it ; while, in virtue even of *his* narrow range of intellectual certainties and participation in Reason, he is often able to calculate what is probable and what is not, and by this means to make expectations and inductive generalisations that are more than " leaps in the dark." All this is perhaps implied, although not expressed, in the account given in the fourth book of the relative spheres of intellectual certainty, and faith in probabilities. Yet it is the vital part of the answer to the question which he proposed to his friends at the memorable reunion nearly twenty years before the ' Essay ' appeared. The subject is approached in the chapter which treats of the " extent " of human knowledge ;[1] in the many passages throughout the ' Essay ' which treat of the relation of the secondary to the primary qualities of the things of sense ;[2] and also in other passages which maintain the impossibility of absolute certainty in any " general propositions regarding matters of fact which man can make."[3] Here are some examples of sentences in which it is referred to :—

[1] Book IV., chap. iii.
[2] Book III., chap. viii. ; Book IV., chap. iii. ss. 10-17, &c.
[3] Book IV., chaps. vi.-viii.

" As to actual relations of agreement or disagreement of our ideas in their coexistences [*i.e.*, as to our certainties about the qualities of *individual substances*], in this our knowledge proper absolute certainty is very short ; though in this consists the greatest and most important part of what is to be known concerning substances. For, our ideas of the species of substances being, as I have showed, nothing but certain collections of simple ideas, united in one subject, and so coexisting together [*i.e.*, nothing but collections of qualities which we refer to individual things according to their kinds] —*e.g.*, our idea of gold that of a body heavy, yellow, malleable, and fusible,—these, or such complex ideas as these, does the general name of the substance gold stand for. Now, when we would know anything *further* concerning this or any other sort of substance, what do we then inquire but what *other* qualities or powers such substances have or have not? which is nothing other but to know what *other* simple ideas [*i.e.*, unanalysable qualities] do or do not coexist in nature with those that make up this complex idea [bundle of qualities] of gold. And this, however weighty and considerable a part soever of human science, is yet very narrow and scarce any at all [*i.e.*, except in the form of more or less probable presumptions]. The reason whereof is, that the simple ideas whereof our complex ideas of substances are made [*i.e.*, the qualities which we refer to them, in the connotation of the terms by which they are denoted] are for the most part [*i.e.*, in the case of all their qualities that are not primary] such as carry with them in their own nature no visible necessary connection with other simple ideas [qualities or powers] whose coexistence with them we would inform ourselves about."

In language that is now familiar to the philosophical reader, this means, that our synthetic judgments about all things in nature which are not at the moment present in sense are destitute of the element of *a priority* or necessity in reason. For Locke is saying in passages

like this, that human beings can find no necessary connection articulating their sense-ideas, or the intelligible
qualities that are presented to them, through which they
might demonstrate, merely from the present sense-given
qualities of a thing, either its future appearances, or
what all or any of its other qualities *must* be.   In all
such cases, on account of the inevitable absence of the
intellectual perception in which certainty or true science
consists, one can only *presume ;* and as " presumptions
of probability " are not certainties of reason, man can
never construct strict science of nature.

" How far soever human industry may advance useful and
experimental philosophy in physical things, scientifical will
still be out of our reach. There can be no science of bodies,
because we want perfect and adequate ideas of those very
bodies which are nearest to us and most under our command.   Distinct ideas perhaps we may have ; but adequate
ideas I suspect we have not of any one amongst them.   And
though the former of these will serve us for common use
and discourse, yet while we want the latter we are not capable of scientifical knowledge ; nor shall ever be able to
discover general unquestionable truths concerning them.
Certainty and demonstration are things we must not in these
matters pretend to."

All intellectual intercourse with the changing world of
things and persons to which we are introduced through
the channel of immediate sense-perception, can thus
only be tentative, and more or less hypothetical, according to this philosophy.   For men have neither immediate nor mediate intuitions of necessary connections
among the few phenomena which come within the
range of their sense - perceptions.   Hence they can
neither interpret nature *a priori*, nor see an absolute

necessity for phenomena meaning what they are believed to mean in *a posteriori* interpretations of them. Instead of being able to see with the certainty of demonstration what the unperceived qualities or powers of sensible substances are, through a sense-perception of their present appearances, man can only in each case balance objections and probabilities, under the general presumption —as Locke would perhaps in his own way allow, though he would not so express it—of the immanence, throughout experience and its changes, of law, order, reason, or divine direction;—all which forbids us to suppose that our inductive expectations as to events in external nature and in human history turn ultimately on blind chance, or that reason in us may in the end be put to confusion by the essential irrationality of experience.

Accordingly, if we adopt Locke's language, we must say that it is only *probable* that "all men will die," or that "the sun will rise to-morrow"; for we cannot demonstrate the absolute necessity in reason of either of these events, and so our "assent" involves an imperfectly intellectual "presumption." Scientific "verifications" themselves would thus present only probable proof; even in the ideal cases in which the assurance that a special law of nature has been ascertained is as firm as the assurance we have that there is order or reason in nature at all—if "verification," in any instance, rises to such assurance. No physical verification, Locke is bound to say, can exclude the abstract possibility of another solution. This language varies from the ordinary use of the word "probable."[1] It also

---

[1] Hume notes this. "Mr Locke," he says, "divides all arguments into demonstrative and probable. In this view we must say

suggests some of the deepest questions in philosophy, which Locke himself hardly brings up into view.

That the physical and natural sciences, along with all our judgments about absent facts in this ever-changing universe of things or persons, consist only of probabilities—although probabilities many of which exclude reasonable doubt — is a prominent lesson in Locke's philosophy. He is fond of illustrating it in connection with the "secondary qualities and powers" of bodies. The subject is introduced in the eighth chapter of the second book, although it is hardly relevant in a logical analysis of our ideas. But the "simple ideas of sense," treated of in that part of the 'Essay,' Locke identifies with the "qualities and powers" of bodies ; they are the intelligible phenomena in which an existence external to each man manifests itself to his senses. These "qualities and powers," he finds, are of two sorts. A few, inseparable from our complex idea of material substance, are referred by us to the material substances themselves,—the existence of which he assumes. These are practically identical in our perceptions or ideas with what they are in the real substance—whatever " reality " may here mean, for this idea, as already remarked, he does not analyse. On the other hand, most, and those the most interesting, of the qualities and powers which enter into our complex ideas of sensible things, may, he finds, be changed without loss of material substance. They are not (as ideas or intelligible phenomena) attrib-

that it is only probable all men must die. But to conform our language more to common use, we ought to divide arguments into *demonstrations, proofs,* and *probabilities ;* by proofs meaning such arguments from experience as leave no room for doubt or opposition."—'Inquiry,' sect. vi., *Of Probability.*

uted to the material substance itself, but are found on
consideration to be subjective or individual sensations of
the persons who are conscious of them. Things around
us *must* be solid, external, and movable,—it is essential to
our complex ideas of matter that they should be so. They
may or may not be hot, or sweet to taste, or odorous, or
melodious, in any of the innumerable varieties of these
and like qualities. ' This second class of "qualities"
depends upon a person's sense-consciousness of them in
a way that the first does not. When we have an idea
of heat, for instance, it is as of a feeling in *us;* or if
regarded as independent of us, we image it to ourselves
as an unknown modification of motion—which is one
of the necessary qualities — although motion has no
apparent necessary connection with the feeling of heat.
Locke calls the former class primary, original, or essential qualities of matter; the others, in their boundless
variety, its secondary derived or relative qualities. The
primary, which involve mathematical relations, and are
therefore quantities rather than qualities, are, he reports,
inseparable from matter, as matter; and they are in
nature as they appear in our perceptions, being at once
ideas and qualities. The secondary, in our sense-experience of them, are only sensations; they are "qualities"
in material things only through the divinely established connection, or constant law, in respect of which
their quantified atoms occasion in us those sensations
which give positive meanings to the terms expressive of
secondary or relative qualities in matter. If there were
no sentient beings all secondary qualities would cease
to exist, except, perhaps, in the form of their primary
correlatives. For, as Locke suggests, the sensations in

us which give idea or meaning to all secondary qualities, may perhaps, under the laws of nature, all depend on correlative sorts of size, shape, and motion of the primary atoms of the bodies to which they are referred. It is highly probable that heat, for instance, depends on atomic motion. But if this hypothesis regarding the secondary qualities and powers of sensible things is rejected, they must depend, Locke argues, on "something still more obscure." On the other hand, "solidity, extension, figure, and motion," in contrast to the secondary qualities and powers, are simple ideas or qualities of sense, which would be really as they are whether there were any sensible being to perceive them or not."

The outcome of Locke's hypothesis about the "qualities and powers" of material substances,—with which alone the physical and natural "sciences" are concerned,—would be, that, in themselves, they are probably capable of being described and reasoned about in terms of mathematical quantity instead of in terms of subjective sensation. Its tendency is, to insinuate such a correlation between (*a*) the sensations, which give idea or meaning to all terms expressive of secondary qualities and powers of bodies, and (*b*) the corresponding modifications of their primary atoms, as that the goal of all scientific research into nature would be—discovery of what the special modifications of the primary or mathematical qualities of individual things are, on which their secondary qualities and powers depend.

The true scientific idea or law of any external thing would then be found in a knowledge of the mathematical relations of the atoms of which it consists; in which knowledge we should find, deductively by implication, the sensations of colour, resistance, sound, taste, smell, heat, &c., to which such atoms, so correlated, *must* give rise in us; and also the changes which they *must* occasion, by communication of motion, in the atoms of which the bodies around them consist,—followed, of course, by those surrounding bodies "operating" on sentient beings differently from what they did before their atoms were so affected. In this way, in a knowledge of the primary or mathematical qualities of anything, we should have the key to *all* its qualities and powers; and in order to explain scientifically the behaviour of all bodies in the material world, we should only need to know what their respective atomic constitutions are. Science of nature so developed would become throughout applied mathematics. It would all be capable of being evolved by us in necessary demonstrations; provided only that we could get possession of the needful data, in a perfect knowledge of the mathematical relations involved in the atomic constitution of each species of things.

Locke suggests something like this in his own cautious way. He thinks it possible, even probable, that *all* the "powers" of bodies may be conditioned by, and expressible in, terms of those motions of their constituent atoms which are always going on in the extended universe; or, if not dependent on this, changes in nature must, he repeats, arise under some other condition or law "yet more remote from our comprehension," and of which the data of our experience do not furnish us with any idea. So that the supposed correlation is only an hypothesis; seeing that the secondary qualities and powers of bodies, for all that we certainly know, may

be independent of their primary qualities, and may depend on "something even more remote from our reach"
than would be a knowledge, in principle and in details,
of his hypothetical correlation.   But it is only an hypothesis; and even if in those correlations are really contained the secrets of which physical science is in quest,
they must still remain secrets to man.   For our feeble
senses, as he argues, could not put us in possession of
the required data; or if they did, we could not work out
the infinitely complex conclusions.   Physical or natural
science is therefore unattainable by a human understanding;—when "science" means, as Locke means by
it, only what is rationally intuited and what is demonstrable, and when it refuses to admit among its propositions any presumptions of probability.   This favourite
argument Locke seems to value for its moderating influence upon the pride of human understanding.   Take
the following passages in illustration:—

"The reason whereof is, that the simple ideas or qualities
whereof our complex ideas of [material] substances are made
up, are, for the most part, such as carry with them no *necessary* connection with any *other* simple ideas [qualities] whose
coexistence with them [in the same substance] we would
inform ourselves about.   The ideas that our complex ones
of substances are made up of, and about which our knowledge concerning substances is most employed, are those
of the secondary qualities; which, depending all, as has
been shown, upon the primary qualities of their minute
and insensible parts, or, if not upon them, upon something
yet more remote from our comprehension, it is impossible
we should know which of them have a *necessary* union or
inconsistency with the other.   For, not knowing the root
they spring from; not knowing *what* size, figure, and texture
of points they are, on which depend and from which result

those qualities which make our complex idea of 'gold,' it is impossible we should know what other qualities result from or are incompatible with the same, and so consequently *must* always coexist with that complex idea we [already] have of it, or else are inconsistent with it. Besides this ignorance of the primary qualities of the insensible parts [atoms] of bodies, on which as on no other depend all these secondary qualities, there is yet another and more inconceivable part of ignorance which sets us more remote from a certain knowledge [as distinguished from sufficiently probable presumption] of the coexistence or incoexistence, if I may so say, of different ideas [qualities or perceived phenomena] in the same subject,—and that is, that there is no [by us] discoverable connection between any secondary quality and those primary qualities it depends on. That the size, figure, and motion of one body should cause a change in the size, figure, and motion of another body, is not beyond our conception. These and the like seem to have some connection with each other. And if we knew these qualities of bodies, we might have reason to hope we might be able to know a great deal more of these operations of them one with another. But our minds not being able to discover any connection between the primary qualities of bodies, and the sensations that are produced in us by them [*i.e.*, their secondary qualities], *we* can never be able to establish certain and undoubted rules [laws of nature] of the consequences. We are so far from knowing *what* particular figure, size, or motion of parts, produce a yellow colour, a sweet taste, or a sharp sound, that we can by no means conceive how *any* size, figure, or motion of any particles can possibly produce in us the idea of any colour, taste, or sound whatsoever ; there is no conceivable connection between the one and the other. In vain, therefore, shall we endeavour to discover by our ideas [*i.e.*, by the data of actual sense] what other ideas [qualities] are to be found *constantly* conjoined with those contained in our present complex idea of any substance ; since we neither know the real constitution of the minute parts on which their qualities do depend, nor, did we know them, could we discover any *necessary* connection between them and any of the secondary qualities."

Our knowledge, in short, in all these inquiries, reaches very little further than the fluctuating data of our experience. A few of the primary qualities have a necessary and visible connection with one another;—for figure necessarily supposes extension; receiving or communicating motion by impulse necessarily supposes solidity. But we can thus discover the necessary coexistence of very few of the absent qualities that are united in substances; we are on the whole left only to the present and remembered experience of actual sense for our certainties about things.

" Thus, though we see the yellow colour, and upon trial find the weight, malleableness, fusibility, and fixedness that are united in a piece of gold ; yet, because no one of these ideas has any evident dependence or necessary connection with the other, we cannot certainly know that where any four of these are, the fifth will be also—how highly probable soever it may be, because the highest probability amounts not to certainty, without which there can be no true knowledge. For this coexistence can be known no further than it is perceived ; and it could be perceived only in *particular* subjects, by the observation of sense ; or, in *general,* by the *necessary* connection of the ideas (qualities) themselves."

As connections of phenomena in nature can never be seen by the eye of man's reason to be necessary, and therefore universal, Locke concludes that all judgments about them can only be presumptions of probability; and therefore absolute certainty regarding natural coexistences (and by analogy of reasoning, natural successions) must be confined to the instances now and here present to the senses, and can never enter into, or constitute,

universal propositions. It follows that a scientific inquirer can never have more than probable assurance that
he has discovered a law of nature; or that any law,
ascertained by induction, may not be suspended by the
interposition of a higher law; or even by some unexpected originating cause,—in a system of things like
that of nature, in which physical law is subordinate to
a yet higher order. Pure mathematical judgments of
universality, Locke would grant, have absolute certainty; and so too would also say of our mathematical
judgments when applied to things of sense, — if the
things as perceived by sense corresponded to the mathematical conceptions. But then we know too inexactly
and too little of the contents of space and time, and
of the forces at work among them, to be ever absolutely
certain that this correspondence exists; so as to be
justified in carrying our certainty beyond the present
data, into universal propositions about the qualities and
laws of the things which our senses perceive. "It is
(certainly) true of a triangle, that its three angles are
equal to two right ones, *wherever the triangle really
exists.* But whatever other figure really exists that is
not exactly answerable to that idea of a triangle, is not
at all concerned in that proposition" (iv. 4, 6).

Mixed mathematics can thus be only hypothetically
certain. The abstract truths of pure mathematical certainty that may be latent in nature, are not in it as it
is sensibly revealed to us, and so we cannot identify in
our reasonings the concrete and imperfect "triangles"
that we actually see and touch with the abstract or
perfect triangle of pure mathematics. By analogy, too,
Locke might so argue as to the abstract causal relation,

and *its* application to the imperfectly known concrete causes or powers on which changes in nature ultimately depend. In contrast with this he finds that abstract moral truths are intuitively necessary. We cannot conceive a lie or an unjust act to be virtuous, but we can conceive the actual laws of nature to be different from what our inductions make them out to be. Fire may cease to burn, but cruelty cannot cease to be criminal. Locke does not ask whether a chaotic universe (emptied of physical law and order) would not be as irrational and impossible as a universe in which moral and mathematical truths were reversed, on the ground in both cases that it would be a universe emptied of God.

Locke does not go much further than this into the philosophy of probability, and the (partly blind) presumption on which he makes it rest. His implied philosophy of natural science and induction may be gathered from what has been already said. It brings us to the margin only of the metaphysics of mathematics and physics. The nature and origin of the order latent in the original constitution and progressive evolution of physical phenomena, is a question which lies outside his inquiries; along with the still more general question *why* human understanding necessarily presupposes order or reason, as existing in the heart of the things and events which it investigates. Natural science does not entertain those purely philosophical questions. It does not seek to determine what is meant by "an agent" in the material world, nor whether in truth any so-called "law" in nature—be it gravitation or evolution by natural selection or any other—can truly be said to explain anything at all—philosophically. It leaves untouched the question of the cause of physical causality, —the reason why the universe "is assumed to be a cosmos and not a chaos." Mere natural science is ready dogmatically to supersede all such questions, by the assumption that "forces" in nature are independent, self-existent, and necessary causes; not merely contingent, because dependent, modes of action of infinite, ever-active Reason or Will, that is at once immanent in nature and supernatural. When we remember the question which gave rise to the 'Essay,' we perhaps expect more than Locke has told us about the *rationale* of the probable presumptions by which our limited "certain knowledge" is supplemented, and by which human life has to be guided. The critic of the 'Essay' is ready to ask, how we are justified in reason, when we pass as we daily do beyond the narrow bounds of sense-perception of the qualities of things present, and possess ourselves, in merely probable "presumptions," of so much of the universe as we seem to conquer of the unperceived past, distant, and future. Locke contributes less perhaps than we might have anticipated to the philosophy either of induction or of faith.

The remaining chapters of the fourth book[1] contain judicious advice for human beings, whose lives thus turn upon probabilities or presumptions, as to the best means for avoiding those risks of error to which the narrow boundary of their certain knowledge makes them liable, —for human errors arise mainly within the sphere of probability, and hardly ever occur, except by defect of

[1] Chaps. xiv.-xxi.

memory or confusion of thought, within the limits of
absolute certainty or knowledge. Locke rejects the syl-
logism as an organ of discovery ; but without adverting to
its proper function, as a formula for guaranteeing the self-
consistency of reasonings. Another question, one which
touches the root of academical scepticism, is not raised
by him. Could there be even probability, if nothing
that is absolutely certain can enter into our mental
experience ? He registers a few absolute certainties in
classes, without showing their philosophical *rationale*,
or their mutual relations, and then contrasts with this
the immense extent of probabilities in their different
degrees. But he does not show any connection between
the two, nor consider whether there *could* be an aggregate of probabilities that rested at last on a mere probability nor inquire whether so resting it could truly be
said to " rest " at all. Hume's ' Sceptical Solution of
Sceptical Doubts' carried modern philosophy afterwards
into these questions,—by his attempt to resolve Locke's
few concrete certainties themselves into illusions, thus
making *every* judgment about reality only probable, and
attaching a " perhaps " to every proposition that can be
formed by man,—including the proposition itself that
all so-called knowledge *is* (perhaps) only probable.

This defect in the 'Essay' was not long unnoticed.
Bishop Butler, in the Introduction to his ' Analogy,'—in
explaining that it was not within his design " to inquire
into the nature, the foundation, and the measure of probability ; or whence it proceeds that *likeness* should *beget*
that presumptive opinion and full conviction which the
human mind is formed to receive from it, and which it

does *naturally* produce in every one,"—adds, that "this is a part of logic which has not yet been thoroughly considered," and that "little in this way has been attempted by those who have treated of our intellectual powers and the exercise of them. Probable evidence in its nature affords," he goes on to say, "but an imperfect kind of information, and is to be considered as relative only to beings of limited capacities. For nothing which is the possible object of knowledge, whether past, present, or future, can be probable to Infinite Intelligence, since it cannot but be discovered absolutely as it is in itself, certainly true or certainly false. But to us, probability is the very guide of life. And a man is as really bound in prudence to do what, upon the whole, *appears* according to the best of his judgment to be for his happiness, as what he *certainly knows* to be so." Hume, with a still humbler theory as to the extent of human knowledge than that advocated by Locke, or by Butler after Locke, proposed, as we saw, for a subject worthy of curiosity,—indeed, as the theme of his 'Inquiry into Human Understanding,'—to investigate "what is the nature of that evidence which assures us of any real existence or matter of fact *beyond* the present testimony of our senses, and the testimony of memory to what has been present to our senses or in our experience." The issue of Hume's investigation is, that blind inexplicable custom, determined by the associative tendency at work in each man, is a sufficient practical explanation of the formation of physical experience and science, and the only guarantee we have of their probability;—and that beyond this there can be neither certainties nor probabilities. All that lies beyond the data of present sense and memory becomes belief by custom and habit through association, of which blind and mechanical process, as ultimate for us, we can find no explanation. It was thus that Hume "solved" the "sceptical doubts" that had been expressed in his 'Treatise of Human Nature.' The "sceptical" solution,—association generated by custom, extended, since Hume's days, through law of heredity, from the individual to the race and its physical surroundings—is now accepted, by many to whom a scientific understanding of life and the universe seems adequate and final, not merely as the scientific but even as the ultimate explanation of moral and spiritual experience.

Locke himself has been classed with the "English association philosophers." Yet the first edition of the 'Essay' contained no express reference to mental association or its consequences, in vogue with Hobbes, and in the following century with Hume and Hartley. The short chapter on "Association of Ideas," now included in the second book, was introduced (in the fourth edition) not to explain philosophically the practical certainties of probability, which play so large a part in Locke's philosophy, far less to explain the few absolute certainties which he recognised,—but for the opposite purpose of warning against the blind tendency mechanically to connect ideas, on the ground that it is the potent manufacturer of prejudices and errors which he had assailed under the name of "innate principles." As Dr Fowler remarks, in his admirable account of Locke, the 'Essay' offers "no natural explanation of the various mental tendencies and aptitudes which it describes, or of the extraordinary facility of acquiring simple and forming complex ideas, so far as the individual is concerned." The principle of Heredity, and the law of Evolution, which now play so large a part in the merely physical explanations of human nature and the universe, were of course not then anticipated. The essence of the 'Essay' is that human knowledge and opinion are not *innate* in each man, but a *growth*. Yet there is no attempt at scientific explanation of the laws under which they grow. At the most, however, such "explanations" could only express the empirical conditions under which the essential principles of Universal Reason are consciously developed in an individual or in mankind. Reason is inexplicable, or at least can only be explained by itself,—by unfolding articulately its essential constitution. To ask for a physical explanation would be to ask for a physical cause of God's existence.

The drift of the 'Essay' is, on the whole, against abstract principles, but always in the interest of philosophical impartiality, or what Locke calls "indifference." He was apt to regard presuppositions of every kind as prejudices, especially when expressed in the form of abstract principles; and he failed to acknowledge principles that are necessarily involved in our mental operations, but which are not consciously patent, at least in their abstract form, in the experience of most men. He sometimes wrote as if he failed to see that without presuppositions of some sort, intellectual and moral, there could neither be reasoned scepticism nor reasonable faith.

THIRD PART.

ADVANCED LIFE: CONTROVERSY AND CHRISTIANITY
(1691-1704).

————

CHAPTER I.

A RURAL HOME IN ESSEX.

THE 'Epistola de Tolerantia,' the 'Two Treatises on
Government,' and the 'Essay concerning Human Understanding' formed the literary outcome of Locke's cogi-
tations up to his fifty-seventh year. They express his
philosophy as it had been formed by collision with the
contemporary adversaries of free thought and reasonableness.. They were given to the world in the last two
years of that interval of his life, when he no longer had
a home with Lord Shaftesbury, either at Exeter House
or in Aldersgate, and before he had found one elsewhere, more peaceful if less conspicuous. It was then
that he delivered to the world the philosophy that has
been expounded in the foregoing chapters, which had
been ripening in his thoughts in many years of considerate observation, in England, France, and Holland.

He was now almost sixty. Two winters in London had aggravated his chronic ailments. The course of public affairs had disappointed his hopes, for the Revolution Settlement, especially its Toleration Act, fell short of his political ideal.

It was then that the home of his old age, the brightest of all his successive homes,—at Beluton, Christ Church, Exeter House, Aldersgate, Amsterdam, and Rotterdam,—was opened to receive him. It was the secluded manor-house of Oates in Essex, the country seat of Sir Francis Masham, one of the members of Parliament for that county. The second Lady Masham was Damaris, the accomplished daughter of Ralph Cudworth, the Anglican theological philosopher of the seventeenth century. It will be remembered that Locke was intimate with the family before he went to Holland, and the intimacy was maintained by correspondence when he was abroad. When he returned to London, in February 1689, Damaris Cudworth had become the wife of Sir Francis Masham of Oates. Now and then, in the course of the two years spent at Mrs Smithsby's apartments in Dorset Court, "by some considerably long visits to Oates," as Lady Masham afterwards told Le Clerc, "Mr Locke made trial of the air of this place, which is some twenty miles from London, and he thought that none would be more suitable for him. His company could not but be very desirable for us, and he had all the assurance we could give him of being always welcome ; but to make him easy in living with us, it was necessary he should do so on his own terms, which Sir Francis at last assenting to, he then believed himself at home with us, and resolved, if it pleased God, here to end his days—as he did."

It was in the early spring of 1691 that the idyllic life at Oates began, and that Locke in this way found the surroundings amidst which his later life was passed. This place, which must ever be associated with his name, was pleasantly situated among the leafy lanes of Essex, north of the romantic glades of Epping Forest, midway between Ongar and Harlow, and not far from Stanford Rivers. There, amongst the simple peasantry of a rural English parish, he enjoyed for almost fourteen years as much domestic happiness and literary leisure as was consistent with broken health and occasional attention to public affairs. From minute details in his immense published and unpublished correspondence, which abounds in homely humorous touches, and from Masham family letters, one can picture the philosopher in the daily routine of this English country-house, when the shadows of the evening of life were lengthening.

When Locke went to live at Oates, in February 1691, Sir Francis and Lady Masham were both in middle life. The daughter of Cudworth was the second wife of Sir Francis, a devout churchwoman, full of thoughtful piety, refined and accomplished, known afterwards in authorship for her 'Discourse concerning the Love of God,' and 'Thoughts in Reference to the Christian Life,' a correspondent of John Norris, the rector of Bemerton, and mystical disciple of Plato and Malebranche. Their only child Francis was four years old when Locke entered the family. A daughter of Sir Francis by his first wife, Esther Masham, then a bright and clever girl of sixteen, was also one of the family circle. She became Locke's favourite companion; he corresponded with her in his own vein of sprightly

humour during occasional separations, when she was
visiting among her friends, or when she was at Oates
during his occasional visits to London. Locke's ad-
mirers owe something to Esther Masham. I have
read two unpublished volumes of hers, containing copies
taken by her own hand of nearly two hundred familiar letters from her friends, written mostly in the
years when Locke lived at Oates.[1] The fresh and
lively details even of the most commonplace incidents
of the family life, here pictured with pre - Raphaelite
realism, withdraw the curtain from the old Essex
manor-house as it was almost two hundred years ago,
and make the family, with Locke as its principal
figure, live again in fancy. Besides the child Francis and the lively Esther, Samuel, the youngest son
of the first marriage—afterwards Lord Masham, and
husband of Abigail, the noted favourite of Queen Anne
—a boy at school in 1691—was then and afterwards
often at Oates for his holidays. Other sons of Sir
Francis, by the first marriage, most of them in the
army in Flanders or in Ireland, make their appearance
in the home circle now and then on leave; or their
letters from abroad are reported as being read with
eagerness by the winter fireside in the oak - panelled
parlour, with its woollen tapestry, Locke among the
listeners. Once and again there is sorrow in the Essex

[1] These volumes are entitled, 'Letters from Relations and Friends
to E. Masham,' in two MS. volumes (335 pp.), with date "1722,"
when they were copied by her, as she says, that she might "reflect
on past experiences, and thus divert some melancholy hours of a solitary life." They are 179 in number, English and French (some of
her relations being French), the earliest dated in 1686, and the last
in 1710.

home, when the death of a favourite son is announced
from abroad. A picturesque member of the Oates family
circle when Locke entered it was the venerable Mrs Cudworth, Lady Masham's mother, who came to stay with
her daughter in 1688, after the death in that year of
her learned husband, and who continued to live at Oates
till her own death in November 1695. Country neighbours, too, appear now and then on the scene. Matching Hall, two miles from Oates, not far from Down
Hall, afterwards the home of the poet Prior, was in
those years occupied by the mother of Sir Francis. A
mile away in an opposite direction from Matching was
Locke's parish church of High Laver, the church in
which he was often seen ; and near it the rectory,
where he often visited the rector, his good friend
Samuel Lowe. Esther Masham's letters and Locke's
refer to many goings to and fro among these houses,
or to familiar intercourse with the farmers and the cottagers. Locke's favourite walks and rides in the leafy
lanes, or the superintendence and manual labour which
he enjoyed in the garden at Oates, are common incidents of the after part of the day, when the work in the
study was over. Riding was Locke's favourite exercise.
His spare, diminutive figure must have been familiar
to the cottagers, who were used to see " Doctor Locke,"
the studious gentleman who lived with Sir Francis, pass
on horseback, on the rough roads towards Harlow or
Ongar or Epping, or on his way to ask for old Mrs
Masham at Matching, or to the rectory at High Laver
to visit Mr Lowe. Sometimes the afternoon's exercise
was in the old-fashioned garden at the manor-house,
where on warm summer days of the closing years of

that far-off seventeenth century he enjoyed the shade of the yew-trees in company with Esther Masham or her mother, or basked in the sun on the sheltered walks. This routine was relieved by visits to town, or by occasional visits at Oates of illustrious friends—Isaac Newton from Cambridge, or the Lord Shaftesbury of the 'Characteristics,' who in former days was Locke's pupil, or Lord and Lady Peterborough, or William Molyneux the Dublin philosopher, or Peter King, Locke's cousin, afterwards Lord Chancellor, and in the last months of Locke's life, Anthony Collins, afterwards of free-thinking repute, then a young Essex squire. Some years after Locke was settled at Oates, a young Frenchman, Pierre Coste, was added to the home circle, recommended by Le Clerc to be Frank Masham's tutor and Locke's amanuensis, who translated the 'Essay' into French when he was living there with its author.

The old manor-house itself, which in those fourteen years was the scene of so much refined home happiness, is not now to be seen. The Masham family disappeared on the death of the last lord in 1776, when the lands of Oates passed into other hands. Thirty years later the manor-house was pulled down by the new possessor. The spot where it once stood, marked by some noble lime-trees, is now part of a green undulating park, one ruined outhouse still bearing witness to the past; near it a spacious pond and the remains of the old-fashioned garden in which Locke meditated, and which he helped to keep. I have seen a picture of the house and its surroundings, as it was when Locke lived in it—a square-looking building, in Tudor style, invested with a peaceful charm, ornamental pond and open lawn in front, barns and trees on one side, a sportsman in the foreground, a turret above the entrance-hall, near it the window of the room in which he studied, that of the room in which he slept adjoining, and beneath both the windows of the snug parlour in which Esther Masham, as she tells, used to read to Locke in the winter evenings "after supper" in 'Astræa,' then a favourite romance, or in some of the books of voyages and travels of which throughout his life he was so fond, where he also charmed the family circle by easy facetious conversation.

Lady Masham says that Locke refused to live at Oates except "on his own terms." The unpublished papers now possessed by Lord Lovelace show what those terms were. He paid 20s. a-week as board for himself and his servant, and 1s. a-week for grass for a horse, or 2s. when, as sometimes happened, he had two horses. The wage of his man was 20s. a quarter, as appears from payments, carefully recorded in the book of accounts, to "James Dorington," and afterwards to "William Shaw" who was his servant when the end came. Locke's books of accounts from 1664 till his death, in two folios, are among the Lovelace treasures. One may infer from them strict personal economy, prudential habits, and a methodical precision almost pedantic. Like the few erasures in his letters and other manuscripts, they bespeak a perfectly well-regulated habit of mind. A few gleanings taken at random from those books help to realise the common manner of life at Oates :—

"1694.—Feby. By six weeks' lodging to Mrs R. Pawling during my stay in London, 36s. By a breast of mutton, 1s. 1d. By 3½ yds. grey cloth, 55s. By 5 yds. silk, for a waistcoat, at 6s. 6d. = 32s. 6d. By one pair worsted hose, 4s. 4d. By

4½ coat buttons, 3s. 4d.   One dozen gold breast buttons, 9s.
By bread, cheese, oranges, and butter, 2s. 6d.   By cherrys
and strawberrys, 2s. 6d.   By Rhenish wine, one quart,
2s. 6d.   By six tarts and three cheesecakes, 3s. 9d.   By two
papers of patches, bought in London for my Lady Masham,
1s.   By a porter for a basket for E. Masham, 8d.   By
gooseberrys and strawberrys, 8s. 2½d.   By milk, 5s. 9d.   By
ten weeks' lodging in London, from April 23 to July 3, £3.
By three weeks' lodging in London, from September 19 to
October 9, 18s.   By two weeks' lodging in London, Dec. 7
to 22, 12s.   By postages, from Feb. 16 till April 23, 33s.
By a pair of worsted stockings, 4s. 8d.   By a box of sugar,
bought for Mrs Cudworth, 23s. 10d.   By a brasse locke for
my Lady Masham, 6s. 6d.   By Thomas Baley for a peruke,
60s.   Oct. 7.   Paid to Awnsham Churchill, bookseller.—By
Norris's 'Letters,' 3s.; Burnett's 'Sermons,' 6d.; 'Assembly's
Confession,' 2s. 3d.; Gassendi's 'Astronomia,' for my Lady
Masham, 4s. 4d.

"In 1696.—March 25.   By a quarter's salary as Commissioner of Appeals, £50.   June 24. Do., £50.   September 29. Do., £50.   December 29. Do., £50 [and so in the
years following].   By two places taken in Bishop Stortford
coach to London, 5s.   To cash paid Sir Francis Masham,
£14, 11s.

"1699.—May 29.   By sixty-six weeks' board for me and my
man, £66.

"1699.—Jan. 11.   James Dorington came to serve me.
April 11.   By a quarter's wages to James Dorington, 20s.
May 20.   Sir Richard Gripps for half-year's interest due to
me for £2000 of my money lent to him on 19th Nov.

"1700.—March 2.   Upon a mortgage in my cousin King's
hands, £50.   Received his declaration of trust.   May 20.
To a year's interest, £100.   July 5.   To money paid Mr
Anthony Collins for mending the coach, £12, 10s."

Many pages might be filled with entries like these.
One of the last in the book was made by some one on
the day after Locke's death :—

" 1704.—Saturday, October 28. By fifteen weeks' board for Mr Locke and his man William Shaw, from July 20 to the time of his death, £15 ; also by fifteen weeks' pasture for two horses, 30s."

There is also a " record of money transactions," from Saturday, January 1, 1689, to Friday, June 30, 1704,— about sixteen pages given to each year. The careful preservation of the most trifling accounts is character- istic,—the bills sent in weekly by the laundress, for example, of which this is one, more or less like all the others :—

" 1697.—Dec. 24. Docktor Lock (*sic*), his bill. Cravat and ruffles, 6d. 1 shirt, ½ shirt, 1 pair stockings, 1 pair drawers, 4d."

In the Lovelace repositories there is a " catalogue of my books at Oates," in Locke's own writing, with " labor ipse voluptas " for the motto. Among them are works of Descartes, Nicole, Malebranche, Gassendi, ' Logique de Port-Royale,' ' Novum Organum,' Newton's ' Principia,' " from the author," with many books of voyages and travels, all in beautiful preservation, and Locke's autograph in most of them. The scrutoire, with its twelve drawers and ten pigeon-holes, which once stood in the study at Oates, is in the Locke library at Horseley Park. It contains many hundreds of let- ters and accounts, carefully docketed, preserved in the order in which they were placed almost two centu- ries ago. In the same interesting repository are rough drafts of several of Locke's published and unpublished works, including one of the projected ' Essay,' in a man- uscript volume, entitled " Intellechy [or] De Intellectu

Humano, 1671; [or] An Essay concerning the Under-
Opinion
standing—Knowledge, ~~Belief~~ (*sic*), Assent.—J. L."

The 'Nynehead Letters' cast light on minute details — expected visits, Locke's careful arrangements
for Sir Francis' " coach " going to meet the incomers
and outgoers, at Bishop Stortford or at Harlow, or
directions for their transit through the dangers of Epping Forest, where "my Lord Peterborough and his
lady" lost their way, and were benighted on their
journey from Parson's Green to the Essex manor-house.[1]
Esther Masham's correspondence paints other scenes.
When she is in London Locke writes to her from
Oates : " It is better to be taken up with business in
London than to freeze in the country. I can scarce be
warm enough to write this by the fireside. You should
therefore be so *gracieuse* as to come home and comfort
your poor solitary *berger*, who suffers here under the
deep winter of frost and snow. The day Mr Coste came
home it snowed very hard a good part of the morning.
. . . I am, of all the shepherds of the forest, *gentile
bergère*, your most humble and faithful servant, Caledon
the Solitary "—*i.e.*, he was as lonely as the shepherd in
' Astræa' was without his mistress.

---

[1] The famous Earl of Peterborough and his wife were warm and
intimate friends during the last sixteen years of Locke's life. He
escorted her, when she was Lady Mordaunt, from Holland to London
in February 1689, and he was always a welcome guest at Parson's
Green, Fulham. She was a daughter of Sir Alexander Fraser of
Durris, in Kincardineshire. In 1713 Berkeley travelled with Peterborough in France and Italy as his chaplain and secretary, when he
was on an embassy to the Duke of Savoy. The brilliant and eccen-
tric Earl, like Lord Pembroke, was thus the friend of Berkeley as
well as of Locke.

We get glimpses into Oates in other unpublished letters addressed to Esther. The brothers in Flanders send their "humble service" to Mrs Cudworth and to "Mr Locke," to whom (in one letter) "pray tell that it would be a difficult matter to find that book here, but when I go into Paris it may be had," and in another, "my humble service to Mr Locke; but as for the book he desires, I have been to twenty booksellers and can hear of no such thing." A letter from one of her French relations inquires as to the success of the great book [1] of their inmate at Oates she had heard so much about: "Vous estes bien heureuse de pouvoir jouer de sa conversation—M. Locque (*sic*), je ne sais si je dis bien le nom du savant homme qui demeure chez vous." The marriage of Francis, the fourth son, to a niece of Bishop Burnet, was an event for a time in the Oates circle. There, in the last years, M. Coste is often referred to, and "humble services" sent to "M. Coste and to Mr Locke." Writing to Esther from Hackney in December 1703, "A. Burnet" refers to the memorable storm of the 26th November which Defoe has commemorated: [2] "One Brown is just come in, and tells me you have had a great deal of hurt done to the house at Oates. Sure this tempest is the heaviest judgment that ever befell poor England. Oh, the poor Bishop of Bath and Wells and his wife, that were broke in a hundred pieces! The bishop's youngest daughter that was at home is fallen distracted." This unparalleled tornado swept over England on one of the

[1] The 'Essay.'
[2] 'An Historical Narrative of the Great and Tremendous Storm which happened on November 26th, 1703.' By Daniel Defoe (187 pp.)

winter nights when Locke, reduced by illness, was a prisoner in his room at Oates.

In the parish records of High Laver, Locke's name appears as a subscriber to parochial and other charities, at the instance of the good rector Samuel Lowe, who was for fifty-seven years incumbent of the parish. Locke's habit in connection with the parish church has been differently represented. The writer of the preface to the quarto edition of the 'Letters on Toleration,' which appeared in 1765, says, that "though he communicated occasionally with the National Church, yet, during his long residence at Oates, he generally attended a lay preacher in that neighbourhood, to assert, as is probable, that liberty in his own person which he had strenuously contended for in behalf of all men." Locke's ecclesiastical ideas might lead him occasionally so to act. His individualism in religion as in philosophy reduced to indifference in his mind, if indeed it did not prejudice him against, the ideal unity of Christendom in one visible organisation; and made him apt to protest in action against exclusive connection with any one of the rival religious societies —shattered fragments of once visibly united Christendom—which in modern times have all assumed the name "Church." He was thus led to protest on behalf of the right of each man, if he found this more for edification, to sustain his religious life even apart from visible ecclesiastical communion. Yet according to records, and to the traditions of High Laver, Locke was habitually seen in the parish church. "Had you been at our church yesterday," he writes in one of his playful letters to Esther Masham,—whom in raillery he used to call his "Laudabridis," as she in turn called him "her John,"—"had you been at our church yesterday, there was one would have put you to it to have kept pace and time with him. He sang the poor clerk out of his beloved 'Behold and have regard,' and made him lose both voice and tune. Would you had been here to have stood up for the credit of our parish which gave up to a stranger! We have had nothing but winter weather since you went, and I write this by the fireside, whither the blustering wind like December has driven me, though it is still August. I hope for a new spring when you come back, and desire to be then as merry as the birds then are when they have their mates, only I desire to be excused from singing; that part shall be yours." And in another characteristic letter to Esther, then visiting in London: "I hope you are not much troubled that you have not your full foddering as you used to have." ["This alludes to Mr Lowe," Esther adds in a note, "then minister of our parish, who had taken a fancy he should die in the pulpit, therefore left off preaching, and for a considerable time got his neighbouring clergyman to give him a sermon."] "As to singing, there be those in the parish will tell you, you lost the perfection of that by your wandering. Had you been at home when I wished, you had had something beyond the ordinary strain of 'Behold and have regard.' But you must be gadding, and so make us sad even under those heavenly strains, for they were heavenly too."

In Locke the rationalising, latitudinarian, or liberal Churchman was still blended with a remainder of the early Puritanism, but always with aversion to the sacerdotal type of Christianity, although it too has sustained many saints and martyrs in the history of Christendom. Lady Masham, in a letter to Limborch after Locke's death, remarks, that "he was born and had finished his studies in a time when Calvinism was in fashion in England. But these doctrines," she adds, "had come to be little thought of before I came into the world; and Mr Locke used to speak of the opinions that I had always been accustomed to at Cambridge, even among the clergy there, as something new and strange to him. As, during some years before he went to Holland, he had very little in common with our ecclesiastics, I imagine that the sentiments that he found in vogue amongst you there pleased him far more, and seemed to him far more reasonable than anything that he had been used to hear from English theologians. But whatever the cause, I know that since his return he has always spoken with much affection, not only of his friends in Holland, but also of the whole society of the Remonstrants, on account of the opinions held by them."

It is now time to watch the work that was going on in Locke's study during those fourteen years of rural happiness in the Essex home. We must let the curtain fall on the incidents of country life in High Laver.

CHAPTER II.

PHILOSOPHICAL CRITICISM AND CORRESPONDENCE.

LOCKE's literary work, disturbed in London by politics and weak health, was resumed in the seclusion of Oates with characteristic industry and method. The five years that followed entrance on rural life in the spring of 1691, were given to the work of authorship; —in defence of the 'Epistola de Tolerantia;' explanation of his opinions on education; improvement of the 'Essay,' in preparation for a second edition; and applications of its principles to an interpretation of Christianity that was meant to show its essential reasonableness and simplicity, and thus promote ecclesiastical comprehension, or at least comprehensive Christian charity. All this was combined with copious correspondence, familiar and philosophical, in which his Dutch friends Limborch and Le Clerc, his Somerset friend Edward Clarke, and a new Irish friend, William Molyneux, figure largely.

Locke's appointment, in 1696, as one of the Commissioners of Trade and Plantations—" a very honourable employment, with £1000 a-year salary annexed to it," as he explains in one of his letters at the time—recalled him for four years to the service of the State, and occasioned frequent, sometimes prolonged, visits to London, during the four years of his commissionership, but with Oates always as his home. Official work did not supersede literary work in the old manor-house, mostly philosophical and theological controversy, during the time he was at the Board of Trade. His published philosophy, and its supposed theological implications, called forth many critics, at a time when Arian and Trinitarian were in collision, and Deism sought to supersede the Christianity of the Church. His manuscripts contain drafts of projected books and pamphlets, which he did not live to publish; and latterly there was the preparation of the 'Essay' for its fourth edition, which appeared in 1700. In that year declining strength and a dangerous illness finally withdrew him from the Board of Trade and from public life. In the four following years he was much engaged when in his study in company with St Paul, whose Epistles were made the subject of reverential yet rational criticism; for Locke was among the first to apply to the Bible those logical processes which, according to the 'Essay,' are the foundation of all reasonable interpretation of facts—natural or supernatural—in this, anticipating later Biblical criticism of the scientific sort.

A little tract on the 'Consequence of Lowering the Rate of Interest and Raising the Value of Money,' which issued anonymously from Oates in 1691, is Locke's argument against depreciation of the currency by Government as a remedy for its illegal depreciation by others. It presents him again as a political economist.

It was followed by two other tracts, a few years after, meant to guide opinion in matters of coinage and finance, an evidently deep interest to Locke at this time.

In the year of his movement from London to Oates, his old adversary, Jonas Proast, produced a rejoinder to the 'Second Letter on Toleration,' which had appeared in the autumn of the previous year. This was met in 1692 by a 'Third Letter' from Locke, in bulk exceeding the other two united. Here he pressed the old lessons with redundant argument and irony, removing one after another the objections to a socially unimpeded exercise of individual judgment in questions of religion. The 'Third Letter' must have filled much of the time spent in the study at Oates during the winter of 1691.

It has been already mentioned that when Locke was an exile in Holland he had written a number of letters to his good friend Edward Clarke of Chipley,[1] about the education of his son. In the spring of 1693, he was busy preparing for the printers the substance of those letters, on a subject which naturally engaged the thoughts of his life, for it was involved in his experimental and practical way of looking at a human understanding. So in the summer of that year the now well-known little book entitled 'Thoughts concerning Education' made its appearance, dedicated to Clarke. It still has its own place among educational classics. It may be read either as an introduction or as a supplement to the 'Essay,' to which its author was giving his last touches, when the letters on education were sent from Holland to Chipley. It breathes the spirit of his philosophy. The

[1] In 1690 and for years after, Edward Clarke of Chipley was M.P. for Taunton.

need for each man forming his knowledge and opinions by the active exercise of his own understanding; revolt against the obstruction of empty idealess words, and against the bondage of dogmatic assumptions; warnings against the abuses to which thinking for one's self is exposed, when unmodified by experience, common-sense, and wisdom,—are considerations never absent from the mind of the writer. In the 'Thoughts concerning Education,' imaginative sentiment is never allowed to weigh against utilitarian prudence; mere book-learning is subordinated to observation of life and its affairs as means to the formation of a manly character; the part which habit plays in unfolding the individual mind, and in the determination of its bent, is, with Locke as with Aristotle, always prominent; the dependence of human understanding, which genuine education is intended to improve, upon the health of that material organism which in this life is practically connected with individual intelligence, is kept in the front along with the relative physiological lessons, and steadily inculcated; while the happiness of those who undergo educational processes is remembered as an "indispensable condition of success;" and mere accumulation of facts in the "storehouse" of memory, without encouragement of efforts to compare and elaborate, is condemned as the besetting sin of teachers. Wisdom more than knowledge, is what Locke desires in the teacher; for only the wise man recognises the "disproportion" between the infinite universe and a finite experience, and the consequent need for selection among the many more or less appropriate subjects which might be presented for study to youth. The first place is felt to be due (in making the selec-

tion) to that sort of experience which might direct to
heaven ; the next place to the experimental acquirement
of "prudence, discreet conduct, and proper management
of ourselves in the several occurrences of our lives, with
whatever most assists one's prosperous passage through
this present life." The "disproportionateness" of human
faculty is made the ground for abandoning studies
which do not increase the power of living prudently,
however much fashion may recommend them. "Custom," he complains, "has misled our teachers, so that
they have drawn us into that maze of words and
phrases, which have been employed only to instruct
and amaze people in the act of disputing, and which
will be found perhaps, when looked into, to have little
or no meaning, . . . words being of no value but as
they are the signs of things and have ideas attached
to them : when they stand for nothing, they are mere
ciphers, and instead of augmenting the value of those
they are joined with, they lessen it and make it nothing." He would confine instruction to useful knowledge, to the exclusion of speculative inquiries. Facts
more than languages, modern before ancient languages,
and all languages by practice in speaking them at first,
their grammar afterwards with its abstract rules and
principles. Home training under a tutor is preferred to a
great school. Information about other people's opinions,
or about the dogmas of sects, without criticism of their
truth, is what Locke everywhere deprecates. "Truth,"
he says, "needs no recommendation of this kind, and
error is not mended by it; in our inquiry after knowledge, it little concerns us what other men have thought.
It is an idle and useless thing to make it our business

to study what have been other men's sentiments in matters where reason only is the judge." In words like these, we trace that exaggerated reaction against authority, and failure to see an unconscious evolution of truth in the history of past opinions and controversies, which was natural to Locke, with his inherited temperament, and in the circumstances amidst which his life had been passed.

The 'Essay concerning Human Understanding' had encountered hostile criticism almost as soon as it appeared. The new spirit which breathed through every part of it communicated a shock to those accustomed either to defer to authority, or to feed their minds on abstractions more than on facts. John Norris, rector of Bemerton, the English Malebranche, had published in 1690 "Cursory Reflections upon a Book called 'An Essay concerning Human Understanding'"—a tract of some forty pages. He blamèd Locke "for proceeding to account for our ideas before he had defined what he meant by ideas, or had explained their nature;" for first "setting himself to prove that there are no innate or natural principles," and then "inconsistently" acknowledging that "there are self-evident propositions to which we give ready assent upon their first proposal," which, if self-evident, must be "universally assented to"; and then assuming that they require conscious instead of potential assent. In relation to the last point, Norris hits a weak point in the 'Essay' thus: "The most that Mr Locke can mean by want of 'universal consent' is, that every individual person does not actually assent to them. This may be granted him from the instance of idiots and children. But the

question will be about the consequence of his argument—whether conscious assent from every individual
be necessary to the supposition of innate principles."
Locke, he means to say, attacks the hypothesis of innate
conscious knowledge, not that of innate power to know.
"It seems to me," the author of the 'Essay' had said,
"near a contradiction to assert that there are truths imprinted on the soul which it perceives or understands not.
That a truth should be innate and yet not assented
to, is for a man to know a truth and be ignorant of it at
the same time."   In opposition to this, Norris argues
that "if there may be impressions made on the mind
whereof we are not conscious, then (by Mr Locke's own
measure) the non-perception of them is no argument
against such original impressions.   And that there may
be such impressions whereof we are not conscious is
what he himself elsewhere expressly does own, as when
he confesses that whilst the mind is intently occupied
in the contemplation of other objects, it takes no notice
of impressions which are at the time being made upon it.
The like is implied in his account of memory, which he
does not make to be a recovery of ideas that were lost,
but a readverting of the mind to ideas that are actually
there, though not attended to, they having been transformed into some kind of unconscious states ; and he
elsewhere supposes that there are infinitely more ideas
impressed upon our minds than we can possibly attend
to or perceive."   This of Norris is interesting as an early
recognition by an English writer of processes of unconscious thought or intellectual activity of which the
individual is the subject, while seemingly not the agent,
—processes afterwards noted in the "unperceived per-

ceptions" of Leibniz, and which play an important part in philosophical speculation in the nineteenth century.

Norris's tract, of which Locke took no notice at the time, was the solitary discord in the chorus of applause which greeted him on the first appearance of his "new philosophy." The 'Essay' rapidly attained a popularity without precedent in the case of an elaborate philosophical treatise. It soon found its way into the universities—especially Dublin and Oxford. The public applause reached Locke at Oates. In December 1692 a book arrived there, presented by its author, then a stranger to him—William Molyneux, a young, but already eminent, member of Trinity College, Dublin. It was entitled 'Dioptrica Nova.' In the dedication of this book, Molyneux said, with reference to logic, that "to none do we owe more for a greater advancement in this part of philosophy than to the incomparable Mr Locke, who, in his 'Essay of Human Understanding,' hath rectified more received mistakes, and delivered more profound truths, established on experience and observation, for the direction of man's mind in the prosecution of knowledge—all of which, I think, may be properly termed logic—than are to be met with in all the volumes of the ancients. He has clearly overthrown all those metaphysical whimsies which infected men's brains with a spice of madness, whereby they feigned a knowledge where they had none, by making a noise with sounds without clear and distinct significations." The arrival of the 'Dioptrica Nova' at Oates was the beginning of a friendly correspondence, which lasted till it was ended by death. "I will confess to you," Molyneux wrote in answer to Locke's grateful acknowledgments, "that I have not in my life read any book with more satisfaction than your 'Essay'; and I have endeavoured, with great success, to recommend it to the ingenious in this place [Dublin]."[1] "You must expect me," Locke replied, "to live with you hereafter, with all the confidence and assurance of a settled friendship. In meeting with but few men in the world whose acquaintance I find much reason to covet, I make more than ordinary haste into the familiarity of a rational inquirer after and lover of truth, whenever I can light on any such." "Mr Norris's unfortunate attempts on your book," Molyneux rejoins, "sufficiently testify to its validity; and truly I think he trifles so egregiously that he should forewarn all men how they venture to criticise your work." Molyneux was at the time the spokesman of many, and his enthusiasm helps us to enter into the admiration of intelligent readers, at a time when the 'Essay' seemed charged with a new revelation, and before its "novelties" had become commonplace by assimilation, in the course of the eighteenth century.

This friendship with Molyneux was formed when Locke was beginning to prepare the 'Essay' for a second edition, the first "being now dispersed"; and during the year and more of preparation that followed, his new Dublin correspondent was the Mentor at his right hand. "I expect," he writes, "a great deal more from any objections you shall make, who comprehend the design and compass of my 'Essay,' than from any one who has read but a part of it, or who measures it from a slight reading by his own prejudices." In the summer

[1] The 'Essay' has since then kept its place in Trinity College, Dublin.

of 1694 the second edition made its appearance. It contained important alterations and additions, on which the correspondence with Molyneux in the interval is an instructive commentary. "If there be anything," Locke writes to Dublin, "in which you think me mistaken, I beg you to deal freely with me. For I flatter myself that I am so sincere a lover of truth that it is very indifferent to me, so I am possessed of it, whether it be by my own or any other's discovery. For I count any parcel of this gold, not the less to be valued, because I wrought it not out of the mine myself." Locke regrets " prolixity and many repetitions " in the ' Essay,' in all which Molyneux sees an added charm,—" that strength of thought and expression that everywhere reigns in it," making him "sometimes wish that it was twice as long." One thing he urges in almost every letter, and that is that Locke would oblige the world with " a treatise on morals, drawn up in demonstrations, according to the mathematical method," agreeably to hints often given in the ' Essay,' which places abstract ethics along with mathematics, among the absolute certainties ;—an enterprise which Locke then postponed, and which was never accomplished. A proposal to turn the ' Essay ' more into the scholastic form of logic and metaphysics, " in order to get it more readily introduced into the universities," " which love to learn according to the old forms," is set aside because, "if in this book of mine they have the matter of these two sciences, or what you will call them, I like the method it is in, better than that of the schools." A new chapter, on " Personal Identity," " writ at your instance," was sent for criticism to Dublin before it was introduced into the 'Essay,' where it now stands in the second book;[1] but their joint efforts fail to relieve it of eccentricity and paradox, due probably to the difficulty of presenting this mysterious idea with the distinctness at which Locke always aimed. The original chapter on the idea of "Power"[2] was transformed on its way into the new edition. The correspondence with Molyneux, and a comparison of the first and second versions of this celebrated chapter, show how much Locke was perplexed to reconcile the spiritual fact of moral freedom from natural causality with the merely scientific conception of a caused or phenomenal cause. The coexistence of divine and human agency added to the perplexity, confessed in his dissatisfaction with this chapter after all the changes it underwent. "I own freely to you the weakness of my reasoning, that though it be unquestionable that there is omnipotence and omniscience in God, and though I cannot have a clearer perception of anything than that I am free, yet I cannot make freedom in man consistent with omnipotence and omniscience in God, and yet I am as fully persuaded of both as of any truths I most firmly assent to." Resting in this wise conclusion, he says he "has long since given off consideration of that question." That God in forming man can *make* organised matter think, while "unthinking matter cannot be this Almighty God;" that "the ideas which are ingredient in the complex idea of God" are got from external or internal sense; while the fact of the real existence of this God, or that "really there are united in one Being all these ideas, is had not from sense, but from demonstration;"

---

[1] Chap. xxvii.   [2] Book II. chap. xxi.

the " *æternæ veritates,*" and the "*principium individua-tionis,*"—are matters on which the correspondents gener-ally agree, but as to which Locke promises to make his meaning clearer. A "jocose problem" of Molyneux, as to whether one born blind, who had been taught "by touch alone to distinguish between an ivory cube and sphere," would be able, when first made to see, to distin-guish from one another, "by sight alone, which was the globe and which the cube," interested Locke so much, that he introduced it into his chapter on "Perception." [1] It afterwards suggested to Berkeley his famous theory, that our power to see surrounding things is really power to interpret significant signs in the universal sense-sym-bolism of nature.

Malebranche's hypothesis, that we "see all things in God," proposed as an explanation of our perception in sense of the qualities of matter, made Locke project a chapter in refutation of it for the new edition. The chapter was partly written, and "would make a little treatise of itself"; but it was held back, "because I like not controversies, and have a personal kindness for the author," and was left unfinished, "lest I should be tempted by anybody to print it." In this little essay, which made its way at last into the world among its author's posthumous works, he has to his own satisfac-tion, "laid open the vanity, inconsistency, and unintel-ligibleness of that way of explaining human understand-ing." Locke and his Dublin friend were agreed in this view of "Malebranche's notions, or rather Plato's in this particular." "What you in your 'Essay' lay down," says Molyneux, "concerning our ideas and

[1] Essay, Book II. chap. ix. sec. 8.

knowledge, is founded on, and confirmed by, the experience and observation that any man may make on himself, or the children he converses with, wherein he may
note the gradual steps that we all make in knowledge."

The 'Examination of Malebranche' is now interesting,
chiefly as evidence of Locke's indifference to any hypothesis in explanation of the fact that "ideas of the
things of sense have been introduced into the storehouse of memory." He accepted the fact without pro-
posing a philosophical theory of sense-perception to account for it. In such theories words are apt to be taken
for things, and men who make them fancy they know
what after all they know not. The organic motions in
our bodies which accompany perception of bodies at a
distance, may perhaps be accounted for by "the motion
of particles of matter coming from them and striking on
our organs." But this is only motion explained mechanically by other motion. It throws no light at all on the
spiritual act of perception which accompanies or follows
the intra-organic and extra-organic affections ; it merely
reveals conditions made necessary to the realisation of
that spiritual act, under the established laws of nature in
our embodied conscious life. The rise of the percipient
act in an individual is "incomprehensible, and can only
be resolved into the good pleasure of God. The ideas (or
sense-perceptions) it is certain I have, and God is the
original cause of my having them ;—but how it is that
I perceive, I confess that I understand not." "How,"
Locke asks, "can any one know, on Malebranche's explanation, that there is any such real being as the sun ?
Did he ever see the sun ? No ; but on occasion of the
presence of the sun to his eyes, he has seen the idea of

the sun 'in God'; but the sun, because it cannot be united to his soul, he cannot see. How, then, does he know that there *is* a sun which he never saw? What need is there that God should make a sun only that we might see its idea in Him, when this might as well be done without any real sun at all? . . . The ideas or perceptions we have, all arise in our minds by the will and power of God,—though in a way that we are not able to comprehend." To call our sense-perceptions "modifications of the mind," or to say that ideas are "modifications of mind," does not mend the matter. It is only substituting one term for another term, without adding to our philosophic insight. "It is plain, sensation and modification stand for the same idea, and so are but two names of one and the same thing. All we can say is, that there is some alteration in our mind, when we perceive or think of something that we were not thinking of a moment before. What Malebranche says of universal reason, whereof all men partake, seems to me nothing new, but only the power we find all men have to find out the relations that are between ideas; and therefore if an intelligent being at one end of the world, and another at the other end, will consider twice two and four together, they *cannot but* find them to be equal. God knows all these relations, and so His knowledge is infinite; but individual men are able only to discover more or less of them gradually as they apply their minds. If he means that this universal reason, whereof men partake, is the reason of God, I can by no means assent; for I think we cannot say that God reasons at all, for He has *at once* a view of all things; but (human) reason is a laborious and gradual progress in the knowledge of things. . . . I should think it presumptuous to suppose that I shared in God's knowledge; there being some proportion between mine and another man's understanding, but none between mine and God's." Man's sense-perceptions and God's knowledge, in short, are both incomprehensible; human philosophy can offer no theory of either,—far less explain the former by means of the latter.[1]

Although Locke took no notice of Norris's 'Reflections' upon the 'Essay,' when they appeared in 1690, he wrote some critical comments upon them three years after, which, like those on Malebranche, were published posthumously. They are to the same effect. To say that *our* ideas are the *divine* ideas, is not to explain the nature of our ideas; and indeed, no words which any one can use can "make known to another what his ideas, that is, what his perceptions, are, better than what he himself knows them to be; which is enough for affirmations or negations about them"—*i.e.*, for our perceptions and judgments of their agreements or disagreements. But if by "nature of ideas" is meant "their causes and manner of production in the mind" —*i.e.*, in what alteration of the mind this perception consists,—Locke answers that "no man can tell what alteration is made in the substance of our mind when we see what we did not see a minute before. . . . Wherein this change called perception consists is, for aught I see, unknown to one side as well as the other; only the one have the ingenuity to confess their ignorance, and the other pretend to be knowing." Norris

[1] I am glad to be confirmed in this interpretation by Mr Abbott, in 'Hermathena,' No. vii.

" explains " perception — like Malebranche — by the power of God enabling us to perceive the divine ideas; so that our power is lost in God's, and with it our responsibility. "This," Locke sarcastically says, "is the hypothesis that clears doubts, and brings us at last to the religion of Hobbes and Spinoza; by resolving all, even the thoughts and will of men, into an irresistible fatal necessity.[1] This, therefore, may be a sufficient excuse of the ignorance I have owned, of what our ideas are, any further than as they are the perceptions we experiment, or are conscious of, in ourselves; and of the dull unphilosophical way I have taken of examining their production, only as far as experience leads me." They are, he means to say, what reflection shows them now to be, no matter in what way they were caused.

The second edition of the 'Essay' appeared in the summer of 1694. The third, which was only a reprint of the second, was issued in the following year, almost contemporaneously with the "Abridgment" of the 'Essay' by Dr Ashe of Oxford, "for the use of young scholars, in place of the ordinary system of Logic," which was long used for this purpose.

In the winter of 1694-95, Locke was busy in theological authorship. His deep-seated sentiment of religion, his early Puritan training, and the circumstances of his life, especially intercourse and constant correspondence with Limborch, made questions of theology and Biblical

---

[1] This is one of Locke's few references to Spinoza, whose "Unica Substantia," absorbing into itself all substance and power, was proposed to explain the dualism left unresolved by Descartes. The theory of "occasional" causality in Malebranche and Geulinx was a half-way stage to a one-sided development of Cartesianism in the monism of Spinoza.

interpretation increasingly interesting to him. The result was a book, published anonymously, in 1695, on the 'Reasonableness of Christianity.' It was an attempt, in the spirit of the 'Essay,' to recall religion from verbal reasonings of dogmatic theologians, which had destroyed the peace and unity of the Church, to the original simplicity of Christianity, as delivered in the Scriptures, when interpreted in the spirit of modern inductive inquiry.

But Locke's new departure in Christian theology, including excursions in Scripture criticism, which formed, perhaps, the distinctive feature of his literary life at Oates, deserves more particular consideration in a separate chapter.

The 'Reasonableness of Christianity' had hardly awakened controversy when Locke returned to the perplexing question of the coinage, on which he had published an argument in his first year at Oates. In 1695 he issued two tracts in further development of his views. One of them was occasioned by an 'Essay for the Amendment of Silver Coins,' by William Lowndes, Secretary for the Treasury. In his reply Locke further anticipated recent doctrines on economics. These tracts brought him once more back into public life.

In 1696 Locke accepted office as a Commissioner of Trade, and for more than four years he was an active officer in this important department of the administration. The Secretary of the Board was William Popple, the translator of the 'Epistola de Tolerantia.' Locke's attendance at the Board is thus summarised by Mr Fox Bourne: "1696. 25th June–13th November (absent three days). 1696–97. 13th–17th February. 1697. 21st

June–22d November. 1698. 11th July–20th October
(absent two days). 1699. 6th June–20th November
(absent two days). 1700. 17th May–20th June, when
he resigned." The Council met almost daily. Notwithstanding indifferent health he was the most efficient, and
among the most regular, of the commissioners. But those
new duties encroached upon his rural retirement, and
its opportunities for literary labour, in the five summers
in which he held office; in the winters he was relieved
from attendance, his advice being always ready. More
than once, " with health impaired by the air of London,"
he asked leave to resign, but was prevailed on by the
king to continue his services. " Riches may be purchased too dear," had been his reply to the congratula-
tions of Molyneux on his appointment. " My age and
health demand a retreat from bustle and business; and
the pursuit of some inquiries I have in my thoughts
makes it more desirable than any of those rewards which
public employments treat people with. I think the
little I have enough, and do not desire to live higher or
die richer than I am. And therefore you have reason
rather to pity the folly than congratulate the fortune
that engages me in this whirlpool." Indeed his life was
more than once in danger through his loyalty to the
service. " He had been kept a close prisoner within
the doors at Oates for more than a month, when, on the
23d of January 1698, he received an urgent summons
from King William to present himself at once at Ken-
sington. It was a dismal winter morning, cold and raw.
Lady Masham begged him to send back the messenger
with word that he was too ill to make the journey.
But he insisted upon going. So he rode through the

snow and wind of Epping Forest in the coach that had
been despatched for him. On Monday afternoon he
returned more dead than alive." More than one such
dangerous adventure on the rough bridle-roads of the
Forest, and an increasing aversion to promiscuous
society, made him long for relief. " My temper," he
wrote to Lord Somers, " always shy of a crowd of
strangers, has made my acquaintances few, and my conversation too narrow and particular, to get the skill of
dealing with men in their various humours, and drawing
out their secrets." At last, in the summer of 1700, the
king accepted his resignation. "I have read in the
newspapers," Limborch wrote, "that on account of your
increasing age and weakness you have retired from the
honourable office you have filled for some years. I com-
mend your resolution to spend the remainder of your
life freed from the burden of politics, in rest, study, and
holy meditation."

The years of the Commissionership were not years
of literary repose. They were the most controversial
years in his life. The 'Reasonableness of Christianity'
involved him in the theological and ecclesiastical controversies of the time, and the 'Essay,' especially in its
theological consequences, was the object of attacks which
he no longer disregarded. Through means of both he
drew upon himself a share of the *odium theologicum*
in the Trinitarian discussions then going on in England.
The chief and centre of these collisions was with Stillingfleet, who was now Bishop of Worcester. It deserves
a place among the really memorable philosophical controversies of the modern world. It was brought about
in this way. John Toland, an Irishman, in a deistical

book entitled 'Christianity not Mysterious,' had exaggerated some opinions in the 'Essay,' and then adopted certain inferences from them of his own, under cover of Locke's authority. In the autumn of 1696, Stillingfleet, who was more an ecclesiastical than a philosophical theologian, in a 'Vindication of the Doctrine of the Trinity,' devoted some pages to Locke as interpreted by Toland, charging him with eliminating mystery and therefore faith in his account of our idea, or no idea, of substance, and in his rejection of all that cannot be reduced to "ideas" as out of all relation to man. Locke replied in January 1697. Stillingfleet's rejoinder came out in May, followed by a "Second Letter" from Locke in August, to which the Bishop replied in the following year. Locke's long and elaborate "Third Letter," in which the ramifications of the questions in dispute are pursued with a needless expenditure of acute reasoning and Socratic irony, was delayed till 1699. The death of the Bishop in that year brought this famous trial of intellectual strength to an end. In the course of the discussion, Locke was drawn further into speculative questions about the rational constitution of human knowledge than he had gone in the 'Essay,' and with a more express concession of presuppositions of reason latent in experience, which awaken into consciousness in individuals with the growth of reflection; and also of the fact that we may have the full certainty of knowledge about ideas that are obscure or mysterious, as well as about those that are distinct.

In 1697 Locke wrote to Molyneux that he had "much rather be at leisure to make some additions to the 'Essay' than be employed in defending himself against the groundless, and, as others think, trifling quarrel of the Bishop." But a storm was rising against the book, which now engaged many adversaries. One of these was John Sergeant, a Catholic priest, whose 'Solid Philosophy asserted against the Fancies of the Ideists' (1697) is a curious criticism of Locke. "Those," he says, "who have in their minds only *similitudes* or *ideas*, and only discourse of them, which ideas are not the thing, do build their discoveries upon nothing. They have no solid knowledge." "I do not wonder at the confusedness of his notions," Locke remarks in a letter, "or that they should be unintelligible to me. I should have much more admired had they been otherwise. I expect nothing from Mr Sergeant but what is abstruse in the highest degree." Sergeant was followed by the noted Thomas Burnet, Master of the Charter House, author of the 'Sacred Theory of the Earth,' and by Dean Sherlock.

A more redoubtable critic than any of these was Leibniz, Locke's greatest philosophical contemporary, whose point of view and method were at the opposite intellectual pole to his own. What Leibniz thought of the 'Essay' was first communicated to him by Molyneux, in a transcript of "reflections" on it, by Leibniz, addressed to Mr Burnet of Kemnay in Aberdeenshire, in the spring of 1697. It anticipates dimly some of the objections which Leibniz afterwards expressed with much elaboration in the 'Nouveaux Essais sur l'Entendement Humain,' which he was preparing at the time of Locke's death. The death of Locke was a bar to the publication, and the 'Nouveaux Essais' was held back till 1765, half a century after its author's death.

Locke made light of the epistolary criticisms of the German eclectic, which were to him "unintelligible." "I see you and I," he writes to Molyneux, "agree pretty well concerning the man, and this sort of fiddling makes me hardly avoid thinking that he is not that very great man as has been talked of him."

Meantime M. Coste was translating the 'Essay' into French, for Continental circulation. Locke himself, as soon as he was freed from the argument with Stilling-fleet, found his chief literary occupation in 1699 in preparing it for a fourth edition. This, as well as Coste's French version, appeared in 1700,[1] followed the year after by a Latin version, by Burridge of Dublin—both in due time republished at Amsterdam and Leipsic. The 'Essay' was now spreading over Europe, impelled by the name of its author, who had become the recognised philosophical defender of religious and civil liberty. Limborch and Le Clerc were his theological and philosophical representatives on the Continent.

The fourth edition of the 'Essay' was the latest production of Locke's mind published during his life. His remaining writings appeared posthumously.[2] He was now in his sixty-ninth year. He had added to the 'Essay' two important chapters, one on "Association of Ideas,"[3] and the other on "Enthusiasm,"[4] besides more

[1] Locke's copy of Coste's French version contains here and there sentences in Locke's hand, afterwards introduced into the second edition of the translation (1729), and now incorporated with the ordinary English editions of the 'Essay.'

[2] Some of them in 1706, under direction of his nephew King and Anthony Collins; several others in 1720, edited by Des Maizeaux, under the direction of Collins.

[3] Book II. chap. xxxiii.   [4] Book IV. chap. xix.

tinkering of the perplexing chapter on "Power." It must be repeated that, although Locke is sometimes ranked in the succession of English "association psychologists," association—word and meaning—makes no appearance in the first three editions of his book, and that the chapter on the subject which it now contains, far from representing the associative tendency as the solution of the ultimate problems of knowledge, treats of it exclusively as the chief source of human errors. Empirical analysis of the certainties of which we are conscious into automatic association, individual or inherited, and *a priori* idealistic analysis of the rational constitution of experience, were both alike foreign to his matter-of-fact report about human understanding as he found it. "Enthusiasm," too, is characteristically brought in, as "a false principle of reasoning often made use of," with ill consequences which his early life among the Puritans probably suggested. Like innate principles, as he understood them, it seemed, in another way, to remove our beliefs from the jurisdiction of reason. What he said on this subject was offered as the substitute for a larger discussion, involving the natural history of enthusiasm, which he excused himself from entering on when the day was so far spent. "To give an historical account of the various ravings men have embraced for religion under the name of enthusiasm, would, I fear, be beside my purpose, and be enough to make an huge volume." [1]

---

[1] This sentence may have suggested the 'Natural History of Enthusiasm' of Isaac Taylor, the recluse of Stanford Rivers, a book written a few miles from Oates, a century and a quarter after Locke's death.

A subject, originally designed for a chapter in the 'Essay,' was prepared, but withheld in order to form the subject of the separate treatise. It appeared among Locke's posthumous works, under the title of 'The Conduct of the Understanding,'—in some respects the most characteristic of all his books. "Your chapter concerning the conduct of the understanding must needs be very sublime and spacious," the admiring Molyneux writes from Dublin. Those lovers of truth who conduct their understandings in what Locke here describes as the "reasonable way," must occupy the point at which "a full view" may be had of whatever question they want to determine. The uneducated majority, on the contrary, seldom reason or think definitely at all; or if they made the attempt, put passion and prepossession in the place of logically regulated thinking. "For want of a large roundabout common-sense, they direct their understandings only to one part of the evidence, converse only with one sort of men, read but one sort of books, and will not come into the hearing of but one sort of notions; and so carve out to themselves a little Goshen in the intellectual world, where alone light shines, and, as they conclude, day blesses them; but the rest of the vast expansion they give up to night and darkness, and avoid coming near it." The intended "chapter" thus became a discourse on the large wisdom needed for the management of a human understanding, so that it may overcome the idols, or tendencies to error, against which Bacon had warned mankind, and which Locke here again explains partly by mental association. Hasty one-sided judgments, bias, want of philosophical "indifference" as to what the evidence may in the end require us to believe, undue regard for custom and authority, indolence, and sceptical despair, are among the states of mind marked as most likely to interfere with the attainment of the harmony of truth as between our individual minds and the universal reality.

The summer of 1698 brought a much-longed-for visitor to Oates. William Molyneux, the loved correspondent of six preceding years, he had not yet seen in the flesh; but after many postponements, the constant correspondents then spent two months together there and in London. Molyneux promised to repeat the visit in the following year; but the letter which reported his return to Dublin, with a promise to repeat the visit to Oates in another year, was followed a few days after by one which announced his sudden death — an unexpected shock to Locke's affectionate nature.

The shades of evening were now fast gathering around him, and he was warned by many signs that " the dissolution of this cottage is not far off."

CHAPTER III.

"WHO, I beseech you, is it that makes sects? Is it
not those who contract the Church of Christ within
limits of their own contrivance?—who by articles and
ceremonies of their own forming separate from their
communion all that have not persuasions which jump
with their model." So Locke wrote in his 'Third
Letter on Toleration.' The words express one motive
of the theological discussions and controversies which
occupied him so much in his retirement at Oates.
Ecclesiastical comprehension was in the air throughout
King William's reign. The Church of England, in
its rejection at the Reformation of the supremacy of
Rome, had never departed from the Catholic traditions,
nor from the continuous organisation of Christendom.
In the sixteenth century opposition to Roman supremacy
substituted faith in the infallibility of Scripture for faith
in ecclesiastical infallibility, with a widespread tendency
at first towards the Puritan extreme. The advance of
the seventeenth century was marked by that return
under Laud to the Catholic spirit and traditions of historic Christendom which was an important factor in the

Civil War. On the other hand, before and after the Restoration, some influential ecclesiastics and religious thinkers were disposed to rest religion and theology ultimately on reason and conscience in man, instead of either on the external authority of the living visible Church, or on the external authority of verbally inspired Scriptures.

Ecclesiastical tradition, and the venerable organisation of the ancient historic Church, had no attraction for Locke. The Visible Society of Christendom was not to him the ideal which it was to the historic imagination of his great contemporary Leibniz, whose comprehensive genius found satisfaction in the unbroken unity of the Catholic Church, with its constitution so adapted to all the dispositions and circumstances of those whom it offers to embrace within its ample fold, resembling that still vaster organisation in which he loved to contemplate the universe under the pre-established harmony of the government of the All-holy and All-wise. Locke's revulsion from his early Puritanism was towards rationalism,—in sympathy with the latitudinarian divines of the Anglican Church in the latter half of the seventeenth century, or their successors, such as Burnet, Tillotson, and Fowler, who held bishoprics after the Revolution. With them comprehension of Dissenters by increased elasticity on the part of the Church was the favoured policy. Locke's theological writings tended to encourage that policy, although, after all, it ended in failure. Its time was not then come.

Locke's intellectual philosophy determined his way of looking at Christianity and the Church; for, like everything in his life, it expressed the delight he took in making use of reason in everything. "The most trifling thing he did must always be seen to have some good reason for doing it," as Coste remarked, in describing his character; he could not therefore part with reason in the supreme beliefs of life. His religion must be reasonable, and could not be accepted on unreasoned authority. He had discovered that in action probability is the guide of life. Religion was with him essentially life and action, and what he looked for in it was reasonable probability, not the absolute certainty of self-evidence or of demonstration. When attainment of certainty was found to be inconsistent with the limits of human knowledge, his philosophy accustomed him to accept the most probable judgment, and then to act as if he were certain. To assume certainty when we are working within the sphere of probability, would appear to him a sign not of strength but of weakness. All that can be done by man in such cases is to see that in reason one belief is more probable than any other that can be supposed; and that accordingly, till it is disproved, or shown to be in reason less probable, he must, as a reasonable being, accept and act upon it.

Locke was predisposed to accept Holy Scripture as infallible with the reverence of a Puritan. It is the reasonableness of Christianity "as delivered in the Scriptures" that he set himself to unfold articulately. "The little satisfaction and consistency that is to be found in most of the systems of divinity I have met with," according to the opening words, "made me betake myself to the sole reading of the Scriptures (to which they all appeal) for the understanding the Christian religion. What from thence, by an attentive and unbiassed search,

I have received, reader, I here deliver to thee." The ground in reason on which he rested his belief was the miraculous physical signs by which he was satisfied that the authority of the Bible was sustained. But he did not, like the Puritans, mean Scripture either as interpreted by his own feelings, or as interpreted by his own sect. He claimed the personal right of interpreting it in the light of historical criticism. Confidence in the infallibility of the sacred literature, to the interpretation of which he was among the first to try to apply the scientific spirit and method, was united in Locke with a deep distrust for what he called "enthusiasm," to which he traced a host of errors. This, with the prominence assigned in his philosophy to the data of external sense, and to the understanding judging according to sense, predisposed him to crave physical miracles as an objective, and therefore solid, test for distinguishing a real revelation from one accepted in blind deference to authority, or under the influence of subjective feeling. "Fancy and strong assurance,"—enthusiastic illumination, without support from positive data of external sense,—sustained by sentiment, but "without proof and examination," were in his eyes sure signs of the absence of the divine spirit of love for truth. Fanatical confidence that one is right, he would say, is no proof that one is right; it is rather a sign that one is wrong. When God, who is true reason, leads our assent to the truth of an alleged fact or of a general proposition in religion, or in anything else, He either exhibits it to us in its intrinsic rationality as self-evident, or else presents miraculous signs in conjunction with the exhibition—signs of whose reality we may be sufficiently assured, if not by the evidence of our own senses, at least by sufficiently probable presumption of the veracity of witnesses. Reasonableness must be our ultimate guide in this as in everything.

Yet Locke's faith in Christianity seems to have rested at last on its moral excellence when interpreted in its primitive simplicity,—combined, however, with the extraordinary physical phenomena which he believed to have accompanied its first promulgation. His Christianity, I think, is something that he accepts because it finds a response in the genuine constitution of man —including human understanding, explained according to his own philosophical report about it—not in man stunted and distorted by traditions, confessions of faith, and ecclesiastical organisations. The response of the spiritual constitution of man to the Biblical revelation, not isolated miraculous signs looked at apart from the moral purpose which they express, seems on the whole to be his ultimate reason for a life of faith in religion as personified in Jesus. "Even in those books which have the greatest proof of revelation from God, and the attestation of miracles to confirm their being so, the miracles," he says, "are to be judged by the doctrine, and not the doctrine by the miracles." Physical miracle, he would probably say, cannot *per se* accredit a verbal revelation; but it may call attention to the books in their divine meanings, and thus get them responded to by what is supernatural in the constitution of man, in this way awakened into consciousness in the individual. When this is so, the physical miracles have a moral meaning; instead of interrupting the order or reason that is latent in the universe, they illustrate the presence of order or reason higher than natural, and to which the customary physical laws are therefore subordinate. They would then be in harmony with the thus correlated physical and ethical order of the universe, as startling occasions, fitted to awaken the spiritual or supernatural faculty that is depressed by sense, but is latent in all men,—being that "inspiration of the Almighty" which, when brought out of latency, gives to the inspired man spiritual understanding of the Infinite Mind, in which he had been unconsciously living and having his being.

Locke, indeed, does not put the subject or the proof in this way. Yet now and then his arguments tend, perhaps unconsciously, to transfer the foundation of Christianity from unreasoned or dogmatic assumption which he always struggled against, to the response which it finds in the conscience and spiritual constitution of man. Still, in his own conception of a human understanding, the lower faculties of sense tended, as we have seen, to obscure the higher faculties which connect man with God or the Infinite. Ecclesiastical dogma and tradition was no doubt a substitute with many for the catholic experience of all round humanity ; but a philosophy which inclines to see in man chiefly a recipient of phenomena presented in sense-experience, is in another way one-sided, and to this narrower faith Locke's argument on the whole inclined. Christian teachers and apologists for Christianity in the eighteenth century, as well as its assailants, alike appealed to the 'Essay concerning Human Understanding' as their philosophical standard, and tested it by the "external and internal evidences" on which it was rested by Locke.

His own Christian belief, sincere and earnest, appears more in the prudential theology of England, in the two or three generations after his death, than in the larger faith, rooted in our whole spiritual being, which showed itself in More, Cudworth, and Leighton in the age preceding; or, since Locke, in the religious philosophy of Law and Berkeley, and still more of Coleridge and Schleiermacher.

The 'Reasonableness of Christianity' was in intention an attempt to recall Christianity from verbal reasonings and dogmas of ecclesiastical schools, destructive of peace and charity among Christians, to its original simplicity. All who are in sympathy of spirit with Jesus as the Messiah or Redeemer of mankind, have accepted what is essential to the simple Christianity of Locke, whatever inferences of their own they may add to this essence of their religion. Personal surrender of life to this simple faith in the Messiahship of Jesus, and a corresponding sympathy with all of whatever name or sect who share in it, was his ideal at once of personal religion and of the Church. "What was sufficient to make a man a Christian in our Saviour's time," he argues, "is sufficient still—the taking Him for our King and Lord, ordained so by God. What was necessary to be believed by all Christians in our Saviour's time, as an indispensable duty which they owed to their Lord and Master, was the believing all divine revelation as far as each could understand it; and just so it is still, neither more nor less. No man has a right to prescribe to me my faith, or magisterially to impose his opinions or interpretations on me; nor is it material to any one

what mine are. It is this which I think *makes me of
no sect,* and entitles me, it seems, in the opinion of my
adversaries, to the name of a Papist or a Socinian."
This "essential Christianity" contains only articles that
the labouring and illiterate man may comprehend; and
nothing can be necessary to be believed by all but what
is suited to ordinary capacities and the comprehension
of ignorant men. "All that is necessary for all to believe about God must be easily understood. There be
many truths in the Bible which a good Christian may
be wholly ignorant of, and so not believe ; which perhaps some lay great stress on, and call fundamental
articles, because they are the distinguishing points of
their sect or communion." But Christianity is with
Locke more than religion as it would be if Christ had
never lived : the revelation of God in Christ, while consistent with the conditions of a human understanding of
the universe, could not have been discovered but for His
miraculous appearance in the world of nature, and His
resurrection after death.

An interesting part of Locke's interpretation of Scripture is the account which he gives of its revelation of
the destiny of men after death. Human immortality
is, he argues, not of the essence of the human spirit, or
necessarily involved in our personality and identity ; nor
is it on the other hand predicable only abstractly of Reason, but also of men in their distinct continuous personal
existence. A life after death was given by God to men
at first, when it might have been withheld, and it has
been lost by the fall of mankind in Adam ; but it may
be recovered through faith in the Messiahship of Jesus,
and sympathy with Him in His divine mission. Anni-

hilation is with Locke the ultimate destiny of all who
do not retain life after physical death as the reward of
the conduct in this life that issues from faith in Christ.
This reward—contrasted with the punishment of annihilation—this conditional offer of immortality is, according
to Locke, the chief motive to goodness of conduct which
Christianity supplies, and which gives it its superiority
to heathen philosophy.

This conditional immortality is accepted by Locke
as the revelation contained in Holy Scripture. The
" death " which is the issue of sin, he would say, must
mean annihilation, and in such matters we should not
seek to be wise above what is written. The idea of
annihilation might also have recommended itself as a
mitigation of the mystery of immoral agency in the
universe being otherwise endless,—when the free agents
who create evil become so confirmed in their habits as
to make their final restoration to goodness impossible.
If moral evil has entered the universe through the creation of agents, who, in virtue of their freedom, may
create either good or evil actions; and if their present
existence is, as facts prove, consistent with the Perfect
Universal System; then their annihilation, after their
" fall " from the divine life, rather than their continued
existence, when they have made themselves permanent
moral failures, might seem to be the outcome of the
universal ethical government. The existence of persons
who can create their own acts is implied in God's moral
government; not necessarily their unending existence,
when they are finally bent on the creation of wicked
acts. But Locke hardly suggests this sort of reasoning, and confines himself to determining the interpreta-

tion of the Biblical terms "life" and "death" in this
relation.

Locke's languid historical[1] imagination made no
account of the continuity of one great ecclesiastical organism, as a miraculous standing evidence of the truth
of Christianity, and a principal means for securing its
victory in the world. Visible ecclesiastical organism,
whether in the form of the ancient historic Church,—
Roman, Greek, and reformed Anglican,—or any other,
he regarded as an accident, and not of the essence of
Christianity—of which those who would might avail
themselves, but visible union with which was not necessary to the communion of those who are united in a
common sympathy with Jesus, and in surrender to his
Messiahship,—"who love all men, of what profession
or religion soever, and who love and seek truth for
truth's sake,"—the one comprehensive communion recognised in Locke's Christianity.

The last years of Locke's life were given to the
exegetical study of the New Testament. The story of
Christ in the Gospels he had studied when he worked
in theology years before. He now turned to the Epistles
of St. Paul, and applied the spirit and methods of the
'Essay' in the critical interpretation of the literature
which he still revered with the reverence of the pious
Puritans who surrounded his boyhood. The same sense
of the need for a reasonable foundation for his beliefs
followed him here as in other investigations; the same

[1] Locke's "historical plain" method, of course, does not refer to
the history of philosophy, or to history at all in that sense, and only
expresses his reverence for the facts and events of nature and of consciousness.

determination to explode unreasoned assumptions, and
to deliver himself from bondage to empty words. This
sort of exegesis implied a revolution in the favourite
methods of the Puritans, who were ready to interpret
texts apart from their context, directed by emotions to
which the words gave rise, or by the tendency to spiritual edification of a meaning which might be read into
the words,—neglecting the context, the circumstances in
which they were written, and the influences at work in
the writers and in the age in which they were produced.
Locke sought, in the spirit of modern historical criticism, to identify himself with the writers, their feelings and thoughts and circumstances, and by regarding
each Epistle as a whole, and in all its relations, to
evolve its rational meaning. He was among the first
in Europe who led towards the large historical exegesis
since practised by the great German critics, which has
now so transformed Christian thought. His dominant
design as a critic was to work his way through the sand
and rubbish of prejudiced interpretations—the presuppositions due to feeling and imagination—the "ideas
and principles," presumed to be "innate,"—which had
previously biassed interpreters.

"The Epistles," he says, "are written upon several occasions; and he that will read them as he ought, must observe
what is in them which is principally aimed at. He must
find what is the argument in hand, and how managed, if he
will understand them right. The observing of this will best
help us to the true meaning and mind of the writer: for
that is the truth which is actually given to be recorded and
believed, and not scattered sentences in Scripture language
accommodated to our notions and prejudices. We must look
into the drift of the discourse, observe the coherence and

connection of all the parts, and so how it is consistent with itself and with other parts of Scripture, if we will conceive it right. We must not cull out, as best suits our system, here and there a period or verse, as if they were all distinct and independent aphorisms, and make these necessary to salvation, unless God has made them so. The Epistles, most of them, carry on a thread of argument, which, in the style they are writ, cannot everywhere be observed without great attention ; and to consider the texts as they stand and bear a part in the whole, that is to view them in their true light, and the way to get the true sense of them."

The application and vindication of these principles in an interpretation of the literature of Apostolic Christianity was the last labour of Locke's life. He nowhere defines his own relation to the theological doctrines that were disputed in the Trinitarian controversy then going on in England, if indeed he had a positive opinion upon questions which seemed to him not necessarily involved in practical Christianity. Doctrines intellectually diffi-cult, and distinctions which demand subtle thought, whatever in them might be true or false, could not, in his view, be essential to a faith that was to be catholic ; so long at least as human understanding was limited in all men to a narrow experience and imperfect faculty, and still more limited in the great majority of mankind by their surroundings, and by the defective education which makes them unable to think for themselves, or even to apprehend the results of subtle thinking in others.

CHAPTER IV.

AFTER 1700, Locke was gathering himself up for the end in the rural repose and family life of Oates. The commission at the Board of Trade was resigned, and the visits to London ceased. The devout spirit and simple piety of one consciously living in the presence of God, appears in the latest acts and expressions of his life, unchecked by that independent exercise of thought which he still vindicated for himself and for others. Religious meditation and Biblical studies engaged much of his remaining strength in the four following years, along with a tract on 'Miracles,' suggested by the essay of his friend Bishop Fleetwood.

The critics of the 'Essay' were not silenced, they were rather multiplied. 'Anti-scepticism; or, Notes upon each Chapter of Mr Locke's "Essay," with an Explication of all the Particulars of which he treats, and in the same order,' an elaborate folio, in four books, by Henry Lee, a Northamptonshire rector, made its appearance in 1702—pleading for "some regard to authority in an age too much given to novelty. 'Tis now become the common mode," the author says, "to go so deep in our inquiries after truth, and to be so warm in our amours, as first to doubt whether there be any such thing as a real truth; for the received maxims of all mankind, which used to be the touchstone by which to try it, must now, it seems, be tried themselves, and in the meantime are to be declared 'purely artificial, and wholly owing to the powerful influence of custom and education.' Our philosophy, our policy, our religion, must be new or none at all." It is in this spirit that Lee addresses himself to his critical work, in which, with some irrelevancy, he touches several ambiguous expressions of Locke, states what is meant by innate ideas and principles not less clearly than Leibniz, and anticipates reasonings of Buffier and Reid in vindication of the common reason that is latent in humanity, implying of any one who opposes this, that—

> "Habit with him is all the test of truth :
> It must be right ; I've done it from my youth."

About the same time the 'Essay' was formally condemned by the authorities at Oxford. "I take what has been done there rather as a recommendation of the book." So Locke wrote to his young friend Anthony Collins, who had now become a frequent visitor at Oates, "and when you and I next meet we shall be merry on the subject." But criticism of the 'Essay' failed to draw its author into controversy, and indeed contributed to its reputation. In the original, or in the French or Latin versions, it was making its way on the Continent, as well as in public opinion at home, and was becoming accepted as the acknowledged standard of English philosophy.

One attack only moved Locke. In 1704 his former adversary, Jonas Proast, unexpectedly revived the old controversy, regarding the principle of religious tolera tion, as logically meaning that, although some modification of theism is necessary to secure the ends of civil government, yet there is "absolutely no such thing under the Gospel as a Christian commonwealth," so that all religious differences short of atheism are foreign to the concerns of the State. Locke in consequence began a 'Fourth Letter on Toleration.' The few pages, ending in an unfinished sentence, which appeared among his posthumous works, seem to have exhausted his remaining strength in the weeks before he died. Thus the idea of religious liberty, which engaged him at Oxford more than forty years before, and had been his ruling idea during the long interval, was still dominant when earthly objects were fading from his view.[1]

Locke's letters to Anthony Collins cast light upon the evening of his life. He was above seventy, and Collins was twenty-six, when their friendship began. The letters express an ardour of affectionate friendship which was natural to Locke. Here are a few extracts :—

"You make the decays and dregs of my life the pleasantest part of it," he writes in May 1703; "for I know nothing calls me so back to a pleasant sense of enjoyment, and makes my days so gay and lively, as your good company." Again : "It is but six days since that I writ to you, and see here

---

[1] I found in the Lovelace collection many letters and other documents regarding the case of Thomas Aikenhead, the youth who was hanged for heresy at Edinburgh in 1697, at the demand of the city ministers. Locke showed much concern in the affair.

is another letter. You are like to be troubled with me.
If it be so, why do you make yourself so beloved? Why
do you make yourself so necessary to me? I thought
myself pretty loose from the world, but I feel you begin
to fasten me to it again. Believe it, my good friend, to love
truth for truth's sake is the principal part of perfection in
this world, and the seed-plot of all other virtues ; and if I
mistake not, you have as much of it as ever I met with in
anybody. Now methinks I begin to see openings to truth,
where a little industry and application would settle one's
mind with satisfaction. But this is at the end of my day,
when my sun is setting. It is for one of your age, I think
I ought to say for yourself, to set about it ; there is so much
beauty and consistency in the prospect. I am a poor ignorant man, and if I have anything to boast of, it is that I
sincerely love and seek truth, with an indifferency where
it pleases or displeases. I take you to be of the same school,
and so embrace you. To be rational is so glorious a thing
that two-legged creatures generally content themselves with
the title, and inform themselves by a tiresome rummaging
in the mistakes and jargon of pretenders to knowledge, not
by looking into things themselves." Then again : " As for
rummaging over Mr Norris's late book,[1] I will be sworn it
is not I have done that ; for however I may be mistaken in
what passes without me, I am infallible in what passes in
my own mind ; and I am sure the ideas that are put together in your letter out of him were never so in my thoughts
till I saw them there. What did I say ?—' put ideas together.' I ask your pardon, it is ' put words together without ideas.' Men of Mr Norris's way seem to decree rather
than to argue. . . . What you say about my ' Essay '—
that nothing can be advanced against it but upon the principle of innate ideas—*in the sense I speak of innate ideas,*
though they make a noise against me, yet they so draw and
twist their improper ways of speaking, which have the sound

---

[1] "Theory of the Ideal or Intelligible World" (1704).

of contradiction to me, that at last they state the question so as to leave no contradiction in it to my 'Essay'; as you have observed in Mr Lee, and Mr Norris in his late treatise. You have a comprehensive knowledge of it, and do not stick in the incidents which I find many do; which, whether true or false, make nothing to the main design of the 'Essay.' That lies in a little compass, and yet I hope may be of use to those that follow the plain and easy method of nature to carry them to knowledge. It was with a design of inquiry into the nature and powers of the understanding that I writ it."

In the spring and summer of 1704, Locke continued to decline, tenderly nursed by Lady Masham and her stepdaughter Esther. The sense of gradual decay finds expression in the letters to Collins. There is correspondence about a chaise which Locke got Collins to have made for him, that he might still enjoy the leafy lanes of High Laver and Epping Forest, and joy expressed for Collins' companionship in his frequent visits to Oates in that last summer, "when your company and kindness have added to the length of my life, which in my way of measuring, doth not lie in counting of minutes, but in tasting of enjoyments. I wish every day the chaise done; not out of impatience I am for the machine, but for the man—the man, I say, that is to come in it. A man that has not his fellow, and for all that, loves me. If I regret my old age, it is you that makes me." Then there are arrangements for Sir Godfrey Kneller coming down to Oates to take Locke's picture for Collins, which, "if it was possible to make a speaking picture, it should tell you every day how much I love and esteem you." The picture was taken, and another of Lady Masham in August 1704,—two months before the end,—the second of Locke by Kneller, who seven years before had made pictures of Locke and Molyneux.[1]

The vanity of mortal life, and the hope of a more spiritual communion with God in the life to come, now absorbed Locke's interest in the controversies and concerns of earth. "All the use to be made of it," he wrote to Collins, a few weeks before the end, in a letter to be delivered to him afterwards, "is, that this life is a scene of vanity that soon passes away, and affords no solid satisfaction but in the consciousness of doing well and in the hope of another life. This is what I say on experience, and what you will find to be true when you come to make up the account." A few days before death came he is pictured by Coste in the garden at Oates taking the air in bright October sunshine, the warmth affording him great pleasure, which he improved by causing his chair to be drawn more and more towards the sun as it went down. They happened to speak of Horace, Coste having repeated to him the verses where the poet says of himself that he was "solibus aptum, irasci celerem, tamen ut placabilis essem." Locke remarked that if he durst compare himself with Horace in anything, he thought it was in these two respects. He loved the

[1] There are several portraits of Locke. The engraving prefixed to this volume is from Kneller's 1697 portrait, when Locke was in his sixty-fifth year. Apparently the portrait here referred to is the one I saw at Holme Park,—thin white hair, weakness and suffering in every feature of the thoughtful countenance, pale, even ghastly. Two of the earliest are at Nynehead, one of·them a companion picture to another which represents his young friend "Betty," Edward Clarke's daughter, beside portraits of Clarke himself and his wife. Locke called Betty his "little wife," and the two used to send the most amusing messages to each other. The Sanfords of Nynehead now represent the Clarkes of Chipley.

warmth of the sun, and he was naturally choleric, but his anger never lasted long; if he retained any resentment, it was against himself for having given way to so ridiculous a passion, which, he often said, "may do a great deal of harm, but never yet did the least good." On the 28th of October he ceased to appear in this world of sense, and passed away, as he declared, "in perfect charity with all men, and in sincere communion with the whole Church of Christ, by whatever names Christ's followers please to call themselves." The last scene is referred to in the homely expressions of the following hitherto unpublished letter,[1] from Esther Masham to a Mrs Smith, who had been housekeeper at Oates :—

"OATES, *November* 17, 1704.

"I am grieved, dear Mrs Smith, you should think I have forgot you; you are very much in my thoughts. You have heard, no doubt, of the death of good Mr Locke. Ever since his death we have been in a continual hurry; for my mother, not being able to settle her thoughts to anything, bustles about as much as she can, and I generally come in for something. Though we could not expect his life a great while, it did, nevertheless, surprise us. His legs were very much swollen, and the day before he died, finding it very troublesome to rise, because of his great weakness that he was hardly able to do anything for himself, he resolved to lie abed, which made the swelling in his legs get up into his body, and immediately took away his stomach and his sleep, for he slept not a wink all that night. The next morning he resolved to rise, and was carried into his study, and in his chair got a little sleep, was very sensible, but soon called to be moved, and was no sooner set elsewhere than he died, closing

---

[1] Preserved among the Birch MSS. in the British Museum. I owe this reference and other particulars to the Rev. R. Rodwell, rector of High Laver.

his eyes with his own hands. He is extremely regretted by everybody. He left Mr King[1] his executor, and has left Frank £3000 and half his books.[2] He left me £10, and like to my father and mother, and several other legacies. He has given to every servant in the house 20s., and Mrs Lane 40s., for which she thought she must have gone into mourning. He has left a great deal for charitable uses. He ordered in his will to be buried in the churchyard, in a plain wooden coffin without cloth or velvet, which cost, he said, would be better laid out in clothing the poor, and therefore ordered four poor men to have coats, breeches, shoes, stockings, and hats. I heard him say, the night before he died, that he heartily thanked God for all His goodness and mercies to him, but above all for His redemption of him by Jesus Christ.—I am, yours, E. MASHAM."

So ended the prudent, moderate, and tranquil life, pious and inquisitive, which began at Wrington and

[1] His cousin, afterwards Lord King, Baron of Ockham in Surrey, and Lord Chancellor (1725), ancestor of the present Earl of Lovelace.

[2] The share of the books, &c., which went to Francis Masham became the property of the Palmers, who bought Oates in 1776. The other part of the library and the MSS. went to Ockham, to Sir Peter King. The Will, as I find on examination of the original record, is dated 15th September 1704, and he describes himself as "John Lock of High Laver." It disposes of £4555 of personal property, besides books, plate, clock, pictures, and manuscripts. The £3000 to Francis Masham, to be held in trust by Peter King and Anthony Collins, with reversion in case of his death to "Dame Damaris Masham." His "ruby and diamond rings," with some books, are left to Lady Masham; £10 to Anthony Collins, £200 and his picture to his "daughter Betty," £100 to the poor of High Laver, and another £100 to the poor of Publow and Pensford in his native Somerset, with souvenirs to the Guenellons, Dr Veen, Furly, and Awnsham Churchill, the publisher. The land and houses in Somerset were divided between Peter King and Peter Stratton. The Will is proved by Peter King, "sole executor" and residuary legatee—"Damaris Masham, Anthony Collins, and Pierre Coste, witnesses," in the winding-up of his affairs. Locke's income when he was at Oates must have kept him in easy circumstances.

Beluton in the stormy years of Charles I. On Tuesday,
the 31st of October, they buried him on the sunny side
of the parish church of High Laver, where, almost two
centuries ago, that serene and pensive face, pale and
tinged with sadness, which Kneller has made familiar to
us all, was often seen. A few chosen friends, including
the Masham family, King, Collins, and Coste, and neighbours at Oates, seem to have formed the little company
who gathered round his grave, when the aged rector read
the beautiful service of the Church of England, on that
autumn day in Essex. The lines of the Latin inscrip-
tion composed by himself, lately traced with difficulty
upon the stone, suggest the pensive language of the
'Essay' about human memory, in which it is suggested
that "the ideas as well as the children of our youth
often die before us, and our minds thus represent to
us those tombs to which we are approaching, where,
though the brass and marble remain, yet the inscriptions
are effaced by time, and the imagery moulders away." [1]
Especially in that remote rural scene, the tomb of
Locke may touch the imagination of the wayfarer. According to tradition, Sir Isaac Newton was one of the
first who visited it. At a little distance are some tombs
of the Mashams, and within the church, those of Sir
Francis Masham, of Damaris, the widow of Cudworth,
and of Mr Lowe the rector. The heads of the Masham
family, with whom he had lived so happily, soon followed him. Lady Masham died at Bath in April 1708,
and rests there in the Abbey Church. Sir Francis died
in 1722, the year in which his daughter Esther collected
and transcribed the letters to which we are indebted,—

[1] Book II. chap. x. sec. 5.

as it seems, on the eve of her departure from the home
of her youth, when, with her treasured memories of her
"Joannes," she disappears finally from view.[1] Locke's
young favourite, Francis Masham, died in 1731, when
Lord Masham, the heir of Sir Francis, and his wife
Abigail were the possessors of Oates. He is buried in
the neighbouring church of Matching. Queen Anne's
favourite died in 1734, and her lord four years after.
The barony expired in 1776, on the death of their only
son, the second lord, who died childless. The estate of
Oates was then sold to Richard Palmer, whose last representative, Miss Palmer of Holme Park, near Reading,
was, at her death, in 1879, in possession of the share of
Locke's books and other possessions that had been left
to Francis Masham. This collection of relics, since dispersed, contained, when I saw it, the chair which Locke
occupied in his last illness, comfortable enough for the
slight and feeble patient, who must have been of low
stature, for the height of the seat is hardly fourteen
inches, occupied in those last years by that slender figure,
wiry but emaciated, calm, yet with signs of suffering.

Locke's writings, which everywhere express his character, have made his intellectual and moral features
not less familiar to Englishmen than his countenance
has been made by Kneller. The reasonableness of taking probability or likelihood for our guide in the most

---

[1] M. Coste, soon after Locke's death, seems to have gone to live
at Chipley with the Clarkes. "Mr Coste is now well settled in Mr
Clarke's family," one of Esther's correspondents writes. Letters
thence from him to Esther Masham refer to Anthony Collins, and
the development of his opinions in the direction of philosophical
necessity and Deism. A few years later Collins was in controversy
with Dr Samuel Clarke about free agency. He died in 1729.

important concerns of human life was his governing principle. The desire to see for himself what is really in harmony with the thought and will of God, in the light of its reasonable evidence, and that all men should do the same, was his ruling passion, if the word may be applied to one so calm and judicial. " I can no more know anything by another man's understanding," he would say, "than I can see by another man's eyes. The knowledge which one man possesses cannot be lent to another." Reluctance to believe in the dark, on blindly accepted authority, instead of faith sustained in the judgment by self-evident or demonstrative reason, or by good probable evidence, runs through his life. He is the typically English philosopher in his love for concrete exemplifications of the abstractions in which more speculative minds delight ; in his reverence for facts— facts in nature, or facts of conscious life ; in indifference to speculation on its own account ; in aversion to verbal reasonings ; in suspicion of mystical enthusiasm ; in calm reasonableness, and ready submission to truth, even when the truth could not be reduced to system by a human understanding ; and in the honest originality which stamped the features of his intellect and character upon all that he wrote. In philosophical discussions he never lost sight of immediate utility ; he esteemed men in proportion to the good they were obviously doing, and thus perhaps unduly disparaged learned scholars and idealistic philosophers. While he practised the severe reasoning that he admired in Chillingworth, he had little patience with those who argue for victory and not for truth, guarding their arguments behind the ambiguity of a word. Large, "roundabout," even prudential and prosaic, common-sense, with occasional help of humour and refined scarcasm, strength of understanding sagaciously directed by a prudent purpose, much more than subtle, daring, comprehensive, or even coherent speculation, are conspicuous in his writings and conduct. His caution approached timidity, and sometimes made him irresolute. His aim was not to explain the universe, but to adapt his life to its actual conditions. The visions of the poet were foreign to his experience; neither Bunyan nor Milton found much response in Locke. Deficiency in speculative imagination, and want of eclectic sympathy with the historical development of human thought are shown when he encounters the vast and complex problem of human knowledge, and the constitution of the reality which it contains. This appears in his indisposition to find elements of truth in systems foreign to his own,—unlike Leibniz, whose ideal of philosophical truth was grander, or at least more pretentious, than that matter-of-fact account of the office and limits of a human understanding which Locke offered in the ' Essay,' in order to bring about an amendment of its operations in the future history of mankind.

CHAPTER V.

PHILOSOPHICAL ISSUES IN THE LAST TWO CENTURIES.

LOCKE'S intellectual philosophy may be interpreted in two ways, as one or other of the two fundamental parts of its constitution regulates the interpreter. Its origin, in reaction against authority and scholastic abstractions, as well as the tendency of opinion in the century which followed its appearance, have favoured one of those interpretations. Accordingly, Locke is commonly associated with the disposition to resolve metaphysics into physics; and our spiritual or supernatural experience, with its elements of reason, conscience, and creative will, into sensuous phenomena.[1]

That we find in our "experience" of the qualities of things and the operations of our own spirits, in their ever-changing variety, the materials which enter into all our knowledge and presumptions of probability;— that man can know, or even have an idea of, nothing that is not clothed in the phenomena thus presented to

---

[1] Yet in Mr Webb's 'Intellectualism of Locke' (Dublin, 1857), we have an ingenious attempt to interpret Locke throughout as even "an Intellectualist in the sense of Reid and Kant." With Reid he has much in common, but from Kant he is surely separated by method and point of view.

him—is one of the two principal lessons of Locke's philosophy of human understanding.

The other is left in the background in those two books of the 'Essay' in which "ideas," not "certainties" and "probabilities," are the subject of analysis.[1] It comes out more when the certainties of common-sense are reported on, in the fourth book; for these involve, not mere ideas, complex and simple, but relations among ideas, intuitively discerned or perceived as true. "It is on intuition or perception," as Locke expresses it, "that the certainty (*i.e.*, the self-evidence and the demonstrableness) of our knowledge depends." Knowledge thus *originates*, according to Locke, in *intuition of relations* among *the data of experience;* and it is on presumptions, involving more or less *likeness* to what we have experienced, as he afterwards shows, that the probability of our opinions naturally depends. Wherever we have an intuitive perception of relations between the subjects and predicates of propositions, we have the absolute certainty of knowledge; and if the perception of relations is accompanied by a common-sense conviction that it corresponds, as one might say, with the order or reason that is latent in experience, then we have some real knowledge of the universe. But he also reports that when we pass out of the world of abstract thought into the world of concrete examples, this certainty never involves universality. Certainty about more than an individual case is "never to be

---

[1] It might be said that the second and third books of the 'Essay' are concerned with Terms and their meanings; the fourth chiefly with Propositions—self-evident, demonstrated, probable, and erroneous.

found except within abstract thoughts or ideas." Whenever we seek it elsewhere—in observation of nature—we find that "our knowledge goes not beyond particulars." It is the contemplation of abstract ideas alone that is able to afford us general knowledge. This confines Locke's ontological certainties to individuals—including God—and withdraws certainty from universal judgments about nature and the attributes of existing realities.

Locke's Epistemology, so far as it goes, might be interpreted in harmony with the formula of Patricius—"cognitio omnis a mente primam originem, a sensibus exordium habet primum,"—with this qualification that Locke puts stress on the "exordium," or the appearance of knowledge in time, and in the consciousness of the individual; he leaves in the background what is implied in its "origo,"—in "perception" or intuitional intelligence of relations, with all involved in this which is latent and so comes out of the mind.[1] Why the 'Essay' and the other philosophical works of Locke make exemplification of the ultimate rational necessities more prominent than the abstract necessities themselves that are latent in the "intuitions or perceptions on which all absolute certainty depends," is partly explained by the motive to which the 'Essay' was due.[2]

---

[1] Yet in a letter to Mr Samuel Bold (16th May 1699), Locke says: "I agree with you that the ideas of the modes and actions of substances are usually in our minds before the idea of substance itself; but in this I differ from you, that I do not think the ideas of the operations of things are antecedent to the ideas of their existence,—for they must exist before they can in any way affect us or make us sensible of their operations, and we must suppose them to be before they operate."

[2] Locke expressly says that his purpose is, not to analyse pure

Locke, we have found, was led to his *via media* philosophy through reaction against *a priori* dogmatism, and
the empty abstractions with which it is apt to be connected ; not by reaction against the sceptical nescience
which would discredit even presuppositions that express
the conditions by which real knowledge must *a priori* be
determined, and by which it is in one sense explained.
The assault in the ' Essay ' upon " innate " ideas and
principles ; its analysis of the metaphysical ideas that
gradually arise in consciousness in the course of the
exercise of our faculties ; its limited and uncritical recognition of self-evident and demonstrated certainties ;
together with the prominence given in it to probability
as the guide of life, were all meant to administer checks
to empty verbal reasonings, and to *a priori* speculation
that is not exemplified in particular facts.   Locke, no
doubt, invited that new philosophical departure, from
the epistemological point of view, which has since drawn
modern philosophy into theories of human, and also of
absolute or divine knowledge, but away from the dogmatic ontologies which those critical theories have
superseded.   His own epistemology was founded upon
the *humanity* of knowledge, showing that man's knowledge, like every aspect of him, is intermediate between
the animal and the divine,—" far short of a universal
or perfect comprehension of what exists."   Philosophy
has, at some periods of its history, been recalled to this
human position by sceptical despair,—in hope of finding relief from doubt in a deeper and truer insight of

reason, or the understanding as such, but "to consider the dis-
cerning faculties of a man *as they are employed above the objects*
(phenomena) *they have to do with* " (Book I., chap. i. s. 62).

man's spiritual being, — as in the Socratic reaction against the scepticism of the Sophists. Locke was brought to a study of the actual facts of a human understanding of the universe with the opposite motive of testing dogmatic omniscience by demanding exemplification of its abstractions in data of experience. He sought thus to convict the dogmatists of their inability fully to realise divine or absolute knowledge of the actual universe, or to substitute a complete rational perception of truth for the presumptions of probability that are appropriate to man.

That Locke was moved by this second motive explains much not only in his own philosophical expressions, but also in that development of philosophic thought, from 1690 till now, which his recall of philosophy to the human or intermediate may be said to have inaugurated. His proposal to try to find what in point of fact a human understanding is or is not able to deal with, was made, not because he found the current of opinion running towards sceptical despair of the power of man's mind to make any way at all in the interpretation of the successively presented data of human experience; or because he wanted men to become more intrepid and comprehensive in their speculations. It was for an opposite reason,—because he suspected that men had been claiming for their knowledge more than could be justified by a true human philosophy. They seemed to have been "letting loose their thoughts into the vast ocean of Being, as if all that boundless extent were their natural and undoubted possession." The 'Essay' is accordingly an inquiry as to whether past failures to reach truth may not have been due

to men having ventured, either as uncritical tradition-
alists or as dogmatic rationalists, to place themselves as
it were at the Divine or central point for viewing the
universal reality; instead of seeing that human individuality necessarily withdraws us from the centre, and
keeps us always at the side; where much that is
actual must remain out of our intellectual sight, and
where things, experienced under the relations of time,
must appear at a different angle from the timeless intellectual vision at the centre. His inquiry was as to what
in point of fact could be seen from the side. So in
the 'Essay' and elsewhere he is fond of returning to
the contrasts between the few points of full light found
within our intellectual horizon; the many points at
which we can have only the dim twilight of probability;
and the boundless realm of darkness which, for us, sur-
rounds both—all suggesting to his reader the moral advantage of habitually pondering the enigma of a human
understanding in the discharge of its necessarily intermediate function, between Nescience and Omniscience.

It was perhaps inevitable that Locke,—disposed by
temperament, as well as by education and his surroundings, to see the danger of dogmatic claims to omniscience rather than the danger of sceptical despair,—
should be more apt to dwell on the weakness of human
understanding, and the narrow limits of human experience, than either on the abstract constitution of Divine
Universal Reason, in which man in a manner shares,
or on the facts that distinguish man as a moral and
spiritual, or supernatural, being. Thus his own philosophy was apt to draw more towards the philosophical
extreme of Empiricism and Nescience than towards

the opposite extreme of transcendental Idealism and potential Omniscience. This was in the spirit of the age in which he lived, of which he was so signally the intellectual representative. In the latter part of the seventeenth century, the assumptions of dogmatic theology that had been supréme in the middle ages, and in the theological ·controversies and religious wars of the sixteenth century and after, were beginning to be subjects of criticism. Simultaneously with this, the astonishing growth of the sciences of observation in England strengthened the disposition to bring every disputed belief before the tribunal of the generalising understanding, which judges only according to the physical categories of sense. Hence the philosophy natural to a representative thinker, at a time when the traditional philosophy was weak, and when leading opinions were reacting even in excess against the pressure of the Past, was apt to be analytic and disintegrative, more than constructive or conservative. This explains how Locke's chief aim was to expose empty verbalism, and to dissolve obstinate prejudices inherited from the Past, which he assailed as " innate ideas " and " innate principles." He wanted to explode verbal forms and dogmas that had usurped the place which was due to experience faithfully interpreted. He did not spare even Bacon and Descartes, pioneers as they were of free inquiry, but not completely freed from the bondage of scholastic abstractions and assumptions. Bacon's too sanguine anticipation of coming sciences of nature which should reveal its " fixed, eternal, universal principles," was probably in Locke's view, when he once and again administered a check to those who vainly hoped for a " demonstrable " science of the laws and qualities of matter; and when he insisted as he did upon man's inevitable ignorance of necessary relations between the innumerable secondary qualities and powers of the things of sense and their few primary or mathematical qualities ; or when he argued for the impossibility of finding universal or necessary propositions in matters concrete. As to Descartes too, when Locke engaged in his 'Essay' Cartesianism was passing into Spinozism; and all along its course it had seemed to Locke, with its teaching about "innate ideas," as he interpreted it, to be too much a "letting loose of thought in the vast ocean of Being."

Accordingly, one need not wonder that Locke, with his early training in natural science and in practical politics, repelled too by the dogmatic theology of the Puritans who surrounded his youth, should unconsciously lean to that narrow and incomplete conception of man which represents him as ending in sense and empirical understanding. Speculative imagination, constitutive reason, moral experience, and thinking will — on all which a deep and spiritual philosophy depends — are either left out of sight or attenuated. An "experience" that ends in sense and empirical generalisation must end incoherently, and therefore contain the seeds of scepticism, if there is (potentially) in man a larger and richer life, due to the factors of his moral and religious experience,—often latent, it is true, in individual men, but found to respond when rightly addressed by words or by miracles. In those supernatural factors in the human mind we have the key to the metaphysical or supernatural interpretation of the universe, at the human or intermediate point of view. From them come to us—

> " Those shadowy recollections,
> Which, be they what they may,
> Are yet the fountain light of all our day,
> Are yet a master light of all our seeing ;
> Uphold us, cherish, and have power to make
> Our noisy years seem moments in the being
> Of the Eternal Silence ; truths that wake
> To perish never."

If this is so, then Locke's philosophy was a common-sense protest on behalf of the right and duty of the understanding to judge according to a somewhat thin and narrow, or at least ambiguous, conception of what enters into human experience. It therefore tended to send the main current of thought in the eighteenth century in the direction of analysis and disintegration, with a preference, healthy in its own way, for concrete and variable examples in sense over abstract and absolute necessities of reason. And so it came to pass that, before the middle of the century, Locke's ambiguously constructed philosophy was transformed into Hume's " sceptical solution of sceptical doubts." [1] The extreme nescience into which Hume resolved Locke called forth Reid and Kant. Reid, in the spirit and according to the "historical" or matter-of-fact method of Locke, sought to penetrate more deeply than Locke had done into the " perceptions " of common reason by which Locke saw that the certainties of knowledge were constituted. Reid traced scepticism to "the Car-

[1] See Hume's ' Inquiry concerning Human Understanding,' *passim*, but especially Lects. IV.-VI.

tesian system of the human understanding," otherwise called "the ideal system," which he attributed also to the 'Essay,' according to which only an image of reality is perceived in sense,—though Locke disclaims any theory on the subject. Kant applied his new critical method to the purely rational side of experience, and to the epistemological problem, which Locke, in an iconoclastic spirit, had tried to solve in the practical interest of man's individual right and liberty to understand things according to positive proof.[1]

The course of British and French philosophy, from the publication of the 'Essay concerning Human Understanding' in 1690, till Reid in 1764 produced his 'Inquiry into the Human Mind on the Principles of Common Sense,' represents on the whole the progress of the disintegrative tendency, which in Britain was only in part and temporarily arrested by Reid. Reid and the psychologists of Scotland were moved to attempt an analysis of the common rational sense deeper than Locke's, by the desire to refute the Hume they saw when looking only at the negative side of Berkeley. But the philosophy which appeals at last to custom and association only was not thus arrested. English and French empirical psychology from Hartley and Condillac to John Stuart Mill and Comte, accepted isolated sensations, emptied of the originating and active Reason which in Berkeley was their necessary constitution and final cause. English psychology from Hartley to Mill continued on the lines of the "sceptical solution of

---

[1] For an able comparison of the Scottish and German answers to Hume, the reader is referred to Professor Seth's 'Scottish Philosophy' (2d ed., 1890).

sceptical doubts;" and "association" is more prominent than the Common Reason in the teaching even of Dr Thomas Brown, who represented Reid's philosophy in its decline, in the second decade of the nineteenth century. Thus for 130 years after its publication the 'Essay' of Locke gave to philosophy in this country its groundwork and its method. The Anglo - Saxon mind cautiously leans to that side of human life which is instinctive and determined by custom, overlooked as outside philosophy altogether by those who would confine its speculations to the ultimate presuppositions, and who despise "axiomata media" as external to the sphere in which it moves.

The German mind, awakened into *a priori* speculation by Leibniz, continued in it on the new lines of Kant, and from Kant to Hegel tended steadily towards the speculative construction and systematic unity of absolute all-explaining Idealism. This philosophy introduced into Britain, at first by Coleridge and by the criticisms of Hamilton, has, within the last forty years,[1] gradually transformed our insular manner of thinking, and inverted for the time Locke's " plain, historical," matter-of-fact procedure.[2] A similar but more transitory dissatisfaction in France with the materialism and theological nescience into which Locke had been there resolved, was represented by Jouffroy and Cousin

[1] It is hardly necessary to mention in this connection Principal Caird, Professors Edward Caird and Green, and Dr Hutchison Stirling,—names prominent in the history of British philosophy in the last quarter of a century.

[2] The most powerful argumentative criticism of this transformation will be found in Professor Veitch's 'Knowing and Being' (1889).

contemporaneously with Coleridge and Hamilton in Britain.

Locke's political philosophy was modified and adopted in France in the eighteenth century by Montesquieu, and many of his opinions on education were modified and adopted by Rousseau.[1] The 'Esprit des Lois' (1748) of Montesquieu,—which in popularity and influence was hardly inferior in the department of political speculation to the 'Essay concerning Human Understanding' in the history of logical and metaphysical thought,—propagated many of Locke's opinions of social polity, in a more attractive form ; while Condillac and the encyclopædists of France unwarrantably associated his name with the sensuous materialism into which their interpretation of the 'Essay' reduced his philosophy.

Notwithstanding the supremacy of Leibniz in Germany, and the natural disposition of the Teutonic mind to *a priori* philosophy and absolute idealism, the influence of Locke even in the universities of the Empire was undoubtedly strong.[2] Locke, directly or through Hume, awakened Kant from his dogmatic slumber, and the 'Kritik of Pure Reason,' in the form which its problem assumes, as well as in some of its main features, bears marks of the parentage of Locke. The 'Essay' and the 'Kritik' differed in the handle by which each took hold of the problem. The concrete data of experience, and their priority in the order of time and natural

---

[1] The 'Sandford and Merton' of Thomas Day is a popular illustration of the educational teaching of Locke and Rousseau.

[2] It may still be traced, for instance in Hartenstein, 'Locke's Lehre von der Menschlichen Erkenntniss' (1861), and Koenig, 'Über den Substanzbegriff bei Locke und Hume' (1881).

evolution, regulate the 'Essay'; the dialectical evolution of presuppositions and principles, the denial of
which would make experience and reasoning impossible, and priority in the order of thought and existence, determine the 'Kritik.'

The connection of Locke's logical enforcement of reasonableness, and independence of authority in theology,
with the history of English Deism, French illuminism,
and German rationalism, is for the student of religious
thought the most interesting issue of his life and
philosophy. But Locke's lasting effect upon religious
thought in these two centuries is seen in the ever-
widening conviction among Christians that religion
and Christianity must, like other beliefs, be exposed to
the test of free criticism, and to the response of the
rational, as well as the moral and spiritual, or supernatural, constitution of man.

In the eighteenth century it was difficult to obtain a
hearing for an interpretation of man and the universe,
other than that attributed to Locke, or of those who in
his name professed absolute empiricism and nescience.
Berkeley, at first trained in the 'Essay,' became at
last in 'Siris' the neglected spokesman of a loftier or
more ambitious creed. Such characteristic utterances of
his as those which follow, for example, were out of place
in his generation, and were overlooked until they came
to be recognised long after :—

"If explaining of a phenomenon be to assign its proper
efficient and final cause, it should seem that mechanical philosophers never can explain anything, their province being
only to discover the laws of nature—that is, the general

rules and methods of motion. We cannot make a single step
in accounting for phenomena without admitting the immediate presence and immediate action of an incorporeal
Agent, who connects, moves, and disposes all things, according to such rules and for such purposes as seem good to
Him. . . . Nothing mechanical either is or really can be a
cause. . . . Strictly, Sense knows nothing. . . . Nature or
sense is reason immersed and plunged into matter, and as it
were fuddled in it and confounded with it.[1] . . . General
rules are necessary to make the world of sense intelligible.[2]
. . . It may not be inferred [from our unconscious reflex
actions] that an unknowing nature can act regularly. The
true inference is only that the human person is not the real
author of these natural motions ; for no man blames himself
if they are wrong, or values himself if they are right.[3] What
is done by rule must proceed from something that understands the rule ; therefore, if not from the human person
himself, from some other active Intelligence. . . . Sense
and experience acquaint us only with the course and analogy
of appearances or natural effects. Thought, Reason, and
Intellect introduce us into the knowledge of their causes.[4]
Sensible appearances, though of a flowing, unstable, uncertain nature, yet having first occupied the mind, they do by
an early prevention render the after task of thought more
difficult — 'sensible' and 'real' being to common apprehensions the same thing. The principles of science are
neither objects of sense nor of imagination, and Intellect
and Reason are alone the sure guides to truth. . . . All
the faculties, instincts, and motions of inferior beings, in
their several respective subordinations, are derived from

---

[1] This adopted from Cudworth.

[2] Compare this with Locke on the unreality of general principles
and universal conceptions.

[3] This implies that the moral or immoral agency of persons is our
one concrete example of independent and creative causality or power.

[4] Mere evolution of phenomena from preceding phenomena, in
short, explains nothing, but itself needs to be explained.

and depend upon Mind and Intellect. . . . Number is no object of sense, it is an act of the mind. . . . Comprehending God and the creatures in one general notion, we may say that all together make one universe or τὸ πᾶν. But if we should say that all things thus make one God, this would indeed be an erroneous notion of God, but would not amount to Atheism, so long as Mind or Intellect was admitted to be the governing part. . . . Sense denotes dependence in the soul which hath it. Sense is a passion, and passions imply imperfection. . . . So far forth as there is real power in the universe there is Spirit. . . . Sense at first besets and overbears the mind. We look no further than to it for realities or causes ; till Intellect begins to dawn, and cast a ray on this shadowy scene. We then perceive the true principles of unity, identity, and existence. Those things that before seemed to be the whole of being, upon taking an intellectual view are seen to be but phantoms. . . . The Mind, her acts, and her faculties, furnish a new and distinct class of objects ; from the contemplation whereof arise certain other notions, principles, and verities, so remote from, and even repugnant to, the first prejudices which surprise the sense of mankind, that they may well be excluded from vulgar speech and books, as abstract from sensible matters, and more fit for the speculation of truth, the labour and aim of a few, than for the practice of the world, or for the subjects of experimental and mechanical inquiry. . . . Sense supplies images to memory. These become subjects for fancy to work upon. Reason considers and judges of the imaginations. And these acts of reason become new objects to the understanding. In this scale each lower faculty leads to one above it ; and the uppermost naturally leads to the Deity, who is rather the object of intellectual knowledge than even of the discursive faculty, not to mention the sensitive. . . . Plato held original ideas in the mind ; that is, notions such as never were nor can be in the sense. Some, perhaps, may think the truth to be this :—that there are properly no *ideas* [mental images, *Vorstellungen*] but what were derived from sense, but that there are also besides these her own acts and operations, such as *notions*. . . . It does not follow that because a thing *is*, it must *actually* exist [*i.e.*, in a consciousness]. . . . That perpetual struggle to recover the lost region of light, that endeavour after truth and intellectual ideas, the soul would neither seek to attain, nor rejoice in, nor know when attained, except she had some prenotion or anticipation of them, and they had lain innate and dormant, like habits and sciences in the mind, which are called out and roused by reminiscence. . . . A Divine force or influence permeates the entire universe. . . . Plotinus represents God as order; Aristotle, as law. . . . As the mind gathers strength by repeated acts, we should not despond, but continue to exert the flower of our faculties, still recovering and reaching on, and struggling into the upper region, whereby our natural weakness may be in some degree remedied, and a taste attained of truth and intellectual life."

Contrast with the philosophy that is implied in these thoughts of Berkeley characteristic sentences of Hume like those which follow,—the issue of Hume's attenuation of Locke, and of his interpretation of Berkeley's subordination of sense and the material world to Mind as virtual scepticism :—

"This theory of the universal energy and operation of the Supreme Being [Mind] is too bold ever to carry conviction with it to a man sufficiently apprised of the weakness of human reason, and the narrow limits to which it is confined in all its operations. We are got into fairyland, long ere we have reached the last steps of our theory. Our line is too short to fathom such immense abysses. . . . Were our ignorance a good reason for rejecting anything, we should be led into denying all energy in the Supreme Being as much as in the grossest matter. All we know is our profound ignorance in both cases. . . . All belief of real existence is derived from a customary conjunction between one object

and another.   Custom is the supreme guide of human
life. . . . Anything may *a priori* be the cause of anything. . . . The whole is a riddle, an enigma, an inexplicable mystery.   Doubt, uncertainty, suspense of judgment,
appear at last the only result of our most accurate inquiry."

These sentences are more in the spirit of the age
in which they were written than those selected from
Berkeley, who habitually realised the constitution and
unity of the universe in supreme immanent Mind, although without critical analysis of this rational constitution.   Hume, taking Locke's simple ideas as isolated
sensations and the essence of knowledge ; and looking
only at Berkeley's negative conclusion that the (independent) existence of sensible things is an absurdity,
dissolved all in the incoherence and contradiction which
would be latent both in Locke and Berkeley so interpreted.   Locke's 'Essay,' under this light, became an
incoherent theory of a "knowledge" resolved into successive sensations blindly connected by custom.   Berkeley
was transformed into a sceptic, on the ground that he
had resolved matter into isolated sensations ; not, as he
really intended, into sense-phenomena charged with
immanent and ever-active Reason, to which they owe
their reality or significance, interpretability, and capacity
for being reasoned about.

The 'Nouveaux Essais sur l'Entendement Humain'
of Leibniz made its appearance in 1765, fully sixty
years after the death of Locke, and about half a century after the death of its author.   The long neglect
of this great work is another illustration of the favourite
modes of thought in last century.   Like Berkeley's
'Siris' it was forgotten till the revolution in philosophy

which followed introduced meaning into its pages.
With his eclectic disposition, Leibniz suggested possi-
bilities of a reconciliation of his own philosophy with
that of Locke, through Locke's "ideas of reflection."
"Perhaps the opinions of this able writer," he says,
"are not so far from mine as they seem to be. For
he grants that there are ideas which do not come from
the senses, and cannot deny that there is much innate
in the mind. The mind is itself innate." But the
' Nouveaux Essais' is in spirit, method, and results at
the opposite pole from the 'Essay' of Locke. The
potential rationality of the universe, and the potential
demonstrableness of true philosophy, are at the bottom
of the ' Nouveaux Essais,' and the ideal which Leibniz
sought to realise was the conversion of this potentiality
into an articulate system. Locke's indifference to the
history of thought in its successive evolutions contrasts with the habitual endeavour of Leibniz to see
the seeds of truth in systems and speculations the most
alien from his own, and by eclectic criticism to absorb
them into his philosophy. Locke's tendency to solve
philosophical difficulties by physical categories is opposite to the spiritual dynamics of his German critic ;
whose "unconscious ideas" contradict the assumption
on which the English philosopher always proceeds,—
that "ideas" and *conscious* intelligence are identical, or
at least two ways of looking at the same thing. With
Leibniz "innate knowledge" is not of necessity conscious knowledge, nor knowledge got independently of
continuous personal exertion, as with Locke ; it may be
unconscious as well as conscious, as far as the individual
is concerned, under laws of the spiritual world to which

there is nothing analogous in nature, which is the realm of caused causes. The 'Nouveaux Essais' advanced upon Locke in the form of anticipations partly of Kant and partly of Lotze.

The ultimate or metaphysical interpretation of the universe which is widely accepted in any age or country, as well as by individuals, depends upon the degree in which faculties, originally latent in each man, are drawn forth into conscious exercise. When, as for the most part in the eighteenth century, external observation, automatic association, and merely generalising understanding are the characteristics, and the spiritual or supernatural faculties are much left in their original latency as at birth,—then the prevalent philosophy naturally tends to self-contradictory scientific agnosticism, which accepts the presuppositions of physical science, and yet argues for theological nescience on the ground that metaphysical presupposition is illusion. On the other hand, in periods when reflective thought is so exaggerated as to leave the sense faculties comparatively dormant—as with medieval and modern schoolmen—abstractions come to supersede concrete things and persons, and the resulting philosophy becomes a web of subtle speculation spun out of the philosopher's thought,—in disregard of facts in experience which, if recognised, would destroy the unity of the subtle system, and make its thought "abrupt." The philosophy that corresponds to the experience of the complete man acknowledges the need and value of the empirical elements and methods of knowledge, and also their subordination to the universalising reason, which connects man with the infinite and eternal. As Leibniz himself says, " those who give themselves up to the details of sense and to the natural sciences are led to despise abstract speculation and idealism, 'while those who habitually live among universal principles, rarely care for or appreciate individual facts. But," in his own eclectic spirit, he adds, " I equally esteem both." Bacon, in a like spirit, profoundly remarks that " those who have handled knowledge have been too much either men of mere observation or abstract reasoners. The former are like the ant; they only collect material and put it to immediate use. The abstract reasoners are like spiders, who make cobwebs out of their own substance. But the bee takes a middle course ; it gathers its material from the flowers of the garden and the field, while it transforms and digests what it gathers by a power not its own. Not unlike this is the work of the philosopher. For true philosophy relies not solely on the power of abstract thinking ; nor does it take over the matter which it gathers from natural history and mechanical experiments, only to lay it up in the memory as it found it ;—for it lays it up altered and digested by the rational understanding. Therefore from a closer and better considered alliance between these two faculties—the empirical and the rational— such as has never yet been fully realised, much may be hoped for philosophy in the future."

It is thus that from Locke to Lotze the modern philosophical world has for two hundred years been engaged in attempts to solve the speculative problem that is involved in Locke's practical ' Essay.' The two intervening centuries have witnessed a struggle between two antithetical conceptions of man's intellectual relation to life and its realities, which may issue in the end in a deepened philosophical knowledge both of the changing phenomena and of the mysterious permanent implicates of his physical and spiritual experience. One seems to hear three conflicting voices in the course of those centuries. The response to the philosophic questions made by one of them is—that "nothing can be known because nothing may be presupposed, except indeed the mechanical presuppositions of physical science." An opposite philosophic utterance comes from another quarter : "The universe may be seen through and through, and its secret is revealed in the light of the Divine Reason that is immanent in it." These two voices are apt to overhear the third, which pleads that man may see enough to justify the faith that he is living and moving and having his being in a universe in which Nature is in harmony with, yet subordinate to, the ethical and spiritual Order with which his higher faculties connect him ; and that the more his latent faith or inspiration is made to respond, by reflection and by the facts of history, the more clearly each man can see the little that is intellectually visible at the human point of insight, and the more wisely and religiously he can direct his life.

APPENDIX.

LOCKE'S WORKS IN CHRONOLOGICAL ORDER OF PUBLICATION.

WHEN IN HOLLAND.

1. Contributions to the 'Bibliothèque Universelle'—(*a*) Methode Nouvelle de dresser des Recueils ; (*b*) Review of Boyle's 'De Specificorum Remediorum cum Corpusculari Philosophia Concordia' ; (*c*) Epitome of the 'Essay,' &c., ... 1686-88

WHEN IN LONDON.

2. Epistola de Tolerantia,[1] . . . . . *March* 1689
3. Two Treatises on Government, . . . *February* 1690
4. ESSAY CONCERNING HUMAN UNDERSTANDING, . *March* 1690
5. Second Letter for Toleration, . . . *October* 1690

WHEN AT OATES BEFORE THE COMMISSIONERSHIP.

6. Some Considerations on the Consequence of Lowering the Rate of Interest and Raising the Value of Money, ... 1691
7. A Third Letter for Toleration, ... 1692
8. Some Thoughts concerning Education (dedicated to Clarke of Chipley), ... *July* 1693
9. Second Edition of Essay concerning Human Understanding, ... 1694
10. Third Edition of Essay concerning Human Understanding, ... 1695

1 Popple's translation in the following summer.

When at Oates during the Commissionership.

Posthumous.

Some writings which have been published as Locke's are not sufficiently authenticated—among others an 'Introductory Discourse to Churchill's Collection of Voyages,' containing a history of Navigation, with a Catalogue of Books of Travels (1704), 'The History of our Saviour Jesus Christ, related in the Words of Scripture' (1705), and 'Select Moral Books of the Old Testament and Apocrypha Paraphrased' (1706). No. 28 of the preceding has also been doubted, although it was included by Des Maizeaux in his " collection " (1720), under the direction of Anthony Collins.

END OF LOCKE.

DATE DUE

DEC 8 '77			
APR 8 '80			
OCT 1 6 '80			
APR 20 '82			
DEC 9 1985			
AP 26 '88			
OC1 1 '88			
AP 3 '90			
MAR 0 7 1991			
MAR 1 6 1992			
APR 06 1993			
APR 2 1 1994			
MAY 0 3 1997			
MAR 3 1 1998			
DEC 2 1 2001			
YLORD			PRINTED IN U.S.A.